$49.95

Mail Orders:

Order additional copies of the **California Building Performance Guidelines for Residential Construction.**

Each copy	$49.95
CA sales tax	$4.12
Shipping & handling.	$3.95
Total	$58.02

$53.95 per CD-ROM version includes 8.25% CA sales tax. Shipping and handling is free.

Online Orders:
www.cabuildingstandards.com

Phone Orders:
800-247-6553 or
(925) 828-7466

Fax Orders:
(925) 829-0714

Homeowners Education Association
P.O. Box 3198
San Ramon, CA 94583

Register Your Book! ▶

Register now... and get free updates, corrections and addenda to the 2004 Edition by e-mail.

❑ Yes, I would like to order additional copies of the California Building Performance Guidelines for F

❑ Send____ copies at $58.02
$3.95 shipping and handling)

MW01621096

❑ Send____ copies of the CD-ROM ❑ MAC or ❑ PC format at $54.07, includes 8.25% CA sales tax (shipping and handling is free).

Enclosed is $____________ payable by check to: Homeowners Education Association, LLC or charge my ❑ VISA or ❑ Mastercard.

Account #________________________________Expires______/__________

Name on account____

Address____

City_________________________ State__________ Zip_______________
(Do not send cash. For privacy of your credit card account, send this card in a separate envelope).

❑ Yes, I would like to order additional copies of the California Building Performance Guidelines for Residential Construction (2004 Edition).

❑ Send____ copies at $58.02 per copy (includes 8.25% CA sales tax and $3.95 shipping and handling).

❑ Send____ copies of the CD-ROM ❑ MAC or ❑ PC format at $54.07, includes 8.25% CA sales tax (shipping and handling is free).

Enclosed is $____________ payable by check to: Homeowners Education Association, LLC or charge my ❑ VISA or ❑ Mastercard.

Account #________________________________Expires______/__________

Name on account____

Address____

City_________________________ State__________ Zip_______________
(Do not send cash. For privacy of your credit card account, send this card in a separate envelope).

Yes, I want to register my 2004 Edition of California Building Performance Guidelines for Residential Construction and Homeowner Maintenance Guide and receive free updates, corrections, and addenda to the 2004 Edition.

Name____

Address____

City_________________________ State__________ Zip_______________

e-mail address ____
(Important. All information will be sent only by e-mail).

PLACE
STAMP
HERE

HOMEOWNERS EDUCATION ASSOCIATION LLC
PO BOX 3198
SAN RAMON CA 94583

PLACE
STAMP
HERE

HOMEOWNERS EDUCATION ASSOCIATION LLC
PO BOX 3198
SAN RAMON CA 94583

PLACE
STAMP
HERE

HOMEOWNERS EDUCATION ASSOCIATION LLC
PO BOX 3198
SAN RAMON CA 94583

$49.95

CALIFORNIA BUILDING PERFORMANCE GUIDELINES FOR RESIDENTIAL CONSTRUCTION

▲▼▲▼▲▼▲▼▲▼▲▼

A practical guide for owners of new homes

- **Construction Performance Guidelines**
- **Important Maintenance Items**
- **Information on Home Construction**

Published by:
The Building Standards Institute
Sacramento, California
www.buildingstandardsinstitute.org

The *California Building Performance Guidelines for Residential Construction and Homeowner Maintenance Guide*, is published by the Building Standards Institute, a private non-profit corporation under license from Homeowners Education Association, LLC. This book is not a publication of the State of California nor any other government agency.

ISBN 0-9711969-1-5. Printed in the United States of America.

First Printing: March 2002
Second Printing: August 2002
Third Printing: May 2003
Fourth Printing: January 2004
Fifth Printing: April 2004

Subsequent Editions

It is the intent of the authors to revise and update the contents of this book every three years. As a result, the 2004 Edition is valid in successive years until a subsequent edition is published.

Building Standards Institute
4629 Whitney Avenue, Suite 3
Sacramento, CA 95821
www.buildingstandardsinstitute.org

Illustrations: Joe Bologna, AIA
Graphic Design: David Grandin
Editorial Assistants: Sarah MacLellan
Jayne Jergentz

TABLE OF CONTENTS

Chapter Four

Roofs

Chapter Five

Exterior Components

Chapter Six

Interior Components

Chapter Six (continued)

Chapter Seven

Utility Systems

Chapter Eight

Grounds

Chapter Nine

Miscellaneous

Preface

Despite a significant need, uniform standards of performance and quality in the California homebuilding industry do not exist. While numerous books have been written about construction quality, few books, publications, or other materials dealing with building performance standards or guidelines have been published. The various Uniform Codes, adopted by governing agencies in the State of California, cover building, plumbing, electrical, mechanical and other house component systems. They derive their language from a health and safety viewpoint, and not necessarily from a construction quality or workmanship standard.

Historically, the definition of quality in home building has largely been a matter or personal and subjective opinion. One person's "minimum quality standards" may be another person's "overbuilding". Should disputes arise regarding issues of construction quality and workmanship, both homeowners and builders are often frustrated by the absence of a written, unbiased reference to deal with these issues. It is the intent of this Manual to provide that written reference.

The ***California Building Performance Guidelines for Residential Construction and Homeowner Maintenance Guide*** is available as a primary reference to both qualify and quantify residential construction issues. The authors have taken steps to prepare this Manual in a style that can be easily understood by a typical Homeowner. The book is not a technical manual written for the construction industry nor is it a "how to do it" manual describing specific methods to build or repair a house. There are numerous books on the market today describing the best methods and best practices for residential construction, and several of these books are noted in the Bibliography.

Introduction

The Purpose of This Manual

The primary purpose of this Manual is to provide the reader with Guidelines for the performance of his or her new house. The authors have been engaged in the business of research and analysis of construction practices for the past 20 years. The Performance Guidelines flow from their own knowledge and from construction industry data and publications (Refer to the section on Limitation on Liability on page 9). The authors have attempted to quantify nearly all of the possible conditions arising from new house construction and then apply a Performance Guideline to each condition. To put it simply, a guideline for construction is nothing more than the consensus of those persons or trade groups involved in the homebuilding business who have agreed upon a set of "rules" for fit and finish of houses. To accomplish the purpose of reasonable uniformity of guidelines, the authors have incorporated comments and changes from more than 70 industry professionals including homebuilders, specialty contractors, architects and engineers. Further reviews of the manuscript were conducted by government building officials, trade organizations and consumer interest groups. Ten California law firms, whose practices range from representing homebuilders to representing homeowners, have provided review and comments on this book. The process took three years.

A secondary purpose of the Manual is to set forth a guide for the Homeowner to perform certain essential maintenance items at his or her house. The Builder may provide this Manual to a Homeowner as part of an express limited warranty connected with the purchase contract. Accordingly, the purchase contract may also require that the Homeowner perform certain maintenance items as a condition of keeping the warranty in good standing. Homeowners should check to see if (and what) maintenance is expected of them to maintain their warranty, and if any conditions in this Manual are specifically excluded from their Builder's limited warranty.

If this Manual is given by the Builder to a Homeowner as part of a limited warranty document, the Homeowner is likely to have the right to contact the Builder regarding the non-performing condition and use this Manual as a point of reference. This Manual does not track with any particular home warranty program, and in fact warranties provided by homebuilding companies to their customers may specifically exclude or modify certain items that are covered in this Manual.

This Manual is organized by descriptions of common house construction problems, the components of the house possibly affected by the condition, the Performance Guideline, the Builder's Responsibility, and the Homeowner's Responsibility. If a Homeowner believes that a particular component or system of the house may not meet the Performance Guideline, the condition is likely to be found either in the chapter relating to that component of the house, or in the Index at the end of the Manual.

Codes

Many years ago, governmental officials decided it was appropriate for builders of houses to adhere to certain construction standards that affected the health, safety and welfare of the general populace. As a result, the first *Uniform Building Code* was published in 1927. The latest *Uniform Building Code* was published in 1997. These codes, in the past, present and future, are the minimum building requirement to which a Builder must build. As stated previously, the codes typically deal with health and safety issues in construction and do not deal with "fit and finish" or maintenance. The authors have been careful in producing the subject matter of this Manual, so as not to create a conflict between any applicable codes and the following Performance Guidelines. Codes are continuously changing, therefore if there are any conflicts between the subject matter of this Manual and the standards set forth in any current or future codes, the code standards should take precedence.

Definitions

The following definitions shall apply in this Manual:

- **After Market Contractor:** A person or company who constructs features and structures at the house after the Builder has completed his work. Examples of after market work are: swimming pools, landscaping, sidewalks and patios, decks, and trellises. In an attached multifamily project such as a townhouse or condominium, the Builder typically performs this work; in a single-family development, this work is usually performed by after market contractors who likely have no business relationship with the Builder.
- **Builder:** A person or company who has the primary responsibility for the construction of the house. This person or company typically has entered into a contract to build the house for the Homeowner, or conveys title to the original Homeowner upon completion of the house. For purposes of this Manual, a Builder does not have to be licensed by the Contractor's State License Board, but in the event that the Builder is not licensed, all construction work performed to build the residence must, by law, be performed by licensed contractors.
- **Performance Guideline:** A tolerance or level of reasonable expectation for the components of a house to be constructed so as to meet certain objectives relating to appearance, function, and longevity.
- **Contractor's State License Board:** An agency of the State of California, headquartered in Sacramento, that licenses, regulates, and disciplines the activities of contractors in the building industry.

- **Homeowner:** A person or entity that purchases a house from the Builder; may also be a person or entity that subsequently purchases a house from a previous Homeowner.

- **Homeowners Association:** A mutual benefit association (usually a non-profit corporation) of owners of residential property (most often a condominium or townhouse) who wish to have their common ownership interests managed according to their financial and maintenance objectives. The association is governed by an elected board of directors, and each member (Homeowner) pays monthly, quarterly or annual fees to the association in exchange for financial and maintenance services.

- **House:** Any single-family dwelling including a stand alone single-family house, a condominium, or attached townhouse. Specifically excluded from this definition are apartments.

- **Maintenance:** Work to be performed by Homeowners and Homeowners Associations to preserve the integrity of buildings and grounds so that neither shall fall into disrepair.

- **Warranty (Limited):** A contract or pledge given by a Builder to a Homeowner or Homeowners Association that describes, among other things, the covered components, the standards to which the house was built, what the Builder will do if the standards are not met, how long the standards will apply, and what the Homeowner must do in the form of maintenance to keep the warranty intact. Some components are not warranted by the Builder but may have the component manufacturer's warranty assigned to the Homeowner. Most warranties are limited and not all inclusive. The Homeowner should read the warranty carefully to understand its limitations.

- **Warranty Administrator:** Any person or entity that administers the Builder's warranty. This may include an independent third party, or it may be a designated and qualified person within the Builder's organization.

- **Weather (normal and extreme):** Long-term average ("normal") weather conditions can be determined by NOAA (National Oceanic and Atmospheric Administration) from most stations reported in NOAA's publications Climatological Data or Local Climatological Data. The definitions of wind speed and special wind regions are also defined in Section 1616A of the 1998 California Building Code. The great diversity of California climate contrasts is not fully represented by NOAA sites, and may require supplemental data and information determined to be suitable by NOAA and state experts in climate and hydrology, such as the California Department of Water Resources.

  For purposes of this Manual, extreme weather conditions shall have these two characteristics:
  1) The local weather event shall be classified as extreme by NOAA according to data taken from the nearest (to the occurrence) and most representative reporting weather station deemed suitable and reliable by the National Weather Service and other NOAA climate experts; and
  2) The local weather event shall also be classified as a 25-year return interval for the particular event in question (e.g., wind, precipitation, snowfall or snow depth, temperature) at that locale.

  Reports can be obtained from the NOAA website: http://lwf.ncdc.noaa.gov/oa/ncdc.html

Other industry terms appear in this Manual in ***blue, boldface, and italicized*** type. Definitions for these terms and phrases are found in the Glossary.

The Authors

David E. MacLellan

David MacLellan has been a California homebuilder since 1969. He has constructed nearly all types of housing including apartments, condominiums, townhouses, mobile home parks, planned unit developments, semi-custom homes, and custom homes. Mr. MacLellan is an engineering graduate from Penn State University with both bachelor's and master's degrees. He is licensed in California as a general building contractor and a real estate salesperson. As a frequent speaker on the subject of construction problems and their remedies, Mr. MacLellan has lectured to numerous professional groups, including the Pacific Coast Builder's Conference. He has founded 17 homeowner associations, and he served for nine years as president of the homeowner's association in the community where he lives. He has provided testimony in more than 200 lawsuits or disputes involving construction problems. Mr. MacLellan has been appointed as a Superior Court Referee concerning matters of land use and construction defects. His consulting firm, MacLellan Wolfson Associates, operates in California, Oregon and Washington.

George E. Wolfson, AIA

George Wolfson is a licensed architect, general building contractor, and real estate broker whose professional career spans more than three decades. Mr. Wolfson holds both bachelor's and master's degrees in architecture from the University of Houston and Columbia University respectively. His professional interest area with The American Institute of Architects includes Codes and Practices. As a principal in the consulting firm MacLellan Wolfson Associates, Mr. Wolfson has engaged in over 300 operations including field investigations, destructive testing, providing remedial architectural drawings and mediating disputes between owners and builders.

William J. Jorgensen

William Jorgensen has been active in residential and commercial construction in southern California for the past 26 years. Mr. Jorgensen is a licensed California general building contractor and is certified as a Phase 1 environmental inspector, certified deflooding specialist, as well as a federal and CAL/OSHA certified inspector. For the past five years, Mr. Jorgensen has worked as a construction defect expert for two of the largest underwriting insurance carriers in California. He has investigated in excess of 750 construction defect matters where he has given expert testimony in mediation and arbitration cases. Mr. Jorgensen's "hands on" experience includes framing, concrete, drywall and finish work. Mr. Jorgensen has recently co-authored a book entitled *Residential and Light Commercial Construction Standards*, which has been published by The RS Means Publishing Company.

How to Measure for Performance Guidelines

If a Homeowner believes a condition exists in his or her house that does not meet a Performance Guideline set forth in this Manual, the Homeowner should first make a measurement. In order to make the measurement, the following measuring tools and devices are typically needed:

1. A tape measure that has at least 1/16 inch markings, and that is 25 feet or longer;
2. Dividers (this tool looks like a compass except it has a point at the end, instead of a point and a pencil). Dividers can be purchased at most stationery stores or at a drafting supply store;
3. A carpenter's level at least 3 feet long;
4. A plumb bob and string at least 10 feet long;
5. A straight edge 8 feet long.

TOOLS TO MEASURE FOR PERFORMANCE STANDARDS

Items 1, 3, and 4 can be purchased at any hardware store. Item 5 can be any piece of material that is 8 feet long and perfectly straight. A good straight edge is a piece of dry, ¾ inch thick plywood that is 6 inches wide and 8 feet long. Make sure the factory or mill cut edge is the one used for measurement. Avoid using a piece of scrap that someone has cut with their own saw. CAUTION: Do not use a standard 8 foot 2 x 4 ***stud*** for this purpose because studs can warp so that they look straight, but really are not truly straight. If measurement of small cracks becomes necessary (such as separations of hardwood flooring), a good measurement tool is a set of feeler gauges. These can be purchased at any automotive supply store.

Examples of Measurement

- → **Concrete crack**: look at the crack and locate the widest point. Take the points of the dividers and place them just inside the edges of the crack. Without opening or closing the arms of the dividers, transfer the measurement to the tape measure and write it down.
- → **Wall out of plumb**: make a loop about 8 feet down in the string attached to the plumb bob (this assumes the wall being measured is 8 feet high. For walls greater or lesser, adjust the loop to the height of the wall). Using a nail or push pin, tack the string tight to the ceiling 2 inches out from the wall / ceiling intersection. Let the plumb bob hang freely so it almost touches the floor. When the plumb bob stops swinging, measure the largest gap along the string using the dividers. Transfer the measurement to a tape measure. Don't forget to

deduct 2 inches plus the thickness of the string. For walls that tilt out, tack the plumb bob string to the ceiling and let the side of the plumb bob barely touch the wall near the floor. Measure from the point of the plumb bob to the wall.

Responsibility of the Builder

Builders have the legal obligation to build a home in conformity with the representations that it makes to the Homeowner in writing and those that are implied by law. Representations or promises are usually contained in a Builder's warranty and may be subject to terms and conditions such as the time periods, Homeowner responsibilities, and the occurrence of naturally caused conditions. The law may also imply the house be constructed within certain performance tolerances, such as those contained in building codes and other standards.

This Manual works to assist in the identification of common conditions sometimes found in new home construction and help in the resolution of any disputes over the performance of new homes. Builders want to work with Homeowners to assure many years of problem free ownership. This is why Builders and other industry professionals have assisted the authors of this book to define these Performance Guidelines.

If a deviation from the Performance Guidelines is found to exist, either by acknowledgment of the Builder or through the various steps in a dispute resolution process set forth in the Homeowner's warranty, the Builder should correct the non-performing condition in a manner that brings the condition into conformance with the Performance Guidelines.

Responsibility of the Homeowner

This Manual also works to help Homeowners understand their new house, under what conditions they may get help from their Builder, what to expect as being normal performance of their house, and what obligations they face in terms of proper maintenance and use.

Since a house is a complex structure, it is important that the Homeowner and Builder work together in a cooperative fashion to prolong the performance of the house. If a Homeowner observes **any** condition that appears to be unusual or threatening regarding construction, he or she has a duty to notify the Builder immediately. Further if the condition is an emergency and a potential life safety situation, and the Builder cannot be contacted (such as a weekend or holiday), the Homeowner has a duty to mitigate his or her damages. That is to say, rather than allow the condition to continue, and possibly worsen because the Builder could not be reached, the Homeowner must contract with others to make temporary emergency repairs. Many Builders offer 24 hr. emergency repair numbers for this purpose. Failure to provide timely notification could lead to a worsening condition for which the Builder may not be responsible.

The Homeowner also has a duty to maintain the surrounding grounds and structures, whether or not they were installed by the Builder. Maintenance should be performed in accordance with the maintenance manual provided by the Builder with the warranty, or in the absence of a maintenance manual, in accordance with generally accepted homeowner maintenance procedures, several of which are included in this Manual.

The Walkthrough

The Walkthrough is the event where the Builder delivers and demonstrates the new House to the Homeowner. The Walkthrough is sometimes referred to as "taking delivery" of the House. Regardless of what it is called, the Walkthrough is one of the single most important events that requires participation by the Homeowner. Adequate time must be reserved by both the Builder and Homeowner to learn about the care, maintenance, and use of the House, as well as to inspect the condition and "fit and finish" of the House. A general rule of thumb is that one hour of Walkthrough time should be allowed for every 1,000 square feet of house. Taking the time to make a comprehensive Walkthrough is especially important to the Homeowner because non-performing conditions that are readily observable during the Walkthrough may become the Homeowner's responsibility if they are not noted at the time of Walkthrough. Typically, areas such as countertops, finish flooring, doors, walls, windows, and mirrors could be damaged with scrapes, scratches, and marrs that result from the moving in of household goods. For these reasons, it is essential that all Homeowners participate with the Builder during this important step in home ownership.

It should be noted that most Builders do not allow early Walkthroughs or partial Walkthroughs prior to the completion of the House for the following reasons:

1) Potential liability resulting from construction conditions;
2) Last minute items will be completed as part of the normal "punch list" process;
3) Disruption to the production schedule of the Builder.

Limitation on Liability

The intent of the ***California Building Performance Guidelines for Residential Construction*** is to provide information for use by homeowners, homebuilders, subcontractors, and governmental entities in dealing with matters of residential construction, particularly issues regarding workmanship. The Guidelines published herein are based upon research and reports obtained by the authors and the publisher, The Building Standards Institute. The Building Standards Institute, Homeowners Education Association, LLC, and the authors assume no liability for the design or manner of construction utilized by any users of this publication, whether in compliance or not with this publication. Each user should consult with his or her own design professionals for incorporation of any Guidelines or designs in their product. Further, if this publication is given by a Builder to a Homeowner or Homeowners Association as part of a limited warranty offered by the Builder, the Builder assumes no liability for the content of this publication other than to incorporate this publication by reference and be to bound by some or all of the Performance Guidelines as more particularly stated in the Builder's warranty. The authors and publisher are not engaged in rendering legal, accounting, or related professional services or advice.

The authors have diligently attempted to research and quantify conditions commonly known in residential construction. In addition to their own experience, the authors consulted with numerous homebuilding industry organizations and technical support groups. Persons interested in providing additional content are invited to express their comments to the authors at their e-mail address: macwolf@buildingstandardsinstitute.org for possible inclusions in future editions of this Manual. It is important to note that the Building Performance Guidelines set forth in this Manual are effective only beginning with the first date of publication.

The following subjects are intentionally not covered in this Manual because of their specialized characteristics:

1. Swimming Pools
2. Home Theaters
3. Solar Heating
4. Electronic Home Managers
5. Computer and Fiber Optic Systems
6. Regulations of the Americans With Disabilities Act

It is anticipated that future editions of this Manual will include information on the above and other systems as more information becomes known about them.

After Market Contractors

At the time a subdivision of new homes nears completion and Homeowners are beginning to occupy their new homes, business opportunities arise for after market contractors. Typically, these contractors have no relationship with the Builder or the Builder's subcontractors. After market contractors often provide goods and services such as swimming pools, security systems, landscaping, deck, patio and masonry work. After market contractors can perform valuable services that may add to the beauty and enjoyment of the house. Since these contractors were generally not involved in the original design and construction of the house, it is important that special attention is paid to the work performed by these contractors. If the after market work is not carefully integrated into the original construction, problems may arise that could potentially lead to unsatisfactory performance of the new house.

Unfortunately, many after market contractors are not licensed. The State of California requires any person or company performing improvement work on a residence to possess a current contractor's license. A contract for work in excess of $500 must, by law, be in writing. For the most part, ordinary household repair work is exempted from the license requirement. However, nearly all after market work on a new house requires a license. In many cases, it also requires a building permit.

WARNING

Often times an unlicensed contractor's pitch to a new Homeowner is:

- ☒ A license is not needed for the work that we do;
- ☒ We can do it cheaper because we're not licensed;
- ☒ No building permit is needed for this work.

The lure of a cheap price often results in shoddy and incomplete workmanship. An unlicensed contractor typically carries no insurance and does not pay payroll taxes. Further, it is a misdemeanor in the State of California for any person (such as a new homeowner) to enter into a contract, either oral or written, with an unlicensed contractor. This is called aiding and abetting an unlicensed contractor.

A Homeowner should always deal with a licensed contractor. All licensed California contractors are issued a pocket identification card. Out of state contractors may not operate in California without a California license. In addition, the Contractor's State License Board has an automatic telephone response system that enables anyone to check on the validity of a license and any disciplinary action taken against a contractor. The toll-free number is 1-800-321-2752. The same information can be obtained from the License Board's website at http://www.cslb.ca.gov.

Ten Most Common Mistakes Made by New Homeowners

1. **Alteration of Finished Grades.** Alteration of finished grades by the Homeowner or an after market contractor results in some of the most costly claims made in the construction defect arena. Unlike a condominium or planned unit developments where the Builder customarily installs the walkways, patios, landscaping, and drainage systems (and thus may become liable for their performance), a single family residence is often delivered without any of these items except a driveway. At a very minimum, the Building Code requires that the house be delivered to the Homeowner with the surrounding bare lot sloped away from the house at a 2% ***slope***. Several cities and counties in California require slopes greater than 2%. A slight V-shaped impression is cut in the lot, called a ***swale***. Rainwater is intended to flow away from the house, to the swale, and then eventually to the street or some other approved storm water collection system. Unfortunately, the Homeowner or an after market contractor will often pour the sidewalks and patios directly on top of the finished grade thus altering the water flow by trapping it between the walkway and the house. Swimming pool contractors have been known to set their decks and coping too high, causing water to flow back toward the house. Often, the net effect of altering the storm water flow around the house causes it to seep under the foundation. Many California soils that are high in clay content will not permit water to readily pass through. This means that the wet soil can swell (expand) to up to 30% of its dry volume. The swelling soil actually lifts the house foundation upward and can cause extensive interior and exterior damage.

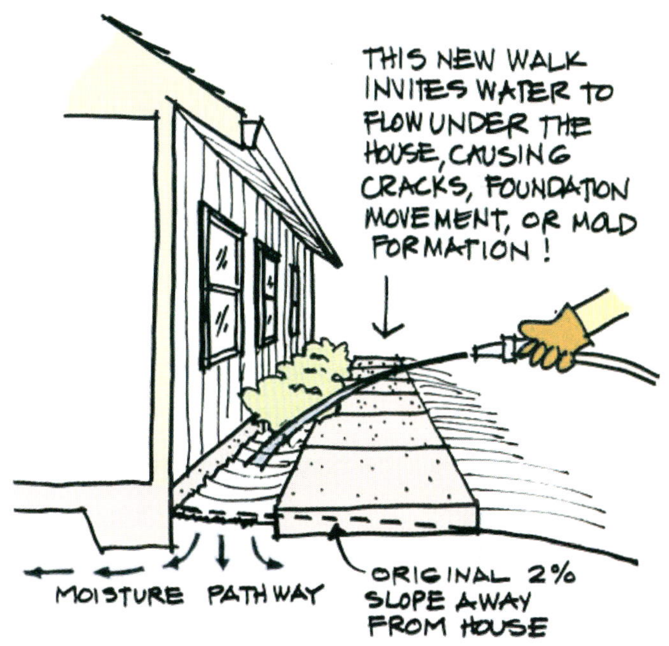

2. **Concrete Patio Poured Too High.** In addition to being poured with a 2% slope, a concrete patio or deck should be poured at least two inches below door thresholds or the stucco weep screed (a weep screed is the metal band at the bottom of the stucco just above the ground). The weep screed allows water that may be behind the stucco to “weep” out and run down the foundation. Pouring the patio or deck too high can result in rainwater being drawn back up into the stucco or behind the siding. As a result, decay of the structure may occur. This condition

also provides an excellent route for termites to enter the building. Since the finished grade should be maintained 6 inches below the house slab, any installed concrete work should not trap water against the foundation. In addition, planters should not be allowed to fill above the required grade.

3. **Deck Trellis, Sunscreen, or Lanai Structure Attached Improperly.** This description includes other structures that are connected to the house. There are many proper ways to create a watertight connection between the deck trellis or the lanai structure and the house. Unfortunately, these "add on structures" are often just nailed or bolted directly to the outside wall of the house. Inevitably, rainwater finds its way into the penetrations and the ***dryrot*** process begins. It is critical that the ledger (the board that is placed up against the side of the house) be either flashed with a metal flashing or caulked in an industry approved manner. If bolts are used to attach the ledger board to the house, the boltholes should be filled with caulk. **Note: Nearly all local governments require a building permit to construct a trellis or lanai that is attached to the house.** A trellis or lanai is considered a structure that could fall down and cause injury; hence a building permit is usually required. Construction of a deck or patio typically does not require a building permit, unless it is 30 inches or more off the ground.

4. **Irrigation Sprinkler Heads Spray Against the House.** Irrigation sprinkler heads that spray against the wood siding, masonry, or stucco walls of a house can lead to rotted walls and leaching of the color from the stucco. Exterior walls are not constructed to withstand the rigors of constant exposure to landscape irrigation. Irrigation water that ponds at the base of a foundation can lead to upward movement of the foundation. It is important that all irrigation spray be directed away from the house rather than towards the house. Spray heads should be checked regularly during the irrigation season to make sure that they have not become twisted and point toward the house. It is also important to recognize that as landscaping grows, spray heads should be raised, relocated, or in some cases eliminated, to keep moisture away from the side of the house. Particularly vulnerable to irrigation spray are posts from overhead decks that have shrubbery growing closely around them.

5. **Bathroom and Laundry Vent Fans Disconnected or Unused.** Bathrooms and laundries are areas of high humidity. Bathroom and laundry fans should never be disconnected (even though the noise may bother the occupant), and the fan should always be turned on during use. Failure to use the vent fans can result in water vapor getting into the drywall, the electrical outlets and even the framing members. Over time, mold, mildew and fungi

may grow in these areas. Water vapor that condenses on walls and windows can eventually find its way into the structure of the house and weaken the structure through ***dryrot***. Rooms where humidifiers are used should also be well ventilated.

6. **Walking on the Roof.** A Homeowner should never walk on his or her roof. Not only can walking on the roof be a slip and fall hazard, but untrained persons are likely to break the roof covering and cause roof leaks. Most houses built today have one of three types of roof covers: concrete or clay tile, wood shakes or shingles, or composition shingles. A few houses today are constructed with "flat" roofs, sometimes known as built up roofs. Cleaning of gutters should be done from a ladder and not by standing on the roof. If an object is thrown on the roof, such as a child's toy, it should be retrieved using a ladder and a telescoping pole rather than by walking on the roof. Most residential warranties exclude damage resulting from unauthorized persons walking on roofs.

7. **Upper Cabinets Overloaded.** While lower cabinets rest on the floor, upper cabinets are hung from a wall using screws or nails. By stacking heavy dishes and glassware in upper cabinets, a Homeowner can load the cabinet beyond its capacity. This can result in sagging shelves, or worse yet, detachment of the cabinet from the wall. Heavy china and cookware should always be placed in the lower cabinets. In a related item, cabinet drawers are often overloaded and then pulled out too far. This action results in the plastic guide being snapped off at the back of the cabinet drawer.

8. **Floor System Overloaded.** Builders have a choice of many wooden floor systems to install in their homes. Regardless of system chosen, all systems must meet the minimum requirements for floor deflection (up and down movement) that are set forth in the Building Code. Many Homeowners are surprised to learn the Building Code permits more deflection than that which they may be comfortable. Household items such as waterbeds, pool tables, and weight lifting equipment can cause significant floor deflection, although the house was built in accordance with the Code. Many houses have a concrete slab first floor and a wooden second floor. It is best to keep heavy items on the first floor, if possible, particularly if the first floor is a concrete slab.

9. **Storage of Household Goods on the Garage and Attic Trusses.** The garage and attic ***trusses*** are designed to support the weight of the roof and ceiling and not the weight of anything else. Unfortunately, many Homeowners view the space in the attic and above the garage ceiling as additional space for storage. Storing household goods in these areas can result in sagging of the roof or possible collapse of the roof. If a Homeowner wishes to use this space for storage, he or she should consult with a structural engineer to determine if additional reinforcement is necessary.

DO NOT USE ATTIC FOR STORAGE
-IT WASN'T DESIGNED FOR THAT USE!

10. **Tinting of Dual Pane Windows.** Many new homes in California are constructed with dual pane windows (also known as double-glazed windows and insulating windows). The two panes of glass are separated by a spacer up to 5/8 inch in thickness. The air space between the dual panes is "dead air". This area is so tightly sealed that air can neither enter nor leave the space. By placing a tinting film on the inside of the window, the sun's rays are reflected back into the dead air space. The temperature in this space can become so hot that it may cause the "rubber-like" seal to rupture, and the insulating value of the window is lost. Windows with broken or ruptured seals are easy to identify: they have moisture between the panes of glass. Homeowners should never tint a dual pane window on the inside unless it is specifically approved by the window manufacturer.

Additional Problems to be Avoided by New Homeowners

☒ **Hanging a Ceiling Fan From a Light Fixture Box.**
Light fixture boxes in the ceiling are not designed to carry the weight of a ceiling fan. Ceiling fans have a special mounting box that requires a different mounting system than a typical light fixture box. If a ceiling fan is hung from a light fixture box, the vibration of the fan and the weight of the fan may cause the box to rip out of the ceiling. Ceiling fans also have special electrical connection requirements that differ from ordinary light fixtures.

☒ **Placing Plastic Deflectors Over Furnace Vents.**
These vents, known as warm air supply grills, are often placed in front of a window or slider door (either in the floor or ceiling). They are designed to sweep the air from these areas and mix it with the air in the center of the room. By placing these deflectors over the grills, the Homeowner creates a space of stagnant air with high humidity during the rainy season. Moisture condenses on the windows and often rots the windowsills and structural members inside the wall. Mold and mildew are likely to grow in these areas. Plastic deflectors should never be used on warm air supply grills.

☒ **Cracking Fireplace Linings.**
Generally, fireplace linings are two types: a cast panel of simulated brick or real brick with mortar between each brick. All fireplaces require a series of low heat fires to "cure" the fireplace lining. By initially building a very hot fire (such as burning sawdust, wax logs, newspapers, or gift wrappings), intense heat can be generated and cause the fireplace lining to crack. Never burn paper or other composite products in the fireplace. Be certain to follow the manufacturer's instructions at all times.

☒ **Placing Rugs or Non-breathable Coverings Over Wood and Synthetic Decks.**
Decks need to breathe, even decks with synthetic coatings. By placing non-breathable coverings (such as indoor/outdoor carpeting) over wood and synthetic decks, moisture will be trapped between the bottom of the covering and the top of the deck. This can result in rot and premature failure of the deck.

☒ **Security Alarm Installation / Penetration of Windows and Walls.**
If an after market alarm is installed by the Homeowner, or by a contractor who has not been hired by the Builder, great care should be taken to seal all penetrations through windows and walls to avoid future dryrot. Never drill into the bottom track of a window or door to install an alarm contact.

☒ **Nailing Fences to House Walls.**
Nailing any part of a fence to a house wall invites two problems: Trapping rainwater between the fence post and the house wall, and the invasion of termites through the fence into the house structure. The terminating fence post should be placed in the ground beside the foundation and should not be attached to or come in contact with the house.

Performance Guidelines

The following nine chapters cover more than 300 Performance Guidelines for residential construction.

When reading a section of particular interest, the following hints are offered to avoid misinterpretation and misunderstanding:

- → Is the condition identified in this Manual*? Check the Index if the condition is not listed in the Table of Contents.
- → If a measurement is necessary to determine the Guideline, have you measured accurately? See **How to Measure for Performance Guidelines** on page 6.
- → Have you allowed the condition to get worse before notifying the Builder?
- → Is the condition covered under the Builder's limited warranty or excluded from the Builder's limited warranty? Check the warranty for exclusions and expirations before notifying the Builder.
- → Is the condition a maintenance item? For example: the eave leaks because the gutters were not cleaned.
- → Is the condition Homeowner caused? For example: the roof leaks because an after market satellite dish installer broke the roof tiles.

(*) If the condition is not identified in this Manual, you may describe it via email to the Building Standards Institute. Contact the Building Standards Institute from their website: http://www.buildingstandardsinstitute.org. In most cases, the Building Standards Institute will reply accordingly. Please note that the Building Standards Institute does not furnish legal advice.

Use of This Manual in Other States

Although this Manual contains the name "California" in its title, most of the guidelines are derived from national standards or guidelines. Further, many of the contributing trade associations are based in other states and have chapters or affiliates in California. Unless specific reference is made to a California Code or a "California only" Guideline, the Manual should serve as a useful reference in other states.

Chapter One

FOUNDATIONS

includes:

Slab on Grade

Grade Beam and Pier

Basements

References for this chapter:

- *Concrete Performance Standards & Maintenance Guidelines*
- *Residential Construction Performance Guidelines*, NAHB
- *Residential Water Problems*, by Alvin Sacks
- *Residential & Light Commercial Construction Standards*, by Don Reynolds
- *Uniform Building Code*, 1997 ed.
- *Workmanship Guidelines*, CA Contractors State License Board

A comprehensive list of references by author and publisher is found in the Bibliography section.

Foundations

General Subject Information: In California, the majority of new houses are built on slab foundations. These foundations consist of reinforced concrete that is poured on a prepared grade. Reinforcing can consist of steel rods called ***rebar*** or welded wire mesh, or the reinforcing can be cables that are stretched tight after pouring the concrete. This is known as a post tensioned slab. Another popular type of foundation is known as the grade beam and pier system. This system consists of ***piers*** drilled into the ground and filled with reinforcing steel and concrete. The piers are connected to low concrete perimeter and interior walls. Another type of foundation is known as the basement foundation and is commonly installed in homes in the East and Midwest. Some older homes and custom homes in California have basements that consist of a room or rooms below the ground level.

Slab on Grade

Condition #1: CONCRETE "SLAB-ON-GRADE" FOUNDATION IS CRACKED

Can Affect:

- Slab foundations
- Garage floors
- Basement floors
- Structural integrity

Performance Guideline: Cracks that occur in slab-on-grade floors should not exceed 3/16 inch in width or 1/8 inch in vertical displacement over any 12 inches in length. For slab floors that are to be covered with vinyl flooring or similar material, cracks should not be visible in the finish floor at a distance of six feet under normal daylight conditions.

Comments: Concrete cracks for many reasons, with the worst cracks caused by expansive (clay like) soils that shrink or expand based upon water content in the soil. Cracking is an inherent nature of a cement product, and no matter how careful the Builder is, it still cracks. Soil expansion related cracks usually appear as vertical displacement rather than horizontal cracks that stay in the same plane. For slab-on-grade floors, a small amount of moisture under the slab is beneficial because it keeps the soil from drying out and shrinking.

Builder Responsibility: Because some concrete cracking is inevitable, the Builder cannot be held responsible for all concrete cracks. However, if the slab-on-grade concrete cracks are greater than the acceptable Guideline, the Builder should repair the concrete in a manner that will meet the above Performance Guideline. Usually the repair consists of filling the crack with a latex fortified cement mixture or epoxy.

Homeowner Responsibility: ***Maintenance Alert!*** The finished grade along the foundation must ***slope*** a minimum of ¼ inch per 1-foot away from the foundation to allow for proper drainage.

→ It is recommended that the Homeowner install ***drip irrigation*** along the foundation for better water control. This will eliminate any over-spray onto the House or concrete foundation.
→ Periodic inspections of the irrigation system, materials, and slopes are necessary for proper and adequate maintenance.
→ If rain is forecast, the Homeowner should put the irrigation controller on "RAIN" setting.
→ If the Builder has not installed gutters and downspouts, it is highly recommended that a gutter and downspout system be installed by the Homeowner and piped away from the foundation.

Condition #2: CONCRETE SLAB IS NOT LEVEL

Can Affect:

- Slab floors
- Basement floors

Performance Guideline: The slab should be level and even, and any deviations should not exceed 1/2 inch of vertical change in 20 feet of length.

Comments: Concrete floors poured in an area that will be ultimately covered with another material should be poured as flat as possible. Some adjustments can be made when setting tile and marble and installing hardwood flooring. Basement slabs may have drains in them, and it is proper for the Builder to slope the slab toward the ***drains***. Garage slabs are intentionally sloped from the inside wall toward the garage door to allow water from wet cars to drain toward the garage door.

Builder Responsibility: Builder should conduct an investigation to determine the cause of the condition. If the condition is a result of improper construction and not a result of improper use or lack of maintenance by Homeowner, Builder should then make the necessary repairs to bring the slab back into conformance with the Performance Guideline.

Homeowner Responsibility: None.

Condition #3: CONCRETE SLAB IS UNEVEN

Can Affect:

- Foundation slab
- Basement slab

Performance Guideline: Concrete floors should not have areas of unevenness of more than ¼ inch over a horizontal distance of 10 feet.

Comments: Except for floors that are specifically designed to slope to drains (such as basement floors or certain decks), unevenness in concrete, known as undulations or "wows", should be avoided during finishing of the slab. Smoothing an uneven concrete slab is not difficult, and many remedies are available.

Builder Responsibility: If the Performance Guideline is exceeded, Builder should, using an industry-accepted method, repair the floor to meet the Guideline.

Homeowner Responsibility: None.

Grade Beam and Pier

Condition #1: EXTERIOR FOUNDATION GRADE BEAM IS OUT OF LEVEL

Can Affect:
- Floor
- Walls
- Roof structure

Performance Guideline: Over 40 feet of length, the top surface of the ***grade beam*** should be no more than 1 inch lower than the highest point, and no more than 1 inch higher than the lowest point. If the length of measurement is shorter, the allowable deviation is reduced proportionately.

Comments: A "benchmark" is a given height for which the Builder and/or designer have agreed for the height of the grade beam to be installed. The term "level" is actually a comparison above and below a theoretical elevation, i.e. benchmarks.

Builder Responsibility: Furnish and install a level ***foundation*** for the House to be built upon. If the Performance Guideline is not met, adjust the foundation or ***mudsill*** to conform to the Guideline.

Homeowner Responsibility: None.

Condition #2: FOUNDATION GRADE BEAM IS OUT OF SQUARE

Can Affect:
- The installation of finish materials such as cabinets, tiles, countertops, i.e. anything that is square or rectangular in shape

Performance Guideline: If measuring the top of the grade beam: from the corner, measure one direction 12 feet. From the original starting point of the wall, measure 90 degrees the other direction 16 feet (*12 feet and 16 feet from the corner should be at a 90 degree angle to one another*). The diagonal distance should be within 1 inch in 20 feet.

Comments: A grade beam that is out of square does not structurally compromise the House. However it may become an appearance issue and create extra work to "custom fit" finish materials.

Builder Responsibility: If the foundation is out of square more than the Performance Guideline and this is materially affecting the performance of the residence, the Builder should correct the out-of-square foundation by making proper adjustments--most likely in the frame.

Homeowner Responsibility: None.

Condition #3: EXPOSED WOOD AROUND PIERS OR GRADE BEAMS

Can Affect:
- Integrity of the wood structure

Performance Guideline: The House should be completed with all wood or paper/cardboard removed from the ***crawl space*** and around the grade beam and piers. The only exception to this is cardboard that is wax treated and used to create a void under the grade beam as part of the construction process. Unless wood is ***pressure treated*** or foundation grade redwood, it cannot be placed within six inches of the ground.

Comments: Wood material is an attraction for termites and encourages infestation within the structure of the House.

Builder Responsibility: If building practices result in wood or paper materials left in the crawl spaces and near the grade beams, Builder should remove the materials.

Homeowner Responsibility: *Maintenance Alert!* Keep all wood or paper products from beneath the House and/or away from the foundation. Avoid attaching anything wooden to the House (such as a fence post) if it makes contact with the earth. Do not store wood or paper products in the crawl space.

Condition #4: EFFLORESCENCE (white powder) APPEARS ON CONCRETE SURFACES

Can Affect:
- Garage floors
- Driveways and walks
- Foundation walls

Performance Guideline: Efflorescence on concrete surfaces is considered acceptable. This condition often occurs when one of the ingredients in the cement reacts with moist air.

Builder Responsibility: None.

Homeowner Responsibility: If the efflorescence is considered unsightly by the Homeowner, it can be removed with a brush and water. For more stubborn areas, brush area with a mixture of one cup of white vinegar to a bucket of water.

Condition #5: CONCRETE APPEARS TO BE DETERIORATING OR DISINTEGRATING (Sulfates)

Can Affect:

- Concrete / foundation slab integrity
- Moisture levels inside structure

Performance Guideline: Minimum Performance Guidelines are met by following general Uniform Building Code requirements regarding sulfates and concrete mix design.

General Subject Information: The effect of sulfates in the soil on concrete has been researched and debated for more than 70 years and is still not totally understood. Sulfate exposure can be a result of an "external" or "internal" source. External sources are the naturally occurring sulfates in the environment. Another external source are those sulfates that are a product of industrial processes or various human activities, i.e. fertilizers used in landscaping. A third external source is and excessive ground water combined with minerals in the surrounding soils that are incompatible with the concrete mix. Internal sources of sulfates may include the sulfates introduced in the concrete; i.e. "dirty aggregate" (rock) from which concrete is made. Despite multiple sources, the potential for sulfate causing structural problems is extremely small.

Comments: The time to eliminate and/or reduce sulfate exposure is during the design and construction phase. Studies have shown that sulfate attack can be greatly reduced by: (1) Conducting lab analysis on soils for specific minerals, i.e. sulfides and sulfates; (2) Incorporating sulfate resistant concrete in the design; (3) Insuring that good clean aggregate is used; and (4) By following the water-cement ratio of the mix design during the pour. These steps will help reduce and/or eliminate the potential for sulfate exposure.

ONLY USE SULFATE-FREE FERTILIZER NEAR THE HOUSE

Builder Responsibility: Builder should conduct adequate testing of the soils to determine the compatibility of the existing soils mineral content and the concrete mix being used. If it has been determined that the soils contain sulfates, the Builder must use (per Code) a concrete mix design with a water-cement ratio that reduces the sulfate attack. The Builder is responsible for concrete installed on soils that have not been thoroughly tested for minerals containing sulfates.

Homeowner Responsibility: ***Maintenance Alert!*** Homeowners should not use fertilizers that are high in sulfates in and/or around foundations. Watering around concrete, specifically foundations, should be kept to a minimum. Do not flood areas adjacent to foundations. Excessive irrigation by the Homeowner will cause problems and is not a Builder's responsibility. Keeping adequate drainage away from the building foundation is a maintenance item.

Basements

General Subject Information: A basement is that portion of the house that extends below the surrounding grade. Basements can be partial (usually found in houses built on hillsides) or full (completely under the first floor). Full basements are not common in new homes built in the western United States. Crawl spaces do not qualify as basements. Additionally, basements are usually constructed for two distinct uses: utility or habitability. Examples of utility are storage, workshop, laundry, and location of mechanical equipment. Examples of habitability are au pair setup, bonus room, bedroom, home theater, and arts and crafts room. It is important to distinguish between the two uses when applying Performance Guidelines.

Typically, basements consist of poured concrete walls or concrete block walls and a concrete slab floor. Because the basement is below grade, care must be taken during construction (and thereafter by the Homeowner) to limit moisture intrusion. A basement that is built and marketed as habitable space (or future habitable space) is likely to have finished wall and floor coverings placed over their concrete surfaces. Code approved heating and ventilation must be installed. Therefore, the Performance Guidelines that apply to basements intended for habitable use are the same Performance Guidelines that apply to the rest of the house. In other words, the slab of habitable basement floor is considered the same as a slab-on-grade floor; habitable basement walls are considered the same as upstairs walls.

The following are Performance Guidelines for basement spaces built for utility purposes with poured concrete walls or concrete block walls and poured concrete floors.

Condition #1: WATER TRICKLES INTO BASEMENT THROUGH WALLS OR FLOOR

Can Affect:

- Usability of the space
- Condition of stored goods
- Moisture levels in habitable areas

Performance Guideline: Water should not trickle or seep through basement walls or floors.

Comments: Because basements are built below grade, they will be damp in winter months. Basements built for utility purposes do not have the same requirements for heating, cooling and ventilation as habitable basements. Condensation on walls should not be confused with an actual leak from the outside.

Builder Responsibility: Assuming that the finished grades have not been negatively altered, or that any Homeowner installed items such as planter beds, flatwork, or irrigation have not altered the flow of water, or the Homeowner has not damaged any installed waterproofing system (if any), the Builder should make the necessary repairs to keep water from trickling or seeping through basement walls or floors.

Homeowner Responsibility: Avoid making any changes to the surrounding grades that would cause rain or irrigation water to flow down the outside of the basement walls. This includes over-watering, constructing planter beds without independent drainage, building "dams" between foundations and raised walkways and failure to keep ***swales*** and yard drains cleaned out. If basement dampness is an issue, the Homeowner should install a dehumidifier. In no event should the moisture barrier on the outside of the basement wall be damaged when planting or irrigation is installed.

Condition #2: BASEMENT WALLS ARE NOT PLUMB

Can Affect:

- Appearance
- Structural integrity

Performance Guideline: Basement walls are considered out of plumb if they exceed more than 1½ inches in 8 vertical feet.

Builder Responsibility: If the Performance Guideline is not met, the Builder should take corrective action to bring the wall into conformance with the Guideline.

Homeowner Responsibility: None.

Condition #3: BASEMENT WALLS ARE BOWED

Can Affect:

- Appearance
- Structural integrity

Performance Guideline: Walls should not bow more than 1 inch in 8 feet (measured either horizontally or vertically).

Builder Responsibility: If the Performance Guideline is not met, the Builder should take corrective action to bring the wall into conformance with the Guideline.

Homeowner Responsibility: None.

Condition #4: BASEMENT WALLS HAVE CRACKS OR HOLES, FLOORS HAVE CRACKS

Can Affect:

- Appearance
- Water tightness

Performance Guideline: Cracks in basement walls should not exceed ¼ inch. Voids should not exceed 1 inch in diameter and 1 inch in depth. Cracks in basement floors should not exceed ¼ inch in width and 3/16 inch in vertical displacement.

Builder Responsibility: Assuming cracks and voids do not leak, the Builder should make a cosmetic repair (such as patching).

Homeowner Responsibility: None.

Landslides and Other Soil Movement

Comments: Landslides and other soil movement, together called subsidence, are mentioned in the Foundations Chapter because that is the first House component likely to be affected by subsidence. However, other components of the House can also be adversely affected, such as the frame, stucco, plumbing, drywall and window and door operations.

Landslides and settling soil are occurrences that begin beneath the soil surface, as opposed to erosion, which is a surface activity. Most soil in California is subject to movement. Subsidence may be caused by construction practices including poor drainage, improper compaction of trenches and foundation pads, building on land that was once a lake bottom or tidal estuary, cutting hillsides, or by other geologic activities that occur deep within the earth and not directly around the neighborhood. Soil movement can also be the result of after market construction such as patios and landscaping improvements, by overwatering, or by drainage changes. Soil movement and drainage should be part of every Homeowner's concern when making after market improvements to their home or during maintenance.

Problems arising from soil subsidence are very complex issues and are not within the scope of this Manual for discussion. These issues are best referred to geotechnical consultants. If a Homeowner notices any abnormal soil movement activity or the results there-from (such as hill slippage, excessive trench or foundation settlement, or large cracks in the foundation, slab, stucco, or drywall), he or she should notify the Builder promptly. It is very likely that the Builder retained a geotechnical consultant as part of the project approval process and may be able to quickly assess whether the movement is cause for concern.

Chapter Two

includes:

Floor Squeaks

Wood Subfloors / Ceilings
Square and Level

Wood Beams / Posts

References for this chapter:

- ***Residential Construction Performance Guidelines*, NAHB**
- ***Residential & Light Commercial Construction Standards*, by Don Reynolds**
- ***Troubleshooting Guide to Residential Construction*, Builderburg Group**
- ***Uniform Building Code*, 1997 ed.**
- ***Workmanship Guidelines*, CA Contractors State License Board**

A comprehensive list of references by author and publisher is found in the Bibliography section.

Floors and Ceilings

General Subject Information: Floors and ceilings begin their formation during the "rough" carpentry stage of house construction. Rough carpentry generally deals with the structural portion of a building that supports the floors, ceilings, walls and roofs. Finish floor coverings are discussed in Chapter Six, Interior Components. Usually the rough carpentry is covered up by an assortment of interior and exterior finishes including, but not limited to: drywall, plaster, paneling, stucco, siding, brick veneer, floor coverings, i.e. carpet, vinyl, hardwood and others. Lumber used for decks that is exposed to the weather will need scheduled maintenance in order to eliminate premature aging and deterioration. The following conditions are issues that seem to show up most often and have become the largest concerns.

Condition #1: FLOOR SQUEAKS

Can Affect:
- Occupant comfort

Performance Guideline: Squeaks that are caused by loose sub-floors, i.e. plywood floor sheathing, loose nails or fasteners, may be considered unacceptable if the subject floor squeaks, noticeably and continuously. NOTE: A squeak-proof floor cannot be guaranteed due to seasonal weather conditions that cause the frame to expand and contract.

Comments: The best method of installation is to glue the subfloor to the ***joists*** and then screw the subfloor to the joists. A wood sub-floor can squeak as a result of an underlying joist coming loose from the plywood sheathing. This in turn may cause a squeak as a result of a nail or fastener working its way loose. As a person steps onto the plywood sheathing, i.e. in a location that the plywood has lost its bond with the floor joist, the plywood may rub up and down on the nail causing a squeak. The squeak can also be a result of the plywood itself flexing. Installing a screw into the wood floor joist through the plywood floor sheathing will generally eliminate a floor squeak.

Builder Responsibility: Any wood sub-floor that does not meet the above Performance Guideline and is a direct result of an improperly installed floor joist, fastener and/or sheathing, should be repaired by the Builder as necessary. Sub-floor squeaks should be repaired to meet the above Guideline.

Homeowner Responsibility: Floor squeaks are likely to occur with seasonal weather changes, and they usually become a maintenance item.

Condition #2: WOOD SUBFLOORS OR CEILINGS ARE NOT FLAT

Can Affect:
- Flooring
- Appearance

Performance Guideline: Any floor or ceiling that exceeds ¼ inch depression or ridge in a 32 inch by 32 inch area should be considered non-performing.

Comments: Because wood is a natural product, some minor framing imperfections can and should be expected.

Builder Responsibility: The Builder should be responsible for any condition that exceeds the above Performance Guideline. The Builder should repair the subject area as necessary including any existing structure or finish materials that may be destroyed and/or damaged because of the repair.

Homeowner Responsibility: None.

Condition #3: WOOD SUBFLOORS ARE OUT OF LEVEL

Can Affect:

- Occupant comfort
- Furniture placement

Performance Guideline: No point on the surface of a wood subfloor should be more than ½ inch higher or lower than any other point on that same surface within 20 feet.

Comments: This Performance Guideline applies to all wood floors in living space only. Decks or other floors that have a predetermined slope for drains and/or drainage are excluded from this Performance Guideline.

Builder Responsibility: The Builder should repair as necessary the non-performing area to meet the above Performance Guideline.

Homeowner Responsibility: Do not store excessively heavy objects on a wood subfloor. *Refer to Preface:* **"Ten Most Common Mistakes Made by New Homeowners",** *Item #8.*

Condition #4: WOOD SUBFLOORS HAVE "SPRINGINESS" OR BOUNCE

Can Affect:

- Furniture placement
- Occupant comfort

Performance Guideline: All floor joists should meet the required size and rating as set forth in the applicable Building Code for the city or county in effect at the time the House was constructed. If manufactured floor trusses are used, the span and spacing should conform to the manufacturer's engineered calculations.

Comments: Floors that are over-spanned or inadequately supported by the wood floor joist or blocking may exhibit a bounce or deflection. This can affect the structural integrity of the subfloor as well as become a nuisance to the Homeowner. Often long spanned floors exhibit this tendency although they meet the deflection standard permitted in the Building Code.

Builder Responsibility: If the floors are over-spanned for the grade of lumber permitted, or if the truss manufacturer's span recommendations were not followed, the Builder should reinforce and/or correct the noted deficiency as necessary to make the condition conform to the Performance Guideline above.

Homeowner Responsibility: None.

Condition #5: *SUBFLOOR* IS OUT-OF-SQUARE

Can Affect:
- Structural integrity
- Finish flooring

Performance Guideline: The diagonal of a triangle cannot be any greater or less than one inch out of proportion of a triangle, with right angle legs of 12 feet and 16 feet. *Example: If a room measures 12 feet one direction and 16 feet in the other direction, a perfect diagonal measurement would be 20 feet. The Performance Guideline does not allow the length of a diagonal to be greater or less than one inch within 20 feet.* Applying this Guideline to rooms of different sizes, the tolerance of the length of the third leg of the triangle (hypotenuse) cannot be more or less than 0.42% of its perfect diagonal length. An exception is an addition or remodel of an existing House, where the Builder and Homeowner agree that it is practical to match the existing out-of-square floor.

Comments: Squareness should be checked before pouring the foundation and again during the frame layout. Out-of-square conditions can easily be corrected before the framing process.

Builder Responsibility: If subfloors (or slab foundations) are far enough out of square that the frame members do not adequately bear on them, the foundation or frame should be repaired to meet the Performance Guideline. If wood subfloors are out of square to an extent that subcontractors installing finish material such as tile, marble or pattern vinyl cannot compensate and a pattern line or grout line is more than one half inch out of square in six feet of length, the Builder should adjust the adjacent wall to bring the out-of-square condition to within Performance Guideline.

Homeowner Responsibility: None.

Condition #6: EXTERIOR WOOD BEAMS OR POSTS ARE WARPED, CHECKED OR SPLIT

Can Affect:
- Appearance
- Structural integrity

Performance Guideline: Exposed wood beams or posts that have splits that exceed 5/8 inch in width are considered excessive and are unacceptable.

Comments: It should be noted that exposed wood posts and beams are a natural material and are thus subject to splitting. This is considered normal. All lumber is grade stamped as to its level of quality. If the lumber is free from heart material, it will most likely resist splitting. The typical material used for post and beams meets the structural requirements, however, not necessarily concerns regarding appearance. It should also be noted that exposed lumber is subject to moisture and will expand and contract accordingly due to moisture levels in the air. Splitting is usually not considered a structural concern, but more of an appearance issue. If it is the intent of the Builder to create a wood beam that is free of splits or checks, composite or laminated architectural grade beams should be used.

Builder Responsibility: The Builder should replace or repair posts or beams as necessary to meet the Performance Guideline.

Homeowner Responsibility: The Homeowner should conduct annual inspections of all exterior wood materials. ***Maintenance Alert!*** If the observed condition is less than the Performance Guideline, the Homeowner can fill the split with any number of commercially available wood fillers. If significant ***dryrot*** is observed, a structural specialist should be consulted to see if the beam or post needs replacing.

Condition #7: WOOD BEAMS OR POSTS ARE TWISTED

Can Affect:

- Appearance
- Structural integrity
- Water tightness

Performance Guideline: Any beam or post that twists more than 3/4 inch in an 8-foot section is considered unacceptable.

Comments: When beams or posts twist in a minor (normal) manner, they generally do not create any potential structural problems. However if a beam ties into a vertical wall and twisting occurs, it may create an opportunity for water intrusion.

Builder Responsibility: The Builder should repair non-performing wood beams or posts as necessary to meet the Performance Guideline.

Homeowner Responsibility: All exterior lumber should be inspected annually for any caulking separation or peeling of paint and be immediately repaired in order to prevent future problems.

Chapter Three

includes:

Stucco

Exterior Insulation and Finish System (EIFS)

Siding:

Hardboard
Panel
Vinyl
Cement Board

Interior Walls

Shear Walls

References for this chapter:

- *Handbook of Construction Tolerances*, by David Kent Ballast
- *Residential Construction Performance Guidelines*, NAHB
- *Residential & Light Commercial Construction Standards*, by Don Reynolds
- *Troubleshooting Guide to Residential Construction*, Builderburg Group
- *Uniform Building Code*, 1997 ed.
- *Workmanship Guidelines*, CA Contractors State License Board

A comprehensive list of references by author and publisher is found in the Bibliography section.

Walls

Stucco Walls

General Subject Information: Stucco is a coating material that is applied to the exterior of the house. It traces its origin to both Europe and the Spanish southwest, where a crude mixture of adobe clay, sand and water was applied over adobe bricks. By the 1920s, stucco consisted of portland cement, sand, and water. It was applied by hand troweling and later by hose nozzles. Wood or metal lath held the stucco to the vertical walls. It was applied in three coats known as scratch, brown, and finish or color coat. Unless otherwise noted in this Manual, the term "stucco" refers to the above-described portland cement three-coat process.

A second finish system, known as the one-coat system, has gained popularity in recent years. This method of exterior finish consists of a foam board applied to the studs or sheathing of the house frame. Next, metal wire lath is stapled to the foam boards, and a fiber cement product is applied with trowels or by spraying. Lastly, a finish coat consisting of colored stucco or acrylic paint is applied. The thickness of the one-coat is about 3/8 inch plus the thickness of the foam board.

A third system, known as Exterior Insulation and Finish Systems (EIFS) was introduced to the United States in the late 1970s. EIFS are a type of cladding for exterior building walls that provide a surface (resembling stucco) in an integrated composite system. EIFS typically consist of a foam board adhesively and/or mechanically attached over a continuous rigid undersurface board-like material, continuous fiberglass mesh embedded in a polymer-based basecoat, and a finish or color coat made of a 100% acrylic paint-like material, provides color and texture.

Condition #1: CRACKS ON STUCCO WALLS

Can Affect:

- Appearance
- Water tightness
- Structural integrity

Performance Guideline: All exterior ***stucco*** covered walls, ***soffits*** and/or garden walls should not have any cracks that exceed 1/8 inch in width or 1/8 inch in adjacent surface displacement. However, cracks less than 1/8 inch covering more than 33% of a one foot square area of a dry surface wall (similar to a spider web pattern), are unacceptable. If the wall is wet, it will show a disproportionate number of surface irregularities and cracks; this Guideline applies to walls measured when dry.

Comments: Why does stucco crack? When new houses are built, the wood framing materials contain up to 19% moisture. As the lumber dries, the wood shrinks, causing stress to the stucco system. As the House ages, components expand and contract at different rates, causing stress on the weaker materials. Expansion and contraction is an inherent characteristic of a wood structure. (*Have you ever noticed that sometimes a wood door sticks, yet other times it opens and closes smoothly? That is because the wood expands and contracts as a result of moisture content in the air*). When the building structure expands and contracts during the settling period, stucco is certain to crack in predictable locations. This condition should be expected and is considered normal.

Stucco can also crack during the application process if it ***cures*** too quickly or if it is not allowed to cure between coats. Stucco is very hard and not very forgiving, as stucco has no elasticity or elongation properties when it comes to movement. Cracking is very common at the corners of door and window frames and/or anywhere there is a hinging effect within the rough framing of the structure. These particular areas are considered "hinge points" in the framing, and induce stress to the hard, but brittle, stucco finish. If and/or when cracks appear in the walls and soffits, this is not something to necessarily be alarmed about. **Always remember: stucco will always crack, the question is "How much cracking can occur before it becomes unacceptable?"**

Builder Responsibility: The Builder has a duty to furnish a House that is free from excessive cracking. If cracks exceed the Performance Guideline listed above, Builder should conduct an investigation, determine the actual cause of cracking, and conduct any needed repairs (if cracks are determined to be a result of improper construction and not from Homeowner misuse).

Homeowner Responsibility: Do not alter the finished grades around the perimeter of the House. Undrained, wet soil can cause foundation movement, which could result in stucco cracking. Expect some normal cracking in stucco. If cracks exceed the Performance Guideline listed above, the Homeowner should notify the Builder.

Condition #2: WATER STAINS OR WATER DAMAGE TO INTERIOR WALLS

Can Affect:

- Appearance
- Water tightness
- Structural integrity

Performance Guideline: All ***lath*** and ***plaster*** should be installed in such a manner that will ensure the House to be watertight and free from any exterior water intrusion.

Builder Responsibility: Upon notification of water intrusion, the Builder should conduct a thorough investigation, determine the exact cause, and then complete the subject repairs as necessary.

Homeowner Responsibility: ***Maintenance Alert!*** If the House has wood trim around the windows and exterior doors, this trim should be inspected for gaps and caulked annually. If a leak appears, the Builder should be notified immediately upon notice of the leak.

Condition #3: COLOR COAT REPAIR WORK DOES NOT MATCH EXISTING COLOR

Can Affect:

- Appearance

Performance Guideline: A poor color match is defined as a visible patch or area that can be seen by a layperson at a distance of 6 feet in indirect light. Any repair work that is necessary should be recolored from one corner to the other corner at full height, or properly "fogged" to acceptably blend the color coats.

Comments: Trying to match color coats on stucco is almost impossible. The manufacturer runs a batch of color compound, which is then labeled according to that lot number. Each lot will have a slight difference to its final color. Other factors (such as temperature and humidity) may cause the same lot, applied on different days, to have noticeable variations in color.

Builder Responsibility: The Builder should match the existing color as close as possible and should complete the repairs by recoloring the entire wall and/or line of sight that needs repair.

Homeowner Responsibility: None.

Condition #4: WEEP SCREED FLASHING IS RUSTING OR RUST MARKS APPEAR ON NUMEROUS PLACES ON THE SURFACE OF THE OUTSIDE WALLS

Can Affect:

- Appearance
- Water tightness

Performance Guideline: ***Weep screeds*** should not become rusted to the point of deterioration. Rust marks on the surface are considered unacceptable, if more than 5 marks measuring over 1 inch long occur per 100 square feet.

Comments: Over time, weep screeds may rust. Unlike roof flashing and other exterior flashing, the weep screed is not primed and/or painted to allow for future protection from the elements. Weep screeds serve three purposes: (1) as a gauge for the thickness of the stucco, (2) to allow the application of the stucco to be in a straight line, and (3) to provide an avenue for moisture that is trapped behind the stucco to exit at the base of the wall. Rust marks on weep screeds usually indicate a ***bleed through*** of rusted lath or nails in the stucco. Some of these rust marks are inevitable.

Builder Responsibility: If the weep screed becomes deteriorated to the point that it has rusted and no longer serves the purpose for which it was intended, the Builder should remove and replace the weep screed as necessary. If the frequency of rust marks exceeds the above Performance Guideline, Builder should seal the rusted areas and recolor the wall.

Homeowner Responsibility: Keep irrigation water from spraying against the stucco. Do not allow vegetation to overgrow in the screed area.

Condition #5: STUCCO COLOR COAT IS SEPARATING FROM THE UNDERNEATH COAT

Can Affect:

- Appearance
- Useful life of exterior coating

Performance Guideline: Stucco color should not separate from the underneath coat.

Comments: Stucco, very simply, is a cement and sand application that is comprised of three coats: scratch, brown and color coat, and is approximately 7/8 inch thick. First, a water-resistant building paper is applied directly to the framing. A chicken wire "mesh", also known as ***lath***, is then applied directly over the building paper. The first coat (scratch coat) is applied to the wall and embeds the wire mesh. The brown coat is applied next and then finally the color coat. Stucco is mixed at the job site and requires certain ratios of sand, cement and water. If the sand or water ratio is too high, the integrity of the product will be compromised, causing the system to fail. All three coats must be mixed with the proper ratios. It is important that the stucco be allowed to "cure" between coats.

Builder Responsibility: The Builder should repair any areas where the coatings have separated.

Homeowner Responsibility: ***Maintenance Alert!*** The Homeowner **should not fasten** any objects to the walls and soffits that are not properly ***flashed, counterflashed*** and sealed. The Homeowner should inspect and perform necessary maintenance in the following areas:

- Around the foundation, the Homeowner should maintain a minimum clearance of 4 inches from finished grade to weep screed and a 2 inch minimum clearance between concrete/asphalt and the weep screed.
- The Homeowner should maintain a minimum ***slope*** of ¼ inch per foot away from the House (foundation) on both soil and hard surfaces.
- The Homeowner should not permit any irrigation sprinklers to spray on any stucco covered surfaces.

Condition #6: WET SPOTS REMAIN ON STUCCO WALLS AFTER A RAIN STORM

Can Affect:

- Appearance

Performance Guideline: This condition is normal and acceptable.

Comments: Stucco is a semi-porous material and hence, will retain water after a storm. The special paper that is behind stucco acts as a water resistant member to prevent moisture from entering the House. The rate of drying of the wall is not uniform.

Builder Responsibility: None.

Homeowner Responsibility: None.

Condition #7: *LATH* IS VISIBLE THROUGH THE STUCCO

Can Affect:

- Useful life of exterior coating
- Appearance

Performance Guideline: *Lath* should not be visible through stucco, nor should any portion of the lath protrude through stucco.

Builder Responsibility: Make necessary repairs so that lath is not visible or protruding through stucco.

Homeowner Responsibility: None.

Condition #8: FOAM BOARD IS VISIBLE THROUGH THE STUCCO

Can Affect:

- Useful life of the exterior coating
- Water tightness

Performance Guideline: Foam boards should not be visible at any surface area of the one-coat system. All foam boards should be covered by at least 3/8 inch of base and finish coat.

Comments: The areas where foam boards butt against exterior openings (such as window and door trim) are often areas where the foam boards do not get completely covered by one-coat stucco. Apart from opportunities for water intrusion, foam will break down when exposed to prolonged sunlight.

Builder Responsibility: Make necessary repairs to coat any exposed foam.

Homeowner Responsibility: None.

Condition #9: WHITE POWDERY SUBSTANCE (efflorescence) APPEARS ON STUCCO WALLS IN WINTER MONTHS

Can Affect:

- Appearance

Performance Guideline: The white powdery substance (known as efflorescence) that appears on stucco walls and bare concrete slabs during the rainy season is caused by lime in the cement reacting with moist air. It is considered acceptable and can easily be removed with water and a brush.

Builder Responsibility: None.

Homeowner Responsibility: This is a Homeowner maintenance item that can be taken care of in the manner set forth in the above Guideline.

Condition #10: WOOD TRIM IS EMBEDDED IN STUCCO

Can Affect:
- Appearance
- Water tightness

Performance Guideline: Wood embedded in stucco is considered acceptable. Water resistant building paper must run continuously behind the embedded wood to prevent moisture from entering the wall cavity. Wood will shrink as it dries out (especially large beams) and a gap may develop between the wood and the stucco. If the gap exceeds ¼ inch at any part or warps more than ¼ inch away from the face of the building, it is considered unacceptable.

Comments: Wood trim is often placed around exterior doors and windows as part of the architectural features of the House. Beams and other structural members are embedded into stucco for the same reason. Much of the trim wood is "keyed" by having the stucco side beveled back or grooved to accept a tight fit between stucco and wood. It is good practice to paint the back of the wood trim before applying, to lengthen its life. Another good practice is to counterflash (see ***flashing***) the head (top) of the window and patio door with sheet metal to avoid water intrusion at this vulnerable point.

Builder Responsibility: Repair or replace excessively gapped or warped wood trim and other pieces that have exhibited these problems.

Homeowner Responsibility: ***Maintenance Alert!*** It is very important to inspect for gaps and if required, caulk around all wood members with a 25-year rated caulk before the rainy season begins. Any old caulking should be removed completely before re-caulking the area.

Condition #11: STUCCO WALL APPEARS "WAVY" DURING SUNSET HOURS OR WHEN LIGHTED WITH LANDSCAPE LIGHTS

Can Affect:
- Appearance

Performance Guideline: Stucco walls that exhibit a wavy characteristic under low light or artificial light are acceptable.

Comments: It is normal for stucco walls to have a wavy appearance under low light or artificial lighting. Stucco is a cement mixture that is applied to walls with a trowel or spray gun. The final finish will not be perfectly flat, and structural elements such as studs or structural panel joints may "reflect" through the finish.

Builder Responsibility: None.

Homeowner Responsibility: None.

Condition #12: PLYWOOD BEHIND STUCCO IS DELAMINATING OR SPLITTING.

Can Affect:

- Appearance
- Water tightness

Performance Guideline: Any sub-surface plywood, i.e. plywood that is installed behind wood siding or stucco, that warps or splits excessively is unacceptable and should be replaced. For this Guideline, "excessive" means that the laminations can be easily separated using hammer claws.

Comments: If plywood has expanded, swelled or is delaminating, this generally means that water has migrated to the backside of the exterior finish. The sub-surface plywood will need to be replaced and the source of water intrusion needs to be determined.

Builder Responsibility: The Builder should locate and seal the source of water intrusion, as well as repair and/or replace any plywood that does not meet the Performance Guideline. Any finishes that have been damaged and/or removed will need to be replaced as necessary.

Homeowner Responsibility: Homeowner should conduct periodic scheduled maintenance, i.e. caulking and painting as necessary to prevent potential problems.

EIFS (Exterior Insulation and Finish System)

General Subject Information: EIFS are exterior applied finish systems that look similar to stucco. However, initial appearance is where the similarities end. EIFS is made up of sheets of EPS (extruded polystyrene) that can be either mechanically or adhesively fastened to solid backing board material. Fiberglass mesh is embedded into a thin layer of cement-like material. A finish coat of acrylic, when combined, creates a waterproofing material and is then applied as the finish coat.

Condition #1: WATER HAS LEAKED INTO INTERIOR WALL CAVITY OR LIVABLE SPACE

Can Affect:

- Interior finishes (drywall, flooring, paint, woodwork, etc.)
- Structural integrity
- Growth of mold / bacteria

Performance Guideline: The entire structure should be watertight. The exterior finish should be installed in such a way as to prevent any kind of water infiltration/intrusion inside the wall cavities or livable space.

Comments: EIFS can fail 1) as a result of inadequate sealing and flashing at and around windows and doors during construction, or 2) through after market activities. Once the skin (acrylic finish) becomes cracked, split, gouged, and/or the caulking separates, water may become trapped behind the system. Trapped moisture has the potential for causing interior wall and/or finishes damage as well as the potential for bacterial and mold growth.

Builder Responsibility: The exterior finish should be installed in such a way as to prevent any water intrusion into either the interior portion of the wall cavities and/or the livable space. Only certified installers should be permitted to install an EIFS product according to manufacturer's recommendations.

Homeowner Responsibility: ***Maintenance Alert!*** The Homeowner should not nail, screw or tie into any portion of the exterior finish. Any fastening into the system must be performed by a certified EIFS installer, for that particular manufactured system. All exterior landscape irrigation must be installed and maintained in such a way as to not permit any water to spray directly onto the wall system. It should be noted that the EIFS system is susceptible to dings and gouges, which may cause water intrusion.

Hardboard Siding

General Subject Information: There are a number of siding products on the market that are made of various wood fiber materials. It is impractical to cover them all individually. The information that follows is generally applicable to these types of products. This section concentrates primarily on siding made of wood particles or other wood based products that are mixed with a resin to bind them together. Most of these siding systems are intended to look like horizontal wood siding and are often embossed to create a wood grain appearance on the surface.

Condition #1: EXTERIOR SURFACE IS BUCKLED

Can Affect:
- Appearance
- Water tightness

Performance Guideline: Hardboard siding should not warp or buckle more than 3/16 inch out of plane when nailed to studs placed at 16 inches on center.

Builder Responsibility: If the above Performance Guideline is not met during original construction, the Builder should make the necessary repairs. There are several conditions that can cause buckling which the Builder can control. Among these are correct fastener spacing, providing adequate space for expansion at the end butts between pieces, providing protective flashing, installing appropriate vapor barriers as recommended by the manufacturer, and protecting siding from moisture during storage on site prior to installation.

Homeowner Responsibility: ***Maintenance Alert!*** The Homeowner is responsible for maintaining the siding system in a sound, water-resisting condition. Among other things this involves painting the siding on a regular schedule (as provided in the manufacturer's recommendations), re-caulking joints periodically, and making sure that exposure to earth, paved surfaces, and water are properly controlled.

Condition #2: DRIP EDGE OF LAP SIDING IS SWOLLEN OR SPLIT

Can Affect:

- Useful life of siding
- Appearance

Performance Guideline: Swelling should not exceed approximately 10% of the original thickness of the drip edge, causing the material to crack and separate.

Comments: Siding materials are subject to swelling at the lower or "drip" edge of each lap when the core material is exposed to and absorbs excessive moisture. This swelling is commonly known as "brooming." In order to avoid "brooming", it is essential to prevent moisture from entering in the hardboard material at the drip edge. This can only be done if the drip edge is properly coated with 100% acrylic paint. This coating should be maintained by the Homeowner as part of a scheduled maintenance program.

Builder Responsibility: The Builder should paint siding systems in accordance with the material and workmanship requirements published by the manufacturer, paying special attention to the complete coating of all drip edges. Drip edges that have deteriorated due to abuse or lack of Homeowner maintenance are not the responsibility of the Builder.

Homeowner Responsibility: ***Maintenance Alert!*** It is important to observe the condition of painted siding surfaces on a periodic basis. An annual inspection is recommended. When paints begin to show signs of wear, this often first occurs in limited areas. Undertaking maintenance and touch up painting before paint degradation proceeds too far will significantly extend the life of the siding system. Homeowner should also prevent irrigation heads from spraying onto siding.

Condition #3: SIDING MATERIAL IS SWOLLEN OR SPLIT AROUND NAILS

Can Affect:

- Useful life of siding
- Appearance
- Water tightness

Performance Guideline: Siding should not visibly swell around nails. The usual pattern of unacceptable swelling is a "donut" shaped thickening of the siding material around the nail head. Nails should not be driven deeper than the surface of the siding.

Comments: Swelling around nails often occurs when the nails are driven too deeply ("overset"), damaging the surface of the siding and creating a path for the entry of water into the siding material. Another cause may be the use of improper nails that deteriorate in the presence of moisture, which can also lead to undesirable water intrusion into the siding material.

Builder Responsibility: The Builder should ensure that nails are not overset, and that the proper types of nails (as recommended by the siding manufacturer) are used in the installation of siding. If nails are not driven more than halfway through the siding, caulking and painting is an acceptable repair. If the nail is driven into more than half the thickness of the siding, another nail must be properly driven in an adjacent location, and the original nail should be caulked and painted.

Homeowner Responsibility: Maintenance of siding surfaces, including painting on an appropriate schedule, will significantly extend the life of the siding and limit the tendency to swell around nails.

Condition #4: SIDING SPLITS, SOFTENS, AND ROTS AT THE BASE OF WALLS

Can Affect:

- Appearance
- Useful life of siding
- Integrity of underlying structural components

Performance Guideline: Siding should not split, soften or rot.

Comments: This condition is often a result of the following situations: 1) siding that terminates less than 6 inches above earth; 2) siding that terminates less than 1 inch above paved surfaces; 3) siding that is in direct contact with storm water flows; and 4) siding that is subjected to direct spray from landscape irrigation systems. Siding may also be damaged by improper after market activity or by improper maintenance.

Builder Responsibility: The Builder should not permit the construction of any condition that will result in siding deterioration at the base of walls. If such conditions exist, the Builder should make necessary repairs.

Homeowner Responsibility: ***Maintenance Alert!*** The Homeowner must guard against introducing conditions that could result in deterioration of siding. For example, the Homeowner must maintain appropriate clearances between siding and earth or paving. When landscape improvements are installed, care should be taken to maintain the original clearances. The Homeowner is also responsible for proper maintenance of systems that can adversely affect siding. Another example: changes in sprinkler head spray patterns that cause irrigation water to spray directly onto siding must be avoided.

Condition # 5: BUTT JOINTS ARE TOO WIDE

Can Affect:

- Appearance

Performance Guideline: Butt joints (the gaps at the end of the board) should not be wider than 3/16 inch.

Comments: Nearly all siding manufacturers require gaps at the butt joints as part of proper installation. The siding boards need to expand and contract with seasonal changes in temperature and humidity. If there is no gap, the boards will often buckle. Butt joints should be covered with a plastic or metal spacer, or caulked and painted.

Builder Responsibility: Butt joints in excess of the Performance Guideline should be brought into conformance with the Performance Guideline.

Homeowner Responsibility: None.

Condition # 6: SIDING IS CROOKED

Can Affect:

- Appearance

Performance Guideline: Siding boards should be within ¼ inch of level over 10 feet of length.

Builder Responsibility: Reinstall any non-performing siding to meet the Performance Guideline.

Homeowner Responsibility: None.

Condition #7: SIDING IS SOFT AND ROTTING AT WINDOW AND DOOR TRIM, RAILINGS, AND OTHER LOCATIONS

Can Affect:

- Appearance
- Useful life of siding
- Integrity of underlying structural components

Performance Guideline: Siding should not be soft, rot, or deteriorate. Joints between adjacent pieces of siding, siding and trim, siding and rail caps, and other such components, should be assembled in such a way that siding deterioration resulting from water intrusion does not occur.

Comments: Water intrusion occurs for two principal reasons: 1) the materials and assembly methods used in the original installation are not correctly selected and integrated into a weather-tight system, and 2) joints and other potential entry points for water are not adequately maintained by the Homeowner. Where caulked joints are used, manufacturers generally specify joints 3/16-inch wide. Smaller joints are difficult to caulk effectively, and the caulk in larger joints will dry up, separate and deteriorate more rapidly. It is a good practice to protect vertical transitions from one type of material to another with metal or equivalent types of flashing.

CHECK FOR GAPS IN WINDOW TRIM CAULKING

Builder Responsibility: Builder should install siding-to-siding and siding-to-trim joints in a sound, waterproof manner that readily sheds water. Non-performing conditions from improper construction should be repaired.

Homeowner Responsibility: ***Maintenance Alert!*** The Homeowner is responsible for periodic maintenance of such items as caulked joints that are essential barriers to unwanted water entry into the siding system. ***Refer to Trim and Siding section in the Homeowner Maintenance Summary.***

Condition #8: SIDING HAS RAISED NAIL HEADS

Can Affect:
- Appearance
- Useful life of siding

Performance Guideline: Nails should be set with the bottom of the nail head flush with the surface of the siding. Use only nails recommended by the siding manufacturer.

Builder Responsibility: The Builder should ensure that nailing is performed in accordance with the requirements of the manufacturer. Nails that protrude at the outset of installation are a result of poor nailing techniques. Nails that protrude progressively over time may be the result of using the wrong types of nails, or installation into framing lumber with high moisture content.

Homeowner Responsibility: None.

Panel Siding

General Subject Information: Panel siding is typically plywood or hardboard that is installed in pieces that are 4 feet x 4 feet or 4 feet x 8 or 9 feet. Often the outer surface of the plywood sheet has been "textured" by resawing or by embossing. Also, the surface may have grooves cut into it to simulate boards or wide channels to simulate ***battens***. This type of siding is often found on the sides and back of the house.

Condition # 1: JOINTS AT PANEL EDGES ARE EXCESSIVELY WIDE OR RAISED

Can Affect:
- Appearance

Performance Guideline: Joints at panel edges should not exceed 3/16 inch in width or 3/16 inch in a plane from the adjacent panel.

Builder Responsibility: Builder should repair or replace any non-conforming panels so that they meet the above Performance Guideline.

Homeowner Responsibility: None.

Condition # 2: PANELS ARE DELAMINATING

Can Affect:
- Appearance
- Structural integrity

Performance Guideline: Siding panels should not delaminate.

Builder Responsibility: Builder should repair or replace any non-conforming panels.

Homeowner Responsibility: None.

Condition # 3: PANELS ARE BOWED

Can Affect:

- Appearance

Performance Guideline: Panel bows in excess of ¼ inch between ***studs*** at 16 inches on center are unacceptable.

Builder Responsibility: Builder should adjust the building frame or the individual panel.

Homeowner Responsibility: None.

Vinyl Siding

General Subject Information: Vinyl siding is becoming popular in California as an alternative to hardboard siding. Vinyl siding is a lightweight, non-wood product that is manufactured with integral color and is resistant to wood destroying insects. Also, many vinyl siding products can be painted.

Condition # 1: VINYL SIDING IS BOWED

Can Affect:

- Appearance

Performance Guideline: Bows in vinyl siding should not exceed ¼ inch between ***studs*** placed at 16 inches on center.

Builder Responsibility: Make the repairs necessary to conform to the above Performance Guideline.

Homeowner Responsibility: None.

Condition # 2: VINYL SIDING IS FADED OR BLOTCHED

Can Affect:

- Appearance

Performance Guideline: Over a period of years, most vinyl siding will fade uniformly. Non-uniform fading (or blotching) is an unacceptable condition and is considered non-performing. Most vinyl siding manufacturers warrant their product against fading and non-uniform discoloration.

Builder Responsibility: If the vinyl siding condition does not meet the manufacturer's warranty standard, the Builder should assist the Homeowner to deal with the manufacturer for repair or replacement of the non-conforming siding.

Homeowner Responsibility: Refer to the manufacturer's warranty on vinyl siding.

Cement Board Siding

General Subject Information: Cement board siding is another popular alternative to hardboard siding in California. Relatively new to the California market, cement board siding offers the advantages of being fire resistant, moisture resistant, and resistant to wood destroying insects. The disadvantage to cement board siding is that because of the physical properties of cement, it is prone to cracking if not properly installed.

Condition # 1: CEMENT BOARD SIDING IS CRACKED OR CHIPPED

Can Affect:
- Appearance
- Water tightness

Performance Guideline: Any cracks in cement board siding less than 2 inches in length or 1/8 inch in width are considered acceptable. Cracks in excess of this Guideline are unacceptable. Chips or full breaks in excess of ½ inch in radius are unacceptable.

Builder Responsibility: Cracks or chips that measure within the above Performance Guideline should be caulked and painted. Cracks or chips that exceed the above Performance Guideline should result in the replacement of the non-performing boards.

Homeowner Responsibility: None.

Siding (General)

Condition # 1: NAILS HAVE STAINED SIDING

Can Affect:
- Appearance

Performance Guideline: Stains that "bleed" into the siding for more than ½ inch in length as viewed from a distance of 20 feet under normal daylight conditions are unacceptable.

Builder Responsibility: If conditions are a result of improper installation, make repairs as necessary to meet the above Performance Guideline.

Homeowner Responsibility: *Maintenance Alert!* Siding nails should be inspected annually. Bleeds can be sealed with a clear aerosol sealer. An exterior painting schedule should follow to ensure proper maintenance.

Interior Walls

Condition #1: WALLS ARE OUT OF PLUMB

Can Affect:

- Door swing
- Appearance

Performance Guideline: Walls are considered out of plumb if they are more than 3/8 inch in any 32 inches of vertical measurement, or they exceed 1/2 inch in 8 foot cumulative vertical measurement. An exception is an addition or remodel of an existing House, where the Builder and Homeowner agree that it is practical to match the existing out-of-plumb wall (provided that the out-of-plumb wall does not pose a structural threat).

Comments: Walls that are out of ***plumb*** can especially affect door performance, such as fit and swing. If a door will not hang without either swinging in or out, the wall is probably out of plumb. It should be noted that any wall that exceeds 2 inches out of plumb might indicate a structural problem with the potential for the wall to collapse.

Builder Responsibility: Make the necessary repairs to meet the Performance Guideline.

Homeowner Responsibility: None.

Condition #2: WALLS ARE BOWED

Can Affect:

- Appearance of interior finishes
- Door opening swing and fit

Performance Guideline: All interior and exterior walls have different finishes. However the allowable tolerance for "rough framed walls" that are bowed should not be greater than ¼ inch in a 32-inch horizontal or vertical measurement, not to exceed ½ inch in 8 feet of length or height.

Comments: Walls that are bowed are generally more an appearance issue and do not compromise the structural integrity of the House.

Builder Responsibility: Any wall that does not meet the Performance Guideline should be repaired. All finishes should be replaced as necessary to complete said repairs.

Homeowner Responsibility: None.

Shear Walls

General Subject Information: Shear walls are specialty walls that can be found in the inside or outside of nearly every house. A shear wall is a structurally reinforced wall that prevents the house from moving back and forth in a catastrophic event such as an earthquake or high winds. For the most part, shear walls are made by nailing structural grade plywood or ***oriented strand board (OSB)*** to the studs (or screwed in the case of steel studs) according to a certain nailing specification provided by a licensed structural engineer or licensed architect. Most houses today, particularly those of two stories or more, have shear walls because of extensive requirements of the Building Code. The moving forces that shear walls resist in upper stories of the house must be transferred to the lower stories and transferred again to the foundation. When completed, shear walls do not look any different from non-shear walls because they are covered with drywall, stucco, siding or other finish material.

Condition #1: SHEAR WALLS ARE INADEQUATE

Can Affect:

- Structural integrity

Performance Guideline: The structural integrity of any shear wall cannot fall below the values set forth in the applicable Building Code. *It is important to note that structural engineers often design shear walls that exceed Building Code requirements.*

Comments: Inadequate shear wall claims normally fall into one of five categories:
1) wrong size nails used; 2) wrong type of nails used; 3) nails are overdriven; 4) nailing schedule (how far apart) not followed; and 5) wrong grade of plywood or OSB used.

Builder Responsibility: Repair the wall to meet Code requirements. If the Builder believes that the wall has been designed in excess of Code requirements, the Builder may obtain the opinion of a licensed structural engineer that the wall in its present condition meets the requirements of the Building Code.

Homeowner Responsibility: None.

Condition #2: SHEAR WALLS OR HOLD DOWNS ARE MISSING

Can Affect:

- Structural integrity

Performance Guideline: Shear walls and ***hold downs*** that are shown on the structural drawings approved by the local governing agency that issues the building permit must be installed as shown.

Builder Responsibility: Meet the Building Code requirements using one of two following methods: 1) retrofit installation of shear walls and/or hold downs as shown on the approved plans, or 2) provide an alternate (and presumably less invasive) plan of repair from a licensed structural engineer that will meet Building Code requirements.

Homeowner Responsibility: None.

Chapter Four

includes:

Structural Components

Ventilation

Eaves

Roof Coverings:

Composite or Synthetic Roof Systems
Wood Shake and Shingle
Clay and Concrete Tile
Composition Asphalt Shingles
Built Up and other Low Slope Roofs

References for this chapter:

- *500 Terrific Ideas for Home Maintenance and Repair*, by Jack Maguire
- *NRCA Roofing and Waterproofing Manuals*
- *Residential Construction Performance Guidelines*, NAHB
- *Residential Water Problems*, by Alvin Sacks
- *Residential & Light Commercial Construction Standards*, by Don Reynolds
- *Uniform Building Code*, 1997 ed.
- *Workmanship Guidelines*, CA Contractors State License Board

A comprehensive list of references by author and publisher is found in the Bibliography section.

oofs

General Subject Information: Many different materials are available for application to residential roofs. Reasons for choosing a particular material include geographic location of the structure, typical anticipated climatic conditions, slope or angle of incline of the roof, appearance considerations, and desired life span of the roof system. All of the different materials encompass a range of performance characteristics, as well as anticipated life spans. Information regarding recommended configurations, installation methods, maintenance practices, and repair procedures, as well as typical anticipated life spans, can usually be obtained from the material manufacturer, or from a recognized industry association.

In the absence of a manufacturer's brochure, how does a Homeowner know who the tile, shake, or shingle manufacturer was, and how the roof cover was supposed to be installed? Some manufacturers stamp their name on the back of their roofing material. If there is no identification, a sample can also be taken to a roofing supply company to obtain the information. Nearly all manufacturers publish information about the proper method for installation of their product.

Roofs can generally be separated into two broad categories: low-slope (often referred to as "flat" roofs), and steep slope (generally having more than 3 inches per foot of ***slope***). Steep-slope roofs are typically fitted with water-shedding roof covering systems, such as asphalt shingles, clay or concrete tile, slate, wood or composite shakes or shingles, or sheet metal panels. Low-slope roofs are typically covered with a waterproof membrane roof system, such as hot asphalt built up roofs (BUR). Low-slope roofs are then surfaced with gravel, embedded mineral granules, or field-applied coatings, modified asphalt roof ***membranes***, and single-ply roof membranes (which are typically smooth surfaced and have water tight, sealed seams).

Except for desert locations, residential roofs are usually built as steep-slope, water shedding systems. At slopes less than 3 inches per foot, special consideration should be given to design and installation of water shedding roof-covering materials.

Flashing and Counterflashing

General Subject Information: Sheet metal ***flashing*** or ***counterflashing*** components provide a mechanical overlap that protects terminations or transitions of roofing materials (e.g., at plumbing vent pipes, skylight curbs, roof edges, the base of walls, etc.) from wind-driven rain or runoff water. Water is conveyed by the flashing past the transition or termination, and passes onto the roof covering downslope, or off the roof.

Structural Components

Condition #1: ROOF *RIDGE* SAGS

Can Affect:

- Structural system supporting the roof
- Interior finishes
- Appearance

Performance Guideline: Roof ridge deflection should not exceed 2 inches in 16 feet of length.

Comments: Roofing materials and the roof structure should be compatible. Use of roofing material that is too heavy for the roof structure can cause excessive deflection and possible structural damage. Snow loads may cause the roof to deflect further.

Builder Responsibility: The Builder should repair any condition caused during original construction that exceeds the above Performance Guideline.

Homeowner Responsibility: Homeowner should not install and/or fasten any products and/or materials on the roof. The installation of materials and/or products by the Homeowner may void any warranty work by the Builder. The Homeowner should contact and/or consult with the Builder prior to the installation of any "add-on" materials and/or products. This includes, but is not limited to, the installation of solar heating panels and TV antenna dishes. Concrete and clay tile roofs are susceptible to breakage and only licensed persons who are qualified to walk on roofs should perform any installation of "add-on" products. The Builder will assume no responsibility for the roof systems when the Homeowner installs anything on the roof or makes any modifications whatsoever without approval of the Builder.

Condition #2: ROOF *SHEATHING* IS BOWED

Can Affect:

- Structural integrity of the roof
- Interior finishes
- Appearance

Performance Guideline: Roof sheathing should have a maximum deflection of 3/8 inch up or down in 2 feet of length. Roof sheathing should conform to the recommendations of the roofing material manufacturer, as well as the specifications of the building designer and the minimum requirements of the Building Code.

Builder Responsibility: The Builder should make the required repairs in order to meet the Performance Guideline.

Homeowner Responsibility: None.

Concrete and Clay Tiles, Slate

Condition #1: ROOF LEAKS

Can Affect:

- Structural framing members
- Interior finishes
- Interior furnishings

Performance Guideline: All roof systems should be installed in a watertight fashion and should not allow any kind of water intrusion under normal inclement weather conditions; *"normal" meaning what is typical for that particular geographic region.* (Refer to definition of normal and extreme weather on page 4).

Comments: Roof tiles and slate are generally not considered the waterproofing membrane of the roof system. Roof tiles serve three purposes: (1) Complimenting the architectural design of the House, (2) Controlling the majority of the roof water by means of shedding water down their overlapping courses and into a gutter, or off the edge of the roof overhang, and (3) Protecting the waterproofing membrane. The felt below the roof tiles, metal flashings, and the tiles themselves comprise the entire roof weatherproofing system. However, under extreme weather conditions (*out of the normal*), i.e. wind-driven rains (*rains that are driven horizontally*), snow and/or ice build-up, the roof system is more susceptible to water intrusion, especially on lower slope and flat roofs. Under extreme weather conditions, water intrusion is considered acceptable.

Builder Responsibility: If the roof leaks under normal weather conditions, the Builder should correct any verified roof or flashing leaks, as well as repair any damages that are a result of the subject leak. The Builder assumes no responsibility for leaks caused by extreme weather conditions or by Homeowner negligence, i.e. improper fastenings and/or penetrations through the roof.

Homeowner Responsibility:
Maintenance Alert! The Homeowner is responsible for periodic maintenance, i.e. cleaning of all roof drains, gutters and downspouts of leaves and other foreign debris and for checking all areas that have a caulking or sealant type material such as vents, pipe penetrations, and sheet metal flashing for cracked sealant, etc. **NOTE:** **Homeowners should not walk on roof tiles**, because concrete and clay tiles are subject to breaking. Generalized inspections can be done by the Homeowner from the ground, from ladders set at the edge of the roof,

and from adjacent properties. Field glasses (binoculars) are often helpful. If more detailed inspections are necessary, it is advisable to hire a qualified, licensed and properly insured roof inspection contractor. Homeowners should be extremely careful when installing products on the roof (such as solar heaters) or fastening items to the roof (such as holiday lights). All after market items attached to a roof should be made by a licensed contractor. The original roof warranty may be voided when someone other than the original contractor makes an addition or alteration to the roof. The painting and caulking of flashings by a qualified roofing contractor is a routine maintenance item.

Condition #2: LOOSE OR FALLING TILES OR SLATE

Can Affect:

- Safety issues related to falling objects
- ***Underlayment*** (*waterproofing membrane*) integrity

Performance Guideline: Tiles should not be loose or fall from the roof. They should be fastened in accordance with the manufacturer's published attachment schedule.

Comments: Tiles generally become loose or slip where the roof meets a wall. Since tiles cannot be fastened with nails through sheet metal flashing, roofers may secure the tiles with roofing cement or other manufacturer's recommended installation material. Loose tiles can slip off the roof and become a serious safety issue. Seismic requirements in the Building Code set forth compliance with specific nailing patterns.

Builder Responsibility: The Builder should remove and/or refasten the non-performing area if caused during original installation. Tiles should be securely attached to the roof by approved methods based upon Codes and the manufacturer's installation requirements.

Homeowner Responsibility: The Homeowner should conduct periodic inspections along all roof-to-wall intersections and look for loose or slipping tiles. A preliminary assessment can most often be accomplished with a visual inspection from the ground or from an elevated portion of the structure. More complete inspections should be done only by qualified roofing specialists.

Condition #3: CHIPPED OR BROKEN TILES OR SLATE

Can Affect:

- Safety issues related to falling objects
- ***Underlayment*** (*waterproofing membrane*) integrity

Performance Guideline: All cracked and broken tiles are considered unacceptable, if installed in that condition. Chips smaller than 3/4 inch are acceptable, providing that the total number of chipped tiles does not exceed more than 10 percent of the square footage of the plane (face) of the roof. Tile with chipped edges that are placed under sheet metal flashing are considered acceptable.

Comments: The Builder is not responsible for any breakage and/or damage caused by Homeowner negligence. The Homeowner and the Builder should conduct a thorough inspection as early as possible in the ownership process (at the ***Walkthrough***). Roof tiles that are made of concrete or clay are fragile and may break.

Builder Responsibility: The Builder should replace any missing, broken, cracked or excessively chipped tiles, which are a result of the Builder's work.

Homeowner Responsibility: *Maintenance Alert!* The Homeowner should inspect the roof for any cracked and/or broken tiles within the first month of occupancy. Homeowners should not walk on the roof, make any roof penetrations, or fasten any objects to the roof. If the Homeowner cannot inspect the roof with a ladder, or by observation from a safe higher vantage point, it is strongly advised that the Homeowner hire a qualified roofing inspector to perform the job.

Condition #4: IMPROPER EXPOSURE, LAPPING AND SPACING OF TILES OR SLATE

Can Affect:

- Useful life of the roof system
- Appearance

Performance Guideline: Exposure should not exceed that of the manufacturer's installation recommendations or Building Code standards.

Comments: Generally speaking, roof tiles and slate are probably "over exposed" if nails are visible and if not installed per the manufacturer's installation recommendations. The exception to this are the ***rake*** tiles along the edge of the roof, which often have exposed nails.

Builder Responsibility: If the tiles have exposed nails, the Builder should make the repairs necessary to meet the manufacturer's installation requirements or Code standards.

Homeowner Responsibility: None.

Condition #5: LACK OF ADEQUATE NAILING

Can Affect:

- Safety issue related to falling objects
- ***Underlayment*** integrity
- Water tightness of structure

Performance Guideline: All roof tiles should be fastened according to the manufacturer's recommendations as well as with Building Code standards.

Comments: Different regions may require different fastening methods. Areas subject to high winds or snow conditions require different fastening or nailing schedules than those with more moderate environments.

Builder Responsibility: If there is a lack of appropriate fastening or nailing, the Builder should make the repairs necessary to meet the Performance Guideline.

Homeowner Responsibility: None.

Condition #6: MISSING OR IMPROPERLY APPLIED SHEET METAL FLASHINGS

Can Affect:

- Water tightness
- Structural integrity
- Interior finishes

Performance Guideline: Roof flashing should not leak under normal conditions. The Builder is not responsible for this condition when the causes of leaks are a result of ice build-up, snow, wind-driven rain or Homeowner negligence.

Comments: Sheet metal flashing and counterflashing are integral parts of a properly designed and installed roof system. Flashings are installed at penetrations through the roof such as plumbing vents, flues, chimneys and skylights. Some other areas that have flashing are ***roof valleys*** and roof-to-wall intersections.

Builder Responsibility: The Builder will repair any flashing deficiencies resulting from improper installation that do not meet the Performance Guideline.

Homeowner Responsibility: ***Maintenance Alert!*** Homeowners are responsible for keeping all sheet metal valleys, gutters and downspouts free from ice build-up, snow, leaves and/or other foreign debris *(see **Chapter 9 Miscellaneous, Ice and Snow**)*. This should be done safely from a ladder without walking on the roof or by a qualified roof maintenance service.

Condition #7: EFFLORESCENCE (Appearance of light colored deposits on concrete tiles)

Can Affect:

- Appearance of roof surface

Performance Guideline: Concrete roof tiles should be uniform in color and free from extensive efflorescence. Minor efflorescence is considered normal and acceptable.

Comments: Water migrating through cracked or porous concrete can carry minerals to the surface of the tile, where evaporation results in minerals being deposited on the tile surface. This is generally not a significant problem, it is mainly an appearance issue.

Builder Responsibility: None.

Homeowner Responsibility: None.

Composition Asphalt Shingles

Condition #1: ROOF LEAKS

Can Affect:
- Structural frame
- Interior finishes

Performance Guideline: All roof systems should, at the time of installation, be watertight and free from any kind of water intrusion under normal inclement weather conditions; *"normally" meaning what is typical for that particular geographic region.* (Refer to definitions of normal and extreme weather on page 4).

Comments: Asphalt composition shingles are the water-shedding cover over the underlayment material of the roof system. Shingles serve two purposes: (1) to compliment the architectural design of the building, and (2) to control the majority of the roof water by means of shedding water down their overlapping courses and into a gutter, or off the edge of the roof overhang. However, under extreme weather conditions (*beyond the norm*), i.e. wind-driven rains (*rains that are driven horizontally*), and snow and/or ice build-up, the roof system is more susceptible to water intrusion, especially on low slope and flat roofs. Under extreme conditions, water intrusion may be unavoidable.

Builder Responsibility: If the roof leaks under normal weather conditions, the Builder should correct any verified roof or flashing leaks, and repair damages that are results of the subject leak. The Builder will not be responsible for leaks caused by Homeowner negligence, such as improper fastening to, installations on, or penetrations of the roof.

Homeowner Responsibility: ***Maintenance Alert!*** The Homeowner is responsible for periodic maintenance, i.e. cleaning of all roof drains, gutters and downspouts of leaves and/or other foreign debris; checking areas that have a sealant type material, i.e. vents, pipe penetrations, and inspecting all sheet metal flashing for deteriorated sealant, etc. Homeowners should also avoid installing products and/or fastening items to or through the roof.

Condition #2: SHINGLES HAVE BLOWN OFF

Can Affect:
- Water tightness
- Appearance

Performance Guideline: Shingles should not suffer damages under normal wind loads for a particular geographic region, as set forth in wind design guidelines.

Comments: All asphalt composition shingles should be installed according to the manufacturer's installation recommendations and local Code requirements.

Builder Responsibility: If shingles are damaged by wind, and wind loads are within the wind design standards of the manufacturer, the Builder should make all the necessary repairs to meet the Performance Guideline. Builder is not responsible for conditions caused by Homeowner misuse or improper maintenance.

Homeowner Responsibility: *Maintenance Alert!* The Homeowner is responsible for periodic maintenance, i.e. cleaning of all roof drains, gutters and downspouts of leaves and/or other foreign debris, checking all areas that have a sealant type material, i.e. vents, pipe penetrations, and inspecting all sheet metal flashing for deteriorated sealant, etc. Homeowners should also avoid installing products and/or fastening items to the roof.

Condition #3: SHINGLES ARE NOT HORIZONTALLY ALIGNED

Can Affect:

- Appearance

Performance Guideline: Unless the Builder is trying to achieve a special architectural effect by staggering the ends or rows of the shingles, shingles should be reasonably straight with even courses.

Comments: If the courses are under exposed this should not affect the integrity of the roof. It should be noted, however, that under exposure might void some manufacturer's material warranties. Conversely, if the shingle is over exposed, this may decrease the life expectancy of the roof system. "Exposure" is an industry term that indicates how much of each shingle or shake can be exposed to the weather.

Builder Responsibility: If the courses are over exposed or under exposed from the manufacturer's installation recommendations, then the Builder should make all the repairs that are necessary to meet the installation recommendations.

Homeowner Responsibility: None.

Condition #4: SHINGLES ARE CURLED OR CUPPED AT EDGES AND CORNERS

Can Affect:

- Roof appearance
- Useful life of roof

Performance Guideline: Asphalt shingle edges and corners need not be flat. Fastener heads should not be exposed. However, the appearance of shingles should be within manufacturer's standards or specifications.

Comments: Between the two types of asphalt shingles (organic and fiberglass shingles), organic shingles have a history of curling and cupping, while some fiberglass shingles have a tendency to crack more easily than organic ones. Cupping and curling shingles can also be caused by inadequate attic ventilation.

Builder Responsibility: If the curling and cupping becomes widespread and is not within the manufacturer's specifications, the Builder should replace shingles as necessary to meet the manufacturer's standards.

Homeowner Responsibility: As roofs age, particular attention should be paid to the condition of curled and cupped shingles. An occasional "tune-up" by a licensed and qualified roofing contractor can extend the life of the roof significantly.

Condition #5: SHINGLES OVERHANG EDGES OF ROOF, TOO FAR OR TOO LITTLE

Can Affect:

- Integrity of eaves
- Water tightness of eaves

Performance Guideline: Composition shingles should overhang the roof edges no less than ¼ inch, and not more than ¾ inch unless the manufacturer's standards and specifications indicate otherwise.

Builder Responsibility: The Builder should replace as necessary any improperly installed shingles that do not meet the Performance Guideline.

Homeowner Responsibility: ***Maintenance Alert!*** The Homeowner is responsible for periodic maintenance, i.e. cleaning of all roof drains, gutters and downspouts of leaves and/or other foreign debris.

Condition #6: ASPHALT SHINGLES HAVE DEVELOPED SURFACE BUCKLING

Can Affect:

- Roof appearance

Performance Guideline: Buckling that exceeds 3/8 inch in height is considered unacceptable.

Comments: The shingle surface does not need to be absolutely flat; in fact, some manufacturers create surface irregularities to enhance the overall appearance of the roof. The determination between buckling and an intended irregular surface is that with a buckling condition, the rest of the roof will be flat with only the affected areas buckled. Buckling is sometimes the result of inadequate ventilation or trapped moisture in the membrane.

Builder Responsibility: If asphalt shingle buckling exceeds the Performance Guideline, then the Builder needs to make the necessary repairs to meet the Guideline.

Homeowner Responsibility: None.

Condition #7: SHADING OR SHADOWING PATTERN APPEARS ON THE SHINGLES

Can Affect:

- Roof appearance

Performance Guideline: Shading or shadowing is considered acceptable.

Comments: Shading or shadowing is a visual phenomenon that in no way affects the performance or longevity of the roofing system. Many manufacturers try to give a "wood shake look" to their composition shingles. The manufacturing operation intentionally produces slight variations in the surface texture. These different textures simply affect the way the surface reflects light, thus creating shadows.

Builder Responsibility: None.

Homeowner Responsibility: None.

Condition #8: EROSION OF SHINGLE SURFACING MATERIALS

Can Affect:

- Useful life of surfacing material
- Fire resistance of the roof
- Reflectivity of the roof
- Appearance

Performance Guideline: At the time of installation, mineral granules should remain adhered to the surface of the shingles and no bare spots should be observable when looking down at the roof.

Comments: Loss of mineral granules from the shingle surface can also occur as a result of 1) rooftop traffic (such as during installation of adjacent roofing materials or other building materials), 2) servicing of rooftop mounted heating and cooling equipment, and 3) as a result of natural weathering of the roof surface. Mineral granule loss can also be a result of poor ventilation or manufacturing defects. Minor loss of granules can be expected over the life span of the roof, and generally will not significantly impact the performance or life of the roof. However, excessive granule loss can cause premature breakdown of the membrane.

Builder Responsibility: The Builder should provide adequate protection to finished roof surfaces during subsequent building component construction (e.g., masonry, siding, etc.) to prevent undue abrasion of mineral granules. The Builder should refer occurrences of significant mineral granule loss to the manufacturer, as this is likely a manufacturing defect.

Homeowner Responsibility: The Homeowner should not permit excessive access to the roof and when access is required, adequate protection should be provided to the roof surface to prevent loss of mineral granules.

Condition # 9: UNSEALED SHINGLE TABS

Can Affect:

- Wind uplift resistance

Performance Guideline: Shingles or shingle tabs should be adhered to underlying shingles.

Comments: Adhesion of shingles to asphalt seal strips on the underlying shingles can be reduced by a number of factors, including contamination of the asphalt seal strips by dust or construction debris, insufficiently driven fasteners, cool air temperatures immediately following shingle application, and improper seal strip manufacture. Manual sealing of shingles to underlying courses can be achieved by "hand-tabbing" or placement of small, evenly spaced beads of asphalt roof cement on underlying shingles.

Builder Responsibility: The Builder should fasten shingles in conformance to recommendations published by the shingle manufacturer, and/or standards published by recognized industry associations. Non-performing installations should be corrected.

Homeowner Responsibility: The Homeowner should retain a qualified roofing professional to perform any addition or repair involving asphalt shingle roofs, hand-tabbing newly installed shingles if necessary to achieve proper seal to the underlying courses.

Wood Shake and Shingle Roofs

General Subject Information: Wood shakes and shingles have been traditional roof coverings (particularly in the West) for decades. Cedar is the primary wood used. The basic difference between a shingle and a shake is the thickness. Shakes are thicker and are often made by splitting the cedar logs with a sharp tool similar to an ax. Additionally, both wood shakes and shingles can be manufactured by cutting the cedar log with a saw. Shakes are typically longer than shingles, and more of the shake is exposed to the weather. Unless they are chemically treated, wood shakes and shingles can pose a significant fire hazard, and some local jurisdictions have prohibited the installation of untreated shingle and shakes. Tile and composition shingles are gradually taking the place of wood shingles and shakes in new homes.

Condition #1: ROOF LEAKS

Can Affect:

- Structural integrity
- Interior finishes

Performance Guideline: All roofs should be installed in a watertight fashion.

Comments: Proper maintenance of a wood shake or shingle roof can substantially extend the expected life of a roof (***Refer to Maintenance Alert below under Homeowner Responsibility***).

Builder Responsibility: The Builder should construct a roof that is watertight. If the House does not meet the Performance Guideline, and the leak is not caused by the negligence of the Homeowner, then the Builder should make all the necessary repairs so that the roof meets the Performance Guideline.

Homeowner Responsibility: *Maintenance Alert!* Gutters, downspouts and valleys should always be kept free of any leaves or other foreign debris. Any penetrations through the roof that exist should be carefully maintained with caulking, asphalt tar, roofing seals, etc. Any Homeowner add-ons, i.e. antennas, satellite dishes, solar collectors, etc. may void the roof warranty. The Homeowner should consult with a licensed contractor and/or the original Builder before making any changes or additions to the roof.

Condition #2: SHINGLES OR SHAKES ARE CUPPED OR CURLED

Can Affect:

- Appearance
- Useful life of roof

Performance Guideline: Newly installed shakes or shingles should be flat within 1 inch of a surface plane.

Comments: Normal exposure to sunlight and rainfall results in loss of natural preservative oils from wood shakes and shingles, leading to some deformation of the wood. In addition, different rates of drying between the top and bottom surfaces of the shake or shingle can contribute to deformation of the wood. These are naturally occurring events and not generally a significant problem, other than an appearance issue.

Builder Responsibility: The Builder should inspect shakes or shingles prior to installation on the roof, segregating those units found to be significantly cupped or curled. Non-performing installation should be corrected. Proper ventilation should be provided for the underside of the roof sheathing.

Homeowner Responsibility: ***Maintenance Alert!*** The Homeowner needs to provide periodic maintenance in order to get a full useful life from a wood roof. Roof "tune-ups" from a licensed roofing contractor are recommended at a minimum of every five years. A "tune-up" can consist of replacing cupped or curled shakes and shingles, separating ridge caps, and blown off shingles. A "tune-up" is not expensive (compared to the cost of a new roof) and it may easily extend the life of the roof.

Condition #3: SHAKES OR SHINGLES ARE LOOSE OR HAVE BLOWN OFF

Can Affect:

- Integrity of the ***underlayment*** (*waterproofing*)
- Interior finishes
- Appearance
- Water tightness

Performance Guideline: Shakes and shingles should not blow off of the roof under normal weather conditions for the geographic region. However, shakes and shingles may blow off as they age and erode. This is normal part of the aging process of the House. Hurricane or gale force winds in regions that do not normally experience these conditions (i.e., extreme) may result in shakes or shingles being blown off the roof; this condition is acceptable.

Comments: Every roof cover product that is installed needs to be carefully selected for that particular region. High wind areas require different fastening methods than those of moderate wind areas and low slope roofs require different and/or additional flashing concerns.

Builder Responsibility: Make repairs necessary to ensure the roof is watertight. Follow the manufacturer's recommended nailing schedule. Visible fasteners are not acceptable, except at ridge caps. Replace any shingles or shakes blown off during normal weather events, unless damage is a result of improper Homeowner maintenance.

Homeowner Responsibility: ***Maintenance Alert!*** Homeowner should remove leaves and other foreign debris from all gutters, downspouts and valleys. Special wood preservatives may be used to enhance and extend the life of such roofs. Older roofs that have not been maintained properly are likely to experience blow off of shakes and shingles.

Condition #4: IMPROPER *EXPOSURE*, EDGE LAPPING, OR SPACING

Can Affect:

- Integrity of structural framing members
- Eave performance
- Water tightness

Performance Guideline: Wood shake and shingle tolerances should not be less than that recommended by the roofing material manufacturer. In general, shingles should extend no less than 1½ inches and shakes should extend no more than 2 inches beyond the rake edge of the roof; and 1½ inches beyond the edge of an eave. The manufacturer's installation recommendations take precedence over this Guideline.

Comments: There are a variety of different shakes and shingles on the market. Each manufacturer has their installation recommendations that need to be followed, in order for the warranty to be valid.

Builder Responsibility: All ***exposures***, edge lapping and spacing should be installed in accordance with the manufacturer's recommendations.

Homeowner Responsibility: None.

Condition #5: JOINTS BETWEEN SHINGLES IN SUCCESSIVE COURSES ARE NOT ADEQUATELY OFFSET

Can Affect:

- Integrity of underlayment

Performance Guideline: No two successive courses (rows) should have joints directly in line with one another. Joint offsets should comply with the manufacturer's recommendations.

Comments: Running any two courses in a direct line, exposes the waterproofing underlayment to the elements, specifically ultraviolet rays of the sun, which leads to deterioration.

Builder Responsibility: The Builder should make the necessary repairs to meet the Performance Guideline.

Homeowner Responsibility: None.

Condition #6: IMPROPER NAIL FASTENING

Can Affect:

- Safety issue related to falling objects
- ***Underlayment*** integrity
- Interior finishes
- Water tightness of structure

Performance Guideline: Each shake or shingle should be nailed with two approved nails or staples. Alternatively, nailing and fastening should be per the manufacturer's installation recommendations.

Comments: The entire roof system should be free of exposed nails and fasteners, except at ridges.

Builder Responsibility: The Builder should make any and all the repairs necessary in order to meet the Performance Guideline.

Homeowner Responsibility: None.

Condition #7: IMPROPER OR MISSING FLASHINGS AND VALLEYS

Can Affect:

- Water tightness
- Interior finishes

Performance Guideline: Flashing and other sheet metal should be furnished and installed per the current Code and in conformance with the approved plans.

Comments: Flashing is often the "weak link" in a roof system. Improperly designed or improperly installed flashing at roof penetrations (such as chimneys, skylights, plumbing vents, flues, or transitions from roof-to-wall) can result in insufficient coverage of the edges of shakes and shingles. Exposed underlayment will quickly deteriorate in sunlight and leaks are likely to occur.

Builder Responsibility: If it is determined that the cause of the roof leak is improperly installed or missing flashing, the Builder should make repairs necessary to meet the Performance Guideline.

Homeowner Responsibility: ***Maintenance Alert!*** Homeowner needs to conduct a yearly inspection (*prior to the rainy season*) to ensure that sheet metal caulking, sealant and asphalt cement have no cracks, voids or splits. The inspection, and any required maintenance, should be performed by a qualified, licensed and properly insured roofing contractor.

Condition # 8: ACCUMULATION OF LEAVES, MOSS, AND ORGANIC DEBRIS

Can Affect:
- Performance and life span of the roof
- Appearance

Performance Guideline: This is a Homeowner maintenance item.

Builder Responsibility: None.

Homeowner Responsibility: ***Maintenance Alert!*** Accumulation of leaves, needles, sediment from dust, etc., and growth of moss or fungi on wood shakes or shingles can lead to premature degradation of the wood. Periodic cleaning with a stiff bristle broom or low-pressure water spray can resolve most occurrences. **DO NOT USE A POWER WASHER**. The Homeowner should retain a qualified roofing professional to perform periodic (annual) cleaning of the roof, removing accumulation of growth or organic materials. Additionally, regular application of moss or fungus inhibiting compounds, or installation of moss or fungus inhibiting materials (such as zinc strips) can reduce the amount of growth. A roofing professional should be consulted for product and application information.

Composite or Synthetic Roof System

General Subject Information: Numerous composite or synthetic materials are now available for steep-slope, water shedding roofs, engineered and manufactured to simulate the appearance of natural materials, such as wood shakes or shingles, slate, or tile, while providing wind uplift and fire resistance. Products include: fiber cement composites, formed metal panels, foil-laminate asphalt shingles, wood fiber based materials, fiberglass and polymer based products, and various recycled materials. Many of these products and their respective installation methods are continually changing. The manufacturer's design and installation recommendations should be consulted for information regarding proper design, installation, and maintenance of these products.

Condition # 1: CRACKED OR BROKEN PIECES

Can Affect:
- Useful life of the roof
- Interior finishes and furnishings
- Safety issues related to falling objects

Performance Guideline: Roof materials should be installed in whole or intentionally cut pieces, sized to fit.

Comments: Cracked or broken pieces may result from flaws in the material undetected prior to installation, from damage occurring during shipping, or from action subsequent to installation, either related to construction of adjacent surfaces (e.g., masonry or stucco cladding above roofs), or external impact (e.g., hailstones or golf balls). New pieces with chipped or broken edges can usually be installed at hips, valleys, rakes, or other locations requiring cut pieces. These pieces should be identified and sorted during the loading process. Fiber cement or wood fiber based materials with pockets of poorly blended components can incur subsequent cracking or breakage.

Builder Responsibility: The Builder should inspect roof covering materials prior to installation, segregating those pieces found to contain visible manufacturing or shipping related defects or damage that would adversely impact the function of the material installed. The Builder may retain those damaged sections for installation in locations that would require cut pieces. Adequate protection should be provided for finished roof surfaces during subsequent work on adjacent surfaces. Non-performing installation should be corrected.

Homeowner Responsibility: The Homeowner should conduct a thorough inspection of the roof at the time of the ***Walkthrough***. The Homeowner should not walk on the roof, or make any penetrations through or fasten any item to the roof. Additionally, the Homeowner should retain a qualified roofing professional on an annual schedule to perform inspections of the roof, noting and replacing any cracked or broken materials.

Condition #2: LOOSE OR DISPLACED PIECES

Can Affect:

- Useful life of the roof
- Appearance
- Safety issues related to falling objects

Performance Guideline: Roof covering materials should be secured according to applicable Codes and manufacturer's recommended fastening schedule, using approved materials and methods. Properly secured materials should not be displaced by normally occurring wind conditions.

Comments: Unsecured pieces can be displaced and create damage by slipping further. Displaced pieces can also result in water intrusion into the structure. At locations where fastening of materials is difficult due to flashing or other impediment, approved adhesive should be used to secure pieces to adjacent ones.

Builder Responsibility: The Builder should install materials secured by approved methods, conforming to applicable Codes and as recommended by the manufacturer. Non-performing installation should be corrected.

Homeowner Responsibility: The Homeowner should conduct a thorough inspection of the roof at the time of the Walkthrough. The Homeowner should not walk on the roof, or make any penetrations through, or fasten any item to the roof. The Homeowner should retain a qualified roofing professional to perform annual inspections of the roof, noting and securing any materials found to be loose or displaced.

Condition # 3: IMPROPER EXPOSURE, LAPS, AND SPACING OF PIECES

Can Affect:

- Useful life of the roof
- Appearance
- Interior finishes and furnishings

Performance Guideline: Roofing materials should be installed, lapped, and spaced according to the manufacturer's published installation recommendations.

Comments: Improperly lapped or spaced materials can result in insufficient coverage of underlying or adjacent materials and roof underlayment material, which may result in intrusion into the structure by water runoff or wind-driven rain, and potential premature failure of underlayment.

Builder Responsibility: The Builder should install materials lapped and spaced as recommended by the material manufacturer. Non-performing installation should be corrected.

Homeowner Responsibility: None.

Condition # 4: MISSING OR IMPROPERLY INSTALLED FLASHING

Can Affect:

- Water tightness
- Structural integrity
- Interior finishes

Performance Guideline: Flashing and other sheet metal should be furnished and installed per the current Code and in conformance with the building designer's specifications.

Comments: Flashing is often the "weak link" in a roof system. Improperly designed or improperly installed flashing at roof penetrations (such as chimneys, skylights, plumbing vents, flues, or transitions from roof-to-wall) can result in insufficient coverage of the edges of shakes and shingles. Exposed underlayment will quickly deteriorate in sunlight and leaks are likely to occur.

Builder Responsibility: If the cause of a roof leak is determined to be improperly installed and/or missing flashing, the Builder should make the necessary repairs to meet the Performance Guideline.

Homeowner Responsibility: ***Maintenance Alert!*** Homeowner needs to conduct a yearly inspection (*prior to the rainy season*) to ensure that sheet metal caulking, sealant and/or asphalt cement are not damaged by cracks, voids and/or splits. The inspection, and any required maintenance, should be performed by a qualified, licensed and properly insured roofing professional.

Roof Ventilation

General Subject Information: Proper ventilation helps dissipate and reduce unwanted moisture in the attic during the winter and hot air during the summer. Vents that are located low on the roof system help bring in cooler air, while vents that are located closer to or on the ***ridge*** help remove warm or moist air. If a roof is not properly ventilated, condensation can develop and may cause mold and mildew growth, water staining to the interior, and deterioration of structural members. Improperly vented roofs will reduce the effectiveness of roof or attic insulation, may cause roofing materials warranties to be voided, and may lead to roof membrane buckling.

Condition #1: ATTIC VENT OR LOUVER LEAKS

Can Affect:

- Structural framing integrity
- Interior finishes

Performance Guideline: Vents and louvers should not leak under normal weather conditions for the geographic region. Some leakage during extreme weather conditions (out of the normal) may occur and is acceptable. (Refer to definitions of normal and extreme weather on page 4).

Comments: It is considered acceptable if water penetrates through the vent or louver during extreme weather conditions for the geographical region. This is considered to be outside the Builder's control. However, if the water intrusion occurs between the vent and the exterior wall finish, the Builder is responsible to meet the Performance Guideline. Also, if leakage occurs during the "normal" rainy season, it is considered non-performing.

Builder Responsibility: The Builder should make repairs that are necessary to eliminate any water intrusion during normal weather conditions. If water intrusion occurs between the vent and the wall finish and is a result of improper installation, the Builder should make the necessary repairs to eliminate leakage.

Homeowner Responsibility: ***Maintenance Alert!*** Keep all vents and louvers free from any obstructions. Do not allow birds to nest in vents.

Eaves

General Subject Information: The "***eave***" is a part of the roof that generally hangs out past the exterior walls. Gutters are often applied directly to the ***fascia*** board of the eaves. Eaves help protect the house by preventing rain from coming directly down the face of the walls, and by reducing direct sunlight into the residence that can damage interior finishes and furnishings. Eaves are generally not the cause of damage to interior finishes or furnishings. However, if there is water blockage (*clogged gutters or valleys*) and/or ice build-up (*ice dams*), there is the potential for water to back up the roof and migrate under the felt (***underlayment***) and cause interior damage.

Condition #1: LEAKS OR STAINS APPEAR AT THE UNDERSIDE OF THE EAVES

Can Affect:

- Water tightness
- Appearance
- Roof performance and structural integrity

Performance Guideline: The roof should be installed in a watertight condition.

Comments: Roof systems are designed for particular regions or geographic areas, i.e. mountainous regions or valleys that have high and/or extreme wind conditions will require materials and fastening methods that are different than areas that have low or no wind conditions.

Builder Responsibility: If the roof eave leaks during normal regional weather and the leaks are a result of improper installation, the Builder should conduct repairs as necessary to meet the Performance Guideline.

Homeowner Responsibility: ***Maintenance Alert!*** The Homeowner is responsible for providing proper maintenance. This includes keeping gutters free from debris, clearing ice dams that may develop, etc.

Condition #2: ROOF SAGS OR BOWS AT EAVES AND FASCIA

Can Affect:

- Appearance
- Water tightness
- Interior finishes

Performance Guideline: Deviation from flatness (a horizontal line) at eaves or fascia board should be no greater than ½ inch in any 8 feet of length

Comments: To understand what flatness is, you must imagine a perfectly straight line between two points. Any difference above or below that line is the tolerance of flatness. If the measurement is equal to or greater than ½ inch above or below that line, then it does not meet the Performance Guideline *(**Refer to "How to Measure" Section of the Preface**)*.

Builder Responsibility: The Builder should correct the out of flatness condition to meet the above Performance Guideline.

Homeowner Responsibility: ***Maintenance Alert!*** The Homeowner should maintain the roof eaves by providing adequate maintenance, i.e. painting, caulking and removal of any debris that might constrict the flow of water. This includes annual gutter cleaning.

KEEPING GUTTERS CLEAN - **BEFORE** THE RAINY SEASON

Built Up Roofing and Other Low Slope Roofs

General Subject Information: A built up roof (**BUR**) system is simply layers of asphalt that serve as the waterproofing medium, sandwiched between various types of roofing membranes known as felts. Even though in residential construction BUR systems are not as common as other roofing materials, they are found where low ***slope*** or flat roof conditions exist. From entry level homes to condominium buildings to expensive desert homes, built up roofs often achieve a particular look that the architect is trying to set forth. There are actually three basic types of BUR that are used today: smooth surface, aggregate surface, and mineral surface. On lower-sloped roof applications, the felt layers should be placed so that the flow of water is not against where the felt laps.

Another type of low slope roof system is the single-ply roof. This system consists of a single membrane layer that is applied (usually with fasteners) over the ***underlayment*** (also called a substrate). The seams are sealed with a special sealant provided by the manufacturer.

It is important that the roofing manufacturer's installation recommendations are closely followed both for the life of the roof and to comply with any warranty by the manufacturer. Finally, the Homeowner should provide preventive maintenance to the roof, as the life span may be greatly influenced by the presence or absence of proper roof maintenance.

Condition #1: STANDING WATER ON ROOF (Ponding)

Can Affect:

- Structural framing
- Interior finishes
- Interior furnishings

Performance Guideline: Minor ponding is acceptable, providing that it does not exceed ½ inch in depth, and is dry within 48 hours after cessation of rainfall.

Comments: All roofs that are considered "flat roofs" should drain either over the edge of the roof, or into an interior roof drain system with an overflow drain. Water that remains on a roof longer than the allowable Performance Guideline is considered unacceptable. Any ponding that exceeds the Guideline may cause premature deterioration to the roofing membrane.

Builder Responsibility: The Builder is responsible for providing drainage with a positive slope for the finished roof. A flat roof should have a minimum slope of ¼ inch of drop to the edge or drain for each 12 inches across the roof surface. Repair or replace as necessary any non-performing condition that is a result if improper construction.

Homeowner Responsibility: ***Maintenance Alert!*** This type of roof system needs a bi-annual inspection and maintenance program, i.e., clearing any debris that may damage the roof membrane, sealing any cracks, tears or rips, and keeping drains, gutters and downspouts free from debris. Also, where the roof turns up to a wall or skylight, the felt material is susceptible to deterioration and may produce leaks if not properly maintained. If the roof has ***parapet*** walls, then all overflow ***scuppers*** or primary and secondary drains must be kept free of leaves, gravel, and debris.

Condition #2: ROOF LEAKS

Can Affect:

- Structural framing
- Interior finishes

Performance Guideline: The roof should not leak under weather conditions that are considered normal for the geographic area. (Refer to definitions of normal and extreme weather on page 4).

Comments: A roof should not leak under normal inclement weather. However, any and all roof systems may leak under extreme or adverse weather conditions, which is acceptable.

Builder Responsibility: The Builder should install a watertight roof. If the roof leaks during normal weather, the Builder should make the repairs necessary to meet the Performance Guideline (unless the leaks are determined to be a result of Homeowner negligence).

Homeowner Responsibility: ***Maintenance Alert!*** After market products such as deck boards, satellite dishes and solar panels should not be fastened directly to the roof system without consulting the original Builder or a licensed roofing contractor. Homeowner should be aware that fastening a product to the roof system could cause the warranty to be voided. Minimize the amount of walking that is done on the roof. Homeowner should also schedule a routine maintenance program.

Condition #3: ROOF *MEMBRANE* HAS BUBBLES OR BLISTERS

Can Affect:

- Integrity of the roof
- Structural integrity
- Interior finishes

Performance Guideline: Bubbles or blisters that exceed 12 inches in diameter are unacceptable. Small and unbroken bubbles/blisters that are less than 12 inches in diameter are considered acceptable. Bubbles or blisters that cover more than 20% of the roof are unacceptable.

Comments: Voids between two waterproof layers of roofing materials can cause bubbles or blisters. When moist air gets trapped between these two layers, the increase in temperature increases pressure, which finally causes the two layers to be pushed apart. Nearly all roofs may experience some bubbles and blisters. If the bubbles and blisters are unbroken and meet the Performance Guideline, they should be left alone. Puncturing and attempting to repair the unbroken blisters can result in leaks where there were none previously.

Builder Responsibility: If bubbles/blisters exceed the Performance Guideline, the Builder should make repairs necessary to meet the Guideline.

Homeowner Responsibility: *Maintenance Alert!* As the roof starts to age, the Homeowner will need to provide periodic maintenance to joints and separations. Areas that have received tar or caulking type materials will also need periodic maintenance due to age and structure movement. The Homeowner should pay particular attention to locations where dissimilar materials meet (i.e., plumbing vents or metal flashing). The joining of dissimilar materials is a prime location for water intrusion, especially as tar and caulking become more brittle and crack.

Condition #4: ROOF *MEMBRANE* HAS SPLITS OR TEARS

Can Affect:

- Integrity of the roof
- Structural integrity
- Interior finishes

Performance Guideline: Splitting and tearing of the roof membrane are unacceptable.

Comments: There are several possible causes of splitting or tearing of a membrane. One cause may be stress from differential movement of the frame of the House. Residential buildings are usually constructed of wood, and will likely expand and contract with changes in the weather. Excessive foot traffic on the roof is another possible cause of splitting and tearing. An invasive testing approach would be necessary to determine actual causes and their origin.

Builder Responsibility: The Builder should inspect the area in question. If the condition is not a result of Homeowner negligence, then the Builder should make the repairs necessary to comply with the above Performance Guideline.

Homeowner Responsibility: A maintenance schedule should be started as soon as the House has been occupied. As the roof ages, maintenance becomes increasingly important. The Homeowner will need to provide maintenance to asphalt cements, joints and separations. ***Maintenance Alert!*** Homeowner should pay particular attention to where the roof ties into dissimilar materials. The tie-in of dissimilar materials (materials that are not of the same kind, i.e. wood in contact with steel, stucco in contact with wood, etc.) are prime locations for water intrusion, especially over time, as roofing compounds like asphalt cement and caulking can crack, separate, and become brittle.

Condition #5: ROOF HAS BARE SPOTS

Can Affect:

- Useful life of roof
- Integrity of underlying felt
- Fire resistance of roof

Performance Guideline: An even layer of gravel or mineral should be firmly embedded into the flood coat, with no bare spots showing. Where the membrane turns up on vertical projections (such as parapet walls, skylights, and plumbing vents), flashing or granular surfacing suitable for exposure should be used to protect membranes.

Comments: Roofs with bare spots are more vulnerable to deterioration than those that are fully covered with gravel. Loose gravel under high wind conditions can also become a hazard. Since it is not possible to attain complete embedment of all aggregate, gravel with sufficient weight to resist wind displacement should be used.

Builder Responsibility: The Builder should furnish a roof that is fully coated or surfaced with gravel or mineral and roofing compounds (if the roof is a surface gravel system). If at the time of installation, the roof does not meet the above Performance Guideline, then the Builder should make the necessary repairs to meet the Guideline. The Builder is not responsible if bare spots have been created by extreme wind conditions or if the condition is caused by improper Homeowner use or lack of maintenance.

Homeowner Responsibility: ***Maintenance Alert!*** The Homeowner has the responsibility of keeping the roof, roof drains, gutters and downspouts free of any foreign debris. Gravel or mineral has a tendency to clog drains and fill gutters. Always make plans to check the roof prior to and after any inclement weather and/or winter rains.

Condition #6: ROOFING MATERIAL AT THE ROOF-TO-WALL INTERSECTION IS SPLITTING

Can Affect:

- Integrity of the roof
- Structural integrity
- Interior finishes and furnishings

Performance Guideline: Splits, tears or rips are not acceptable.

Comments: A common area for water intrusion to occur is at a horizontal location that ties into a vertical surface. Many roof leaks occur at these flashing locations. Any leaking that occurs at these locations is unacceptable and will need immediate attention. At all horizontal to vertical changes, a triangle shaped ***cant strip*** should be installed to allow the 90-degree intersection to be reduced to two 45-degree angles.

Builder Responsibility: If the roof leaks are a result of poor or inadequate flashing, counterflashing and/or the lack of adequate cant strips, and the leak is not the result of Homeowner negligence, the Builder should make all the necessary repairs to meet the Performance Guideline.

Homeowner Responsibility: ***Maintenance Alert!*** As a general rule, avoid walking on the roof. Avoid stepping or walking on locations where materials transition from the horizontal to the vertical.

Condition # 7: UNSEALED LAPS

Can Affect:

- Useful life of the roof
- Interior finishes and furnishings
- Structural integrity

Performance Guideline: All laps of the roof membrane should be properly sealed.

Comments: Unsealed laps or “fishmouths” can occur as a result of poorly constructed overlaps on roof membrane systems. Unsealed laps can result in water migration into the roof system, which can reduce the performance and life span of the roof and installation components. In addition, if the opening lap extends to a lower layer, water can find its way into the structure.

Builder Responsibility: The Builder should install the membrane roof system with all laps properly sealed.

Homeowner Responsibility: The Homeowner should retain a qualified roofing professional to perform annual inspections of the roof.

Condition # 8: FASTENER BACK-OUT

Can Affect:

- Useful life of the roof
- Interior finishes and furnishings
- Wind uplift resistance

Performance Guideline: All fasteners should be properly sized and installed, per the manufacturer’s instructions.

Comments: Fasteners of insufficient length, or fasteners that are improperly installed, can become loose from vibration, from fluttering of the membrane due to wind action, or from the expansion and contraction due to temperature variations. Backed-out fasteners can deform and puncture membranes and contribute to a reduction in wind uplift resistance of the roof system.

Builder Responsibility: The Builder should install the roof system with all fasteners properly sized and securely installed per manufacturer's specifications. Fasteners found to be backing out within the accepted warranty period should be replaced.

Homeowner Responsibility: The Homeowner should retain a qualified roofing professional to perform annual inspections of the roof, noting and repairing any anomalies that are found, such as backed out fasteners.

Condition # 9: ACCUMULATION OF A BROWN RESIDUE FROM ASPHALT ROOFING PRODUCTS

Can Affect:

- Appearance

Performance Guideline: This is an acceptable and normal condition.

Comments: Formation of "tobacco-juice" residue results from migration of surface oils from the asphalt based membrane during initial weathering and once washed away by rainfall or rinsing with water it is unlikely to recur. The only significant affect of this condition is a potential impediment for bonding of any coatings applied to the roof surface. This possible impediment can be resolved by rinsing of the roof surface prior to application of the coating.

Builder Responsibility: The Builder should properly clean and prepare the surface of new asphalt based membrane roofs prior to application of any coating.

Homeowner Responsibility: None, other than annual inspection and maintenance.

Chapter Five

EXTERIOR COMPONENTS

includes:

Walkways and Driveways

Decks and Patios

Garage Doors

Windows and Patio Doors

French Doors/Other Exterior Doors

Chimneys and Flues

Gutters, Downspouts & Flashing

Skylights

Paint and Stain

References for this chapter:

- *The Complete Idiot's Guide to Trouble Free Home Repair*, by David Tenenbaum
- *Concrete Performance Standards & Maintenance Guidelines*
- *500 Terrific Ideas for Home Maintenance and Repair*, by Jack Maguire
- *Handbook of Construction Tolerances*, by David Kent Ballast
- *Residential Construction Performance Guidelines*, NAHB
- *Residential Water Problems*, by Alvin Sacks
- *Residential & Light Commercial Construction Standards*, by Don Reynolds
- *Top 25 Construction Problems and Their Resolution*, BIASD
- *Troubleshooting Guide to Residential Construction*, Builderburg Group
- *Workmanship Guidelines*, CA Contractors State License Board

A comprehensive list of references by author and publisher is found in the Bibliography section.

Exterior Components

Walkways and Driveways

General Subject Information: When it comes to concrete, there is one fact that all Homeowners, Builders, and tradespersons must realize: CONCRETE WILL CRACK. Concrete walkways and driveways are constructed with joints that create a weakened plane or thinner section of concrete. The purpose of these control joints is to control and contain the cracking to specific areas, i.e. the thinner section. Therefore cracks in control joints are a normal occurrence and are considered acceptable. The degree to which concrete cracks or the deviation in vertical displacement are the determining criteria as to whether or not the cracking is unacceptable or within industry standards. There are many reasons that concrete products crack and most are not related to any structural problems.

Condition #1: DRIVEWAY IS CRACKED

Can Affect:

- Appearance
- Safety issues related to tripping hazard
- Structural integrity of the driveway

Performance Guideline: Any crack that exceeds ¼ inch in width or exceeds ¼ inch in vertical displacement is considered unacceptable. Minor cracking is normal. A crack that occurs along a joint that is cut into the driveway when it was poured is considered acceptable, provided the crack does not exceed ¾ inch in width. Further, this Guideline includes spacing control joints in the wet concrete at industry recommended intervals based upon the thickness of the slab. A nominal 4-inch thick slab should have control joints spaced at 12 feet or less.

Comments: When trees are planted in the vicinity of any concrete work, there is the potential for the root system to undermine the concrete, causing the concrete to eventually crack, heave and/or settle (this holds true for the foundation as well). If the driveway is used for large RV storage, it may crack due to the weight of the RV. RVs should be stored on a separate concrete pad that is reinforced with steel and is at least 6 inches thick. Moving vans should be parked on the street. Concrete trucks used by after market contractors for pools and patios should be parked on the street, and their contents should be pumped to the desired location.

Builder Responsibility: The Builder should meet the above Performance Guideline, providing the cracking is not a result of any Homeowner misuse or negligence (this includes Homeowner overwatering of the surrounding area and causing the soils to expand). If the concrete cracking exceeds the Guideline, the Builder should make the appropriate repairs as necessary to meet the above Guideline. The Builder will also be responsible for the replacement of any landscape that was damaged as a result of the repairs.

Homeowner Responsibility: ***Maintenance Alert!*** Cracks that occur at ***control joints*** are to be maintained by the Homeowner. This maintenance consists of filling the crack with a suitable concrete caulk. Also the Homeowner should maintain the area around the driveway in a way that will not allow soils to be washed away from beneath the driveway. Tree roots are a primary cause for concrete to heave and/or crack in landscaped areas. When placing trees in the vicinity of any concrete product, it is important to consider the potential growth of the root system (for example, palm trees have very small root balls, while the root system of a willow is extensive and will cause significant heaving of drives and walks). The Homeowner should seek the advice of a licensed landscape architect or contractor and install a root barrier system in these instances.

Condition #2: WALKWAY IS CRACKED

Can Affect:

- Appearance
- Safety issues related to tripping hazard
- Structural integrity of the sidewalk

Performance Guideline: Any crack that exceeds ¼ inch in width or exceeds ¼ inch in vertical displacement is unacceptable. Cracking that occurs at a ***control joint*** is acceptable, unless the crack exceeds 1 inch in width and ¼ inch in vertical displacement. Minor cracking is considered normal.

Comments: Generally speaking, the further away from the foundation, the less compaction there is within the soils. Concrete sidewalks are much more susceptible to heaving or subsiding than a structural foundation. Not only is the soil potentially not as well compacted, but there may be a flow of irrigation water to the landscape. If the soils are expansive, water will cause the soils to expand; when the soils dry out they start to contract. Both expansion and contraction apply an excessive amount of stress upon concrete.

Builder Responsibility: The Builder should meet the above Performance Guideline, providing the cracking is not a result of any Homeowner negligence. If the concrete cracks exceed the Guideline, the Builder should make the appropriate repairs as necessary to meet the above Performance Guideline. The Builder will also be responsible for the replacement of any landscape material that was damaged as a result of the repairs.

THIS TREE WAS PLANTED TOO CLOSE TO THE SIDEWALK.. ITS ROOTS PUSHED UP THE WALK!

Homeowner Responsibility: ***Maintenance Alert!*** Cracks that occur at control joints are to be maintained by the Homeowner. The Homeowner should also maintain the area around the sidewalks in a way that will not allow soils to be washed away from beneath them. Tree roots generally pose the biggest threat to concrete sidewalks. When Homeowners decide that they want to install a tree, they often make their decision solely on the beauty of the tree. However, when placing trees in the vicinity of any concrete product, the most important consideration should be the potential for growth of the root system.

Condition #3: WATER PONDS ON SIDEWALK

Can Affect:
- Safety issues related to slipping hazard

Performance Guideline: Any standing or ponding water that exceeds 3/8 inch in depth in a circle more than one foot in diameter is considered unacceptable. All water should drain off or evaporate within 24 hours of cessation of rain.

Comments: All sidewalks, or any concrete for that matter, that are subject to the outside elements should slope a minimum of ¼ inch vertically for every one foot horizontally. In other words, if the concrete sidewalk is three feet across, the sidewalk should slope in one direction ¾ inch from level.

Builder Responsibility: If the sidewalk does not meet the Performance Guideline, the Builder should make the repairs necessary to meet such Guideline, provided the unacceptable condition was not caused by actions of the Homeowner. The Builder should repair any landscape that is damaged as a result of the repairs.

Homeowner Responsibility: ***Maintenance Alert!*** The Homeowner should not let any irrigation undermine the sidewalks. Sidewalks need to have a very solid foundation in order to prevent any cracking or damage from occurring.

Condition #4: CONCRETE DRIVEWAY THAT ABUTS THE GARAGE IS HIGHER THAN THE GARAGE SLAB

Can Affect:
- Water tightness of garage
- Safety issues related to tripping hazard

Performance Guideline: A concrete driveway should never be higher than the interior portion of the garage slab that it abuts. A deviation in two adjoining sections of concrete should not be greater than 1/2 inch between the two adjoining surfaces.

Comments: The driveway portion of the concrete should not exceed the height of the garage slab. This can cause a build-up of water at the garage door entry and may present a safety hazard with regards to tripping. A good practice is to pour the driveway slab up to ½ inch lower than the garage slab. This allows for future movement of the driveway slab.

Builder Responsibility: If the driveway does not meet the above Performance Guideline, and the condition is not caused by actions of the Homeowner, the Builder should make the necessary repairs.

Homeowner Responsibility: None, provided that the Homeowner has done nothing to alter the drainage, which could cause the driveway to heave above the garage slab.

Condition #5: DRIVEWAY APPROACH IS TOO STEEP, CAUSING VEHICLES TO SCRAPE OR TO BOTTOM OUT

Can Affect:

- Vehicle integrity and appearance
- Appearance of the driveway approach

Performance Guideline: The driveway approach should meet the standards of the local municipality at the time of construction.

Comments: During design and engineering of the site, the streets and lots are calculated to provide positive water drainage away from streets and residences. These designs are fairly standard, and they take into consideration wheelbase and clearance of most vehicles. However, vehicles with exceptionally long or short wheelbases or vehicles that have been lowered are likely to scrape or bottom out.

Builder Responsibility: If the driveway approach does not meet the local municipal standard, the Builder should make repairs necessary to meet the above Performance Guideline. However, the Builder does not have a responsibility to make driveway approaches suitable for all vehicles.

Homeowner Responsibility: None.

Condition #6: CONCRETE DRIVEWAY IS *SPALLING*, SCALING OR CHIPPING

Can Affect:

- Driveway structural integrity
- Appearance

Performance Guideline: The surface of the concrete should not disintegrate to the point that the aggregate (small rocks) are showing in more than 5% of the driveway surface area.

Comments: Builder is not responsible if the Homeowner spills chemicals, oils, salts, etc. on concrete that can cause premature breakdown. This includes the use of rock salt to remove snow and ice. If the soils contain sulfates that cause concrete degradation over time, the Builder is not responsible.

Builder Responsibility: If surface spalls, scales or chips exceed the Guideline and the condition is not related to Homeowner negligence, the Builder should make the repairs necessary to meet the Performance Guideline.

Homeowner Responsibility: The Homeowner should not spill acidic products or create excessive landscape moisture that may cause damage to the concrete surface. If a Homeowner uses rock salt as an ice-removing agent, the Homeowner is assuming the risk of damage to the concrete (and surrounding landscape as well).

Condition #7: CONCRETE STOOP IS PULLING AWAY FROM THE FOUNDATION

Can Affect:
- Appearance
- Safety issues related to tripping hazard

Performance Guideline: Concrete stoops that join to the foundation should not separate from the foundation by more than ¼ inch.

Comments: When the foundation of the House and steps/stoops are poured at separate times, there is a possibility that they will move at different rates and cause minor heaving, settling and/or separation. The above Performance Guideline will also apply in situations where expansion joints separate concrete.

Builder Responsibility: If the steps or ***stoops*** are separated from ¼ inch to one inch, the Builder may fill the separation or replace the stoop at his option. Stoops that are separated by gaps in excess of one inch should be repaired or replaced as appropriate.

Homeowner Responsibility: Separations up to ¼ inch are the responsibility of the Homeowner to maintain. Concrete caulk may be used to fill the gap.

Condition # 8: DRIVEWAY OR WALKWAY IS NOT A UNIFORM COLOR

This Condition is discussed in the Decks and Patios section of this Chapter, under Condition #6.

Garage Doors

Condition #1: GARAGE DOOR LEAKS WATER / SNOW AT HEAD, JAMBS OR THRESHOLD

Can Affect:
- Contents of garage
- Intended use of garage

Performance Guideline: Install garage doors in accordance with the recommendations of the manufacturer. Some water or snow can be expected to enter around the door under high wind conditions. This is acceptable. The garage slab should ***slope*** toward the door at 3 inches per 20 feet. The driveway surface at the garage door should be sloped to inhibit the entrance of water. There should also be a vertical drop of up to ½ inch between the driveway slab and the garage slab, so as to act as a weather break. If the garage is located at the bottom of a downsloped driveway, the two feet of driveway closest to the garage slab should also be sloped away from the garage slab at the rate of ¼ inch per foot. A drain that runs parallel to the garage door(s) is also acceptable.

Builder Responsibility: Conform to the Performance Guideline. Builder should adjust door in the event that excessive water entry occurs at jambs and head. Garage door weather stripping can be very effective to meet the Performance Guideline.

Homeowner Responsibility: ***Maintenance Alert!*** Homeowner is responsible for adequate maintenance and protection of the garage door. Homeowner damage to the door, frame, and/or guides that results in poor performance of the garage door is a Homeowner responsibility. Proper lubrication of the door tracks and operating mechanism is discussed in the **Homeowner Maintenance Summary, Garage Doors**.

Condition #2: GARAGE DOOR FAILS TO OPERATE PROPERLY OR GETS JAMMED

Can Affect:

- Intended use of door

Performance Guideline: Barring damage caused by Homeowner misuse, garage doors should operate smoothly and completely, as intended by the manufacturer.

Builder Responsibility: Unless the Homeowner has been negligent or abusive in the use of the garage doors, the Builder should be responsible for making adjustments to malfunctioning doors as required to restore their performance to the manufacturer's specifications.

Homeowner Responsibility: Maintain garage doors in accordance with the manufacturer's recommendations and avoid abusive or negligent use of doors that could result in damage. One-piece garage doors may sag with age. It is the Homeowner's responsibility to keep the metal rods that span the top and bottom of the door in a tight condition and in proper alignment.

Condition #3: GARAGE DOOR OPENS "MYSTERIOUSLY"

Can Affect:

- Security of garage, House, and contents

Performance Guideline: Garage door openers should operate only on their own assigned frequencies. Random external signals should not cause the door to open or close.

Comments: The condition of mysterious opening and closing of garage doors sometimes occurs when the door is equipped with an automatic opener. The transmitter may share a radio frequency with other devices, such as another garage transmitter in the neighborhood, or an airplane flying overhead. Signals from these transmitters will activate the automatic door opener. Most openers have programmable code switches that can be changed if the above-mentioned condition occurs.

Builder Responsibility: If a Homeowner reports a problem of random openings or closings of the automatic door opener, the Builder should instruct the Homeowner on the procedure to change the opener code.

Homeowner Responsibility: Read the instruction manual that is furnished with the automatic door opener.

Decks and Patios

General Subject Information: Decks and patios are accessory structures used to enhance the architecture and livability of the house. Most decks and patios are not installed by the Builder, except as part of a planned community such as a condominium or patio house project. Because decks are exposed continually to weather, they require more maintenance and have a shorter useful life than other exterior components. Apart from original construction, the useful life of a deck and patio will depend upon the degree of Homeowner maintenance, the annual rainfall in the area, local weather conditions, and which direction the deck or patio faces.

Condition # 1: WATER PONDS ON DECKS AND PATIOS

Can Affect:

- Useful life of deck
- Safety issues related to slipping hazard

Performance Guideline: There should be no more than 3/8 inch of water standing in a ponded area 24 hours after cessation of rain (assuming that ***deck drains***, if installed, are maintained in a free flowing condition by Homeowner).

Comments: Decks and patios should be constructed with a minimum slope of ¼ inch of drop for every one foot of length away from the House. That is to say, the deck or patio should be one inch lower four feet away from the House than at the edge of the House. Some enclosed decks that are not designed to drain over the outer edge have drains located in the deck surface. Decks constructed in this manner should also have overflow drains. The deck surface should be sloped to these drains so that the deck drains freely within 24 hours after cessation of rain. A wood surface deck (including composite boards made to look like wood) should drain directly through the deck to ground below.

Builder Responsibility: Assuming that condition is a result of original construction, repair the surface of the deck or patio to create the proper slope, i.e. ¼ inch to the foot, so that the deck surface meets the Performance Guideline.

Homeowner Responsibility: ***Maintenance Alert!*** Keep decks clean and free of dirt and debris so that they will not become slippery or plug the deck drains during storms. If deck drains are installed, they should be flushed with a garden hose prior to the start of the rainy season and periodically during the rainy season. Overflow drains should be inspected to ensure that they are not clogged with leaves or

other debris. Potted plants should not be placed directly on the deck surface. They should be placed on stands or spacers to allow air to circulate underneath. Plant stands with metal legs should be avoided or protect the deck surface from penetration by the metal legs.

Condition #2: DECK MEMBERS ARE ROTTING

Can Affect:

- Structural integrity
- Appearance
- Useful life of deck

Performance Guideline: Deck structural members such as ***posts***, ***beams***, and ***joists*** should be ***pressure treated*** wood, or Code approved wood that is naturally resistant to decay.

Builder Responsibility: Construct structural members of decks using pressure treated lumber or Code approved wood that is naturally resistant to decay. If pressure treated lumber is cut on-site, the cut ends should be treated with an approved wood preservative. Treated lumber, fir, cedar and redwood may be used as deck top boards. Man-made composite material may be used as top boards also.

Homeowner Responsibility: *Maintenance Alert!* Perform an annual inspection of the deck and renail all loose boards and raised nails. Recoat the top boards with a good quality deck sealer every one or two years, depending upon the amount of exposure. Keep the underside of the deck free of debris and storage materials so that air can circulate underneath. The bottom of posts should be maintained 6 inches away from the soil. Landscape shrubs should not be allowed to grow around posts, as moisture may dryrot the posts.

Condition #3: DECK IS NOT FLASHED AT HOUSE / DECK CONNECTION

Can Affect:

- Structural integrity of the House

Performance Guideline: Decks attached to a House or other habitable structure should be flashed with an approved flashing material between the House and deck connection. Flashing should cover the top of the ***ledger*** completely and turn down at least one inch to prevent water from running between the back of the ledger and the exterior surface of the House. Building paper is not an acceptable flashing material.

Builder Responsibility: Install deck ledgers with an approved flashing material that runs behind the water resistant membrane, behind the exterior surface of the House, and over the top edge of the ledger.

Homeowner Responsibility: None.

Condition # 4: NAIL HEADS OR SCREWS PROTRUDE ABOVE THE SURFACE OF THE DECK BOARDS

Can Affect:

- Appearance
- Safety issues related to tripping hazard

Performance Guideline: At the time of the Walkthrough, nail heads, screws, or other fasteners that protrude above the deck board surface by more than 1/16 inch are considered non-performing.

Builder Responsibility: Renail or screw fasteners that do not meet the above Performance Guideline at the time of the Walkthrough.

Homeowner Responsibility: After the Walkthrough, renailing or screw tightening of deck boards is a Homeowner maintenance item. Deck boards shrink as they dry out, and they also move up and down with seasonal temperature changes. ***Maintenance Alert!*** If the deck has wooden railings, the rail post bolts should be tightened every 6 months during the first two years of occupancy as a safety precaution.

Condition #5: PATIO SURFACES CRACK AND SEPARATE

Can Affect:

- Appearance
- Life of patio surface materials
- Safety issues related to tripping hazard

Performance Guideline: Patios and decks should be constructed on soils and sub-surfaces that are properly drained and compacted sufficiently to prevent excessive movement. Decks and patios should be constructed to slope away from the House with a slope of ¼ inch to the foot. Cracks in hard surfaces (such as concrete) exceeding ¼ inch in width, or ¼ inch in vertical displacement, are unacceptable. Modular ***pavers*** are subject to individual differential settlement, but should not have surfaces that are vertically offset by more than ¼ inch from one paver to the adjoining one (Refer to Condition # 1 in the Walkways and Driveways section of this Chapter).

Builder's Responsibility: Builder should construct patios in conformance to the Performance Guideline. If modular ***pavers*** are used, Builder should conform to the manufacturer's installation recommendations.

Homeowner Responsibility: Maintain all drainage courses and catch basins so that they are free of dirt, leaves and other debris. Do not apply unreasonably heavy loads on deck surfaces.

Condition # 6: FINISHED CONCRETE SURFACE HAS BLOTCHY / MOTTLED COLOR

Can Affect:

- Appearance

Performance Guideline: Assuming that each batch of concrete has been prepared with the same amount of color additive, non-uniform surface color on concrete is considered acceptable.

Comments: Concrete, whether natural in color, or whether colored by adding agents to the mix, is not likely to dry (cure) in a uniform manner. Many factors influence the surface appearance of concrete that is less than a year old. Factors include the amount of moisture in the underlying soil and the humidity during the first 30 days. The more moisture in the soil and air, the greater the chances for non-uniform surface color. Over time (usually within 2 years) the non-uniform color will gradually become uniform as the surface of the concrete reacts to the air.

Builder Responsibility: None.

Homeowner Responsibility: None. However if the Homeowner wants to speed up the process of equalizing the color, he or she can brush the concrete with a wire broom and allow the air to react with the darker areas.

Windows and Patio Doors

General Subject Information: Windows come in many different types such as side vent, single hung, double hung, and fixed. Patio doors are, for industry purposes, considered a large window. Both window and patio door frames are made of metal (usually aluminum), wood, or plastic (PVC), or a combination of these materials. The installation methods and operation of windows and patio doors are similar. It is not the purpose of this section to provide extensive information on the various types of windows and patio doors, but simply to cover several conditions that may occur with windows and patio doors.

Condition # 1: GLASS IS SCRATCHED OR BROKEN

Can Affect:

- Visibility,
- Appearance
- Occupant comfort

Performance Guideline: At the time of delivery, glass that is visibly scratched or broken from a line of sight from 11 feet under daylight conditions (but not direct sunlight) is unacceptable. Damage to glass after the Homeowner takes delivery of the House is not a Builder responsibility. The same Performance Guideline applies to damaged screens.

Builder Responsibility: Replace broken or scratched glass or screens if noted at the time of delivery of the House.

Homeowner Responsibility: The Homeowner should take care to inspect all windows and patio doors prior to delivery of the House, especially on houses that have stucco as an exterior finish. Sand from the stucco may find its way onto the glass, and window washers can accidentally make small scratches in the glass when they are trying to clean it. Never use an abrasive cleaner on glass.

Condition #2: GLASS HAS IMPERFECTIONS

Can Affect:
- Appearance
- Visibility

Performance Guideline: Imperfections that are part of the manufacturing process (as opposed to scratches), such as waviness and "cat's eye", which are visible from a distance of 6 feet under normal lighting conditions, are considered unacceptable.

Builder Responsibility: Replace glass that does not meet the Performance Guideline.

Homeowner Responsibility: None.

Condition #3: WINDOWS AND PATIO DOORS ARE DIFFICULT TO OPEN AND CLOSE

Can Affect:
- Occupant comfort

Performance Guideline: All windows and patio doors should open and close freely ("freely" defined as without having to exert undue pressure or force by an adult of average strength). All latches and locks should operate in a similar manner.

Builder Responsibility: All window and door operating mechanisms, including latches and locks, should operate smoothly, without sticking or jamming, assuming that there is appropriate Homeowner maintenance. The Builder should adjust and/or otherwise correct malfunctioning mechanisms. Window and patio door operational problems caused by foundation or frame problems are also the responsibility of the Builder. Any damage that is caused by misuse or lack of proper maintenance by the Homeowner should not be the responsibility of the Builder.

Homeowner Responsibility: ***Maintenance Alert!*** Windows and patio doors installed in houses today require little maintenance. Doors and windows have a tendency to "stick" during the winter months because the wood frame of the House takes on moisture, thereby expanding slightly; this is acceptable. Lubricating the rollers and slides with an approved window lubricant (available at any hardware store) and adjusting the rollers on the patio doors are simple and routine maintenance items. In addition, Homeowner should brush and vacuum the patio door tracks and window tracks routinely.

Condition #4: WINDOW IS FOGGED BETWEEN PANES OF GLASS

Can Affect:
- Visibility
- Insulation value

Performance Guideline: Dual glazed window and dual glazed patio door seals should not rupture during the manufacturer's warranty period, providing there is no misuse by Homeowner.

Comments: Most windows and patio doors installed in new or remodeled houses are ***dual pane*** glass: two panes of glass made into a "sandwich" with a dead air space in the middle. The sandwich is sealed so that the air cannot enter or leave the space. This dead air space provides an insulating quality that windows with single pane glass do not have. When the seal is broken, moisture enters between the panes, and the window becomes foggy. Seal materials have greatly improved in recent years, allowing manufacturers to extend their warranties. The warranty on dual glazed windows is likely to be a manufacturer's warranty.

Builder Responsibility: Within the warranty period, the Builder should assist the Homeowner in dealing with the manufacturer to replace windows and patio doors whose seals have failed. This excludes failures caused by Homeowner negligence or misuse (see below).

Homeowner Responsibility: None. However, many Homeowners unknowingly cause window seal failure by tinting the inside pane. This causes excessive heat build up between the panes of glass and the seals are likely to rupture. *Refer to* ***Ten Most Common Mistakes Made By New Homeowners*** *located in the Preface.*

Condition #5: WINDOW GRIDS DISINTEGRATE

Can Affect:
- Appearance

Performance Guideline: Window grids should not disintegrate or drop down inside the dual panes.

Comments: Dual pane windows are often manufactured with a "grid" of plastic or aluminum inside the panes to give an impression of individual panes of glass. It is unacceptable if these grids fail because they were not properly secured or because of disintegration from ultraviolet rays.

Builder Responsibility: Builder should replace windows whose grids have failed. Exception: if the Homeowner has tinted the inside of the windows or otherwise caused the condition, Builder should not be responsible for failed grids.

Homeowner Responsibility: None. However, do not tint the inside pane of dual pane windows.

Condition #6: WINDOW LEAKS AT HEAD (top) / WINDOW LEAKS AT SILL (bottom) / PATIO DOOR LEAKS AT SILL (bottom)

Can Affect:

- Occupant comfort
- Structural integrity

Performance Guideline: Windows should not leak at any point regardless of the location of the leak. (*See extreme weather exception at* ***Condition #7*** *below.)*

Comments: A window or patio door that leaks, apart from being an annoyance to the Homeowner, should not be allowed to go unrepaired. A window that leaks at the top may not be flashed properly at the head or an opening higher up on the wall (such as an attic vent) may not be properly flashed. A window that leaks at the bottom may be leaking because (1) the sides and sill are not properly flashed, (2) the lower corners of the window frame itself are not properly sealed, or (3) the ***weep holes*** are plugged. A patio door that leaks at the bottom may be leaking because of improper sill flashing or because the outside patio or deck is too high.

Builder Responsibility: The Builder should diagnose the cause of the leak and make repairs to eliminate the non-performing condition, if the condition is a result of improper / inadequate construction.

Homeowner Responsibility: ***Maintenance Alert!*** The Homeowner should annually inspect and clean debris from all window and patio door weep holes and caulk all inside corners of the sill. This maintenance is especially important in geographic areas that have trees with small leaves and also areas that experience dust storms. Patios and decks should be constructed 2 inches below the patio door threshold. *Refer to* ***Ten Most Common Mistakes Made By New Homeowners*** *located in the Preface.*

INSPECT AND CAULK TRIM ANNUALLY

Condition #7: WINDOWS LEAK WHEN THE WIND BLOWS HARD

Can Affect:

- Occupant comfort

Performance Guideline: Use of residential windows and doors that are labeled with the appropriate AAMA "R"-rating for the geographical area are the Performance Guideline for rain and wind intrusion. For example, an oceanfront house should usually have windows and doors with a higher "R" rating than a house in a wooded valley.

Comments: Wind-driven rain can sometimes penetrate window weather seals and joints. Wind-driven rain can also blow back through the weep holes into the interior of the House. Windows should be selected in accordance with the American Architectural Manufacturer's Association (AAMA) "R"-ratings that match window systems with weather conditions found in the geographic location of the House. Exception: even a properly selected window may leak if exposed to extreme wind or rain. During a storm it is not unusual to find that the sill track of the window is filled with water; this condition is acceptable. At the conclusion of the inclement weather (wind and rain), the water will drain out of the track. Weather extremes are defined on page 4.

Builder Responsibility: The Builder should install windows and patio doors that meet the appropriate AAMA standards for the geographic area where the House is built. If this standard is met, the intrusion of wind-driven rain during extreme weather conditions is acceptable.

Homeowner Responsibility: None.

French Doors and Other Exterior Doors

General Subject Information: "French" style doors are becoming a popular door style in homes today. Other exterior doors include the front door, rear door and garage pedestrian door. Patio doors, which are actually considered a specialty window, are covered in the "Windows and Patio Doors" Section of this Chapter. Generally, if doors open (swing) into the House, they offer a better degree of weather protection. Many manufacturers will not warrant their doors if they are installed with an outward swing.

Condition#1: WATER ENTERS WALLS AND INTERIOR THROUGH TOP, JAMBS AND THRESHOLD

Can Affect:

- Wall components
- Interior finishes
- Structural integrity

Performance Guideline: Water entering through top, sides, bottom, or under door is considered unacceptable, unless the water is a result of excessive wind-driven rain. Pedestrian garage doors are not covered by this Guideline and are often installed without a sill.

Comments: Proper flashing of head, jambs and sills of doors is essential in preventing water intrusion. All flashing should be installed in the proper sequence, "fish-scale" style, and integrated with the House wrap or building paper so that water is directed to exterior surfaces. Manufacturers of exterior doors generally provide specific installation and maintenance recommendations. These recommendations should be adhered to strictly.

Builder Responsibility: Repair any exterior door that leaks as a result of improper original installation.

Homeowner Responsibility: *Maintenance Alert!* Keep threshold weeps and other drainage paths clean and free of obstructions and debris. If exterior door trim and joints between the door frame and the exterior wall surface are caulked, inspect caulking annually and re-caulk (including the threshold) as necessary to maintain a weather-tight seal. Keep doors closed during wet weather. Depending upon geographic location and exposure, the weatherstrips at the doors will need to be replaced between three and five years.

Condition #2: DOORS ARE WARPED, OUT-OF-LEVEL, NOT PLUMB

Can Affect:

- Door performance
- Weather tightness

Performance Guideline: The vertical and horizontal planes of the door should not vary from a true plane by more than ¼ inch. Doors should not be installed out of true level and plumb by more than 1/8 inch. French door *leaves* should be installed in alignment with each other. Doors should remain in any position in which they are placed without closing or opening by themselves. If doors do move, it is an indication that they are out of plumb.

Comments: Initial door installations should be made in secure, plumb, level and square rough openings of the size specified by the manufacturer. Doors should be set in place within the Performance Guideline specified above. Any interior door manufactured in wood should be painted with a prime coat and a finish coat. Any exterior door manufactured in wood should be painted with a prime coat plus two finish coats. All six sides of a door should be painted promptly after installation to prevent moisture from entering the wood fibers. This will particularly affect the door head, where end grain may be exposed. Sufficient clearance should be left at the door head to prevent any header deflection from transferring a load to the doorframe that may cause the door(s) to bind. The doorframe jambs should be securely attached to the rough frame in order to prevent door sag. With some types of doors, it is advisable to use long hinge screws that will penetrate the rough jambs by at least 1-1/4-inch. Doors that are significantly out-of-plumb will swing open (or closed) by themselves. This is an annoyance and not acceptable workmanship. External forces, such as settlement, can also cause out-of-level and out-of-plumb conditions described above. Look for cracks in drywall radiating outward from the upper corners of door openings (usually at approximately 45 degrees). This is a fairly reliable indicator of movement in the structural frame but not necessarily non-performing.

Builder Responsibility: Install doors within the Performance Guideline set forth above, and in adherence of the door manufacturer's installation requirements. Ensure that door components subject to moisture exposure are completely and effectively protected as soon as possible after the initial installation. The Builder is responsible for correcting any material, workmanship or inadequate design that results in improper door performance.

Homeowner Responsibility: Do not place any load on door *leaves*, as they are not designed for this purpose and may sag over time. Keep door leaves and frames in good condition by repainting and re-caulking on a periodic basis. Adhere to the manufacturer's recommendations. Sometimes it is necessary to correct the fit of wood doors, either because of minor swelling or because surrounding finishes were replaced with materials of different thickness (for example, floor coverings). Any such corrections should be done professionally, and any bare wood should be immediately and completely sealed. If the bottom of a door is cut due to a change in flooring material, the fresh cut should be sealed.

Condition #3: CORROSION OR STAINING OF EXTERIOR HARDWARE

Can Affect:
- Appearance
- Door performance

Performance Guideline: Hardware exposed to exterior atmospheric conditions should be corrosion-resistant. Hardware exposed to salt air in a marine environment, or air containing corrosives from pollutants, should be made of materials suitable for use in such environments (for example, stainless steel).

Comments: Hardware exposed to outdoor conditions requires special attention, both in selection and maintenance. The fact that an item of hardware is corrosion-resistant does not mean, however, that it will not become discolored. For example, bright brass hardware, which is commonly used in exterior applications, has a factory-applied lacquer coating. Consumers are often not aware of this, and when the lacquer finish eventually breaks down (as it almost certainly will) dark spots will appear. The consumer may then conclude that the product is unacceptable; this is not the case. Proper maintenance at this time will restore the finish, but more frequent care will be required thereafter. It is advisable to wait for 2 days after applying varnish, paint, or stain to a door before installing brass hardware to avoid chemical reactions between the brass and the curing finish that could cause staining.

Builder Responsibility: Install appropriate hardware for the specific environmental exposure of the House.

Homeowner Responsibility: ***Maintenance Alert!*** First, read the manufacturer's maintenance and care recommendations. Keep hardware clean and bright by polishing on a regular basis with a clean, soft cloth. Do not allow dust and other deleterious materials to accumulate. To preserve the factory-applied coating, avoid any abrasive products such as cleaners or polishing pads. While good care will extend the life of brass coatings, they will eventually break down and dark spots may appear. When tarnish reaches an undesirable level, the hardware should be removed from the door and the remaining lacquer coating completely removed. Coating removal should be done in accordance with the manufacturer's recommendations.

Chimneys and Flues

General Subject Information: The vast majority of fireplaces and flues that are installed in new homes are metal factory-built assemblies. The traditional masonry fireplace and chimney is relatively rare. Factory-built assemblies will provide good service if properly used and maintained. See **Chapter 6 "Fireplaces"** for further information.

Condition #1: CHIMNEY CAP DOES NOT DRAIN

Can Affect:
- Water resistance of cap
- Life of cap

Performance Guideline: Chimney caps should be built so that tops have sufficient slope to avoid ponding of water.

Builder Responsibility: Builder should correct any improperly installed cap that is non-performing.

Homeowner Responsibility: The Homeowner should include an inspection of the chimney cap and flue termination whenever the chimney flue is maintained by a professional cleaning service. Promptly notify Builder of any problem identified. If the original installation secured the chimney cap through the horizontal surface of the chase cover, the Homeowner must periodically check the caulking of the attachment screws to avoid water penetration.

Condition #2: FLUE ENCLOSURE OPEN FOR ENTIRE HEIGHT (through floors and ceilings)

Can Affect:

- Fire resistance of chimney assembly

Performance Guideline: Flue enclosures should be blocked with sheet metal fitted to the opening and the flue where passing through floors and ceilings. These sheet metal assemblies are called ***draft stops***.

Builder Responsibility: Builder should retrofit any draft stops missing from original construction.

Homeowner Responsibility: Chimneys are supposed to be completely enclosed, and therefore cannot be inspected readily. If missing draft stops are discovered in the course of inspections or other work, the Homeowner should notify the Builder.

Condition #3: IN THE CHIMNEY, WATER RUNS DOWN THE OUTSIDE OF THE FLUE

Can Affect:

- Chimney framing
- Interior finishes

Performance Guideline: Where the flue exits through the chimney cap, a storm collar should be installed to deflect water away from the penetration. Water should not run down the outside of the flue. During periods of high wind driven rain, some leakage is to be expected and is acceptable.

Builder Responsibility: If storm collar is missing or leaks, Builder should make the necessary corrections to meet the above Guideline.

Homeowner Responsibility: Promptly bring any leak to the attention of the Builder; excepting leaks during periods of high wind driven rain.

Condition #4: FIREPLACE DOES NOT *DRAW* PROPERLY

Can Affect:

- Occupant comfort
- Interior air quality
- Ability to keep a fire going

Performance Guideline: Fireplace and chimney assemblies should be sized and installed in a manner that permits smoke and other products of combustion to exit freely through the flue, without putting any smoke into the room.

Builder Responsibility: If the condition is a result of improper installation, Builder should make any necessary corrections to achieve proper airflow in the flue. It is advisable to consult the fireplace manufacturer for their recommendations regarding flue diameter, permissible flue offsets, the shape and size of flue terminations, etc., as these factors may vary according to the type of system installed.

Homeowner Responsibility: See **Chapter 6 "Fireplaces"** for recommendations regarding cleaning of the flue. Dirty flues can cause poorly drawing fireplaces. Also, overloading the fireplace with too much fuel may cause both smoke and fire to enter the room. Never burn newspapers or gift wrappings. If glass doors are installed as part of the House, they must be closed during burning operation. Fireplaces that do not have glass doors should not have them added unless specifically approved by the manufacturer.

Gutters and Downspouts

General Subject Information: The most heavily populated areas of California experience seasonal rainfall, and it is easy to forget the effects of a hard rain when the weather is sunny and warm. Control of rainwater from roofs is important for the long-term satisfactory performance of houses. Significant amounts of water can flow over the edge of a sloped roof during a strong rainstorm. If uncontrolled, this water will flow down wall surfaces and increase the likelihood of leaks at windows, doors and through wall surface coverings. When water from the roof hits the ground next to a house, water and soil can splash onto the lower surfaces of the structure. This may produce unsightly and potentially damaging conditions. Although they are not required by Code, gutters are the best way to control water flow from eaves. Downspouts direct water from the gutters to the ground in a controlled manner. In semi-arid areas of California with little rainfall, it is a frequent practice for Builders not to include gutter and downspout systems with their homes (see **Chapter 8, "Drainage",** for additional information). If installed, downspouts and gutters should be sized according to the Sheet Metal and Air Conditioning Contractors' National Association (SMACNA) guidelines or with International Plumbing Code design criteria.

Condition #1: STANDING WATER IN GUTTERS AFTER RAINFALL

Can Affect:

- Gutter life
- Water-borne insects
- Gutter performance

Performance Guideline: Gutters, if installed, should be installed with a downward slope in the direction of the nearest downspout, if the frame of the House permits such installation. Alternatively, gutters may be installed dead level with downspouts. Gutters and/or downspouts should be installed in a manner that permits water to drain or evaporate completely from gutters within a period of no greater than 24 hours after the cessation of rainfall in summer and 36 hours in winter. No part of any gutter should be installed with a back-slope (sloping away from the nearest downspout).

Builder Responsibility: If the Performance Guideline is not met, the Builder should correct either the slope of the gutter or add more downspouts.

Homeowner Responsibility: ***Maintenance Alert!*** Homeowner should keep gutters free of leaves, toys, or other debris. The slope of a level gutter can easily be unfavorably reversed by allowing debris to accumulate. Further, the acid produced by decaying leaves will, over time, eat through a metal gutter. Gutters should be cleaned annually and more frequently if mature trees are adjacent to the House.

Condition #2: GUTTER JOINTS LEAK / DOWNSPOUT JOINTS LEAK

Can Affect:

- Gutter and downspout life
- Adjacent trim, walls and ground surface below
- Gutter coating (paint, etc.)

Performance Guideline: Gutter and downspout joints should be assembled so that they do not leak.

Builder Responsibility: The Builder should make repairs so that the seams at gutters and downspouts do not leak.

Homeowner Responsibility: None.

Condition #3: GUTTER ENDS ARE EMBEDDED IN WALL SURFACE MATERIAL

Can Affect:

- Moisture resistance of wall

Performance Guideline: Gutters should not be embedded into stucco and should terminate no closer than one inch from the surface of intersecting walls.

Comments: Gutters are sometimes installed before the application of surface materials, such as stucco. If insufficient space is provided between framing and gutter terminations, it may be impossible to obtain complete stucco coverage, resulting in potential wall leaks.

Builder Responsibility: If gutter ends are embedded or are too tight to wall surface materials, they should be rebuilt or corrected to meet the Performance Guideline mentioned above.

Homeowner Responsibility: None.

Condition #4: GUTTERS OVERFLOW

Can Affect:

- House components below the overflow
- Utility of areas below the overflow

Performance Guideline: The Builder should size gutters so that they do not overflow under normal rainfall conditions. The frequency and cross-sectional area of down spouts should be adequate to serve the computed maximum flow of storm water. The shapes of gutters should be selected so that water flowing off the roof is intercepted by the gutter and does not wash over the front edge of the gutter. Water falling from upper roofs directly onto lower roofs without gutters is acceptable.

Comments: Design criteria for gutter size and type is sometimes determined by the architect. Usually, it is determined by the Builder's specialty contractor according to published data including roof area, roof slope, and roof cover material (shake, tile, shingles etc.).

Builder Responsibility: If overflow is a result of improper or inadequate installation and not from inadequate Homeowner maintenance, make necessary adjustments to the rainwater collection system so that gutters do not overflow during periods of heavy rainfall (as opposed to extreme, i.e. not normal, conditions for the area).

Homeowner Responsibility: ***Maintenance Alert!*** Annual maintenance of gutters and downspouts is important to avoid leaks and prolong the life of the system. Gutters should be cleaned thoroughly. If the House is in an area with mature trees, it is a good idea to place gutter screens along the gutter length and in the top opening of each downspout to help minimize leaf debris. If a gutter or downspout leaks, have it repaired at the first opportunity. If gutters are made of galvanized sheet metal (as opposed to aluminum or plastic), their useful life will be greatly reduced if the Homeowner allows acidic bird droppings, eucalyptus leaves or pine needles to accumulate in the gutter.

Condition #5: GUTTERS DO NOT EXTEND FULLY TO THE GABLE ENDS OF THE ROOF

Can Affect:

- House components below the overflow

Performance Guideline: Gutters should provide complete coverage along the roof eave.

Builder Responsibility: Unless the architectural design of the House shows otherwise, gutters should run completely along the eave. An exception to this is the use of a ***dutch gutter***, or diverter, at certain locations to divert rainwater to other areas (i.e. over an entryway).

Homeowner Responsibility: None.

Condition #6: STORM FLOW FROM DOWNSPOUTS DISCHARGES AT HOUSE FOUNDATION

Can Affect:

- Foundations
- Sidewalks and patios
- Landscaping

Performance Guideline: At a minimum, storm water should be discharged on ***splash blocks*** and channeled away from the House foundation to a drainage ***swale*** or storm drain.

Builder Responsibility: The Builder should construct the House as to direct rainwater away from the House foundation. This can be accomplished by grading, use of splash blocks, downspout extensions, or with an underground piping system.

Homeowner Responsibility: ***Maintenance Alert!*** Do not alter the finished grades around the House that were provided by the Builder unless done according to Code and as directed by a licensed landscape architect or civil engineer. Keep all drainage swales free of debris. If the House has one, flush out the underground pipe system with a garden hose prior to the start of the rainy season.

Condition #7: DOWNSPOUT MAKES "PINGING" NOISE DURING RAIN STORMS

Can Affect:

- Occupant comfort

Performance Guideline: Due to many factors beyond the control of Builder, such as architectural design, rainwater collection requirements, and varying degrees of annoyance threshold by the occupants, the Builder is not responsible for downspout noise.

Builder Responsibility: None.

Homeowner Responsibility: If downspout noise exists to the extent and/or in a location that affects the quality of habitability (such as outside a bedroom window) the following suggestions can mitigate the noise:

→ If the bottom of downspout is "kicked out" from the wall and is not inserted into a collection pipe, glue a piece of carpet padding into the kicked out portion. Make sure the metal is clean and dry and use a watertight glue. Inspect the discharge during the rainy season to keep it cleared of any leaves or debris.

→ If the downspout has several twists and turns and the bottom is not accessible, hang a galvanized steel or plastic chain with one inch wide links into the top 3 to 5 feet of the downspout. Hang the top link from a copper or brass rod that is at least 12 inches long. It is important that the chain and the rod be made of a material that does not rust. Inspect the chain frequently during the rainy season and clean it as necessary.

Skylights

General Subject Information: Skylights are simply windows in the roof. Also, like windows, skylights can either be fixed (unopenable) or operable (capable of being opened). The most commonly used skylights are made of acrylic or similar plastics, usually shaped in the form of a dome and set in an aluminum frame. Some skylights have flat plate glass in them. Another type of skylight is in the form of a tube that directs light through attics into a light diffuser at the level of the ceiling. All skylights in California must conform to Title 24 energy regulations and safety provisions contained in the Uniform Building Code.

Condition #1: SKYLIGHT LEAKS

Can Affect:

- Interior finishes
- Roof framing integrity

Performance Guideline: Skylights should be installed so they do not leak. Skylights may leak as a result of failures in the frame or glazing, or more commonly because of incorrect installation.

Builder Responsibility: Improperly installed skylights should be reset and properly waterproofed. The Builder should be responsible for administering any manufacturer's warranty work in the event of a failure of the skylight assembly.

Homeowner Responsibility: None.

Condition #2: MOISTURE CONDENSES ON INTERIOR SURFACES OF THE SKYLIGHT

Can Affect:

- Interior finishes

Performance Guideline: Moisture condensation on the interior surface of skylight glazing is considered acceptable. However, condensation moisture that is excessive and finds its way into surrounding finishes and cavities is unacceptable. Skylight perimeters must be detailed so that condensation water is adequately trapped in an impervious gutter or similar detail, where it can rest until it has a chance to evaporate.

Builder Responsibility: Installation should conform to the Performance Guideline. Improperly detailed skylight perimeters should be reconstructed so that condensation water is adequately trapped and allowed to evaporate.

Homeowner Responsibility: The Homeowner assumes responsibility for the amount of humidity created in kitchens, baths, laundry rooms and other areas or devices that produce water vapor.

Condition #3: MOISTURE APPEARS BETWEEN THE PANES OF A DUAL PANE SKYLIGHT

Can Affect:

- Skylight insulation value
- Appearance

Performance Guideline: Moisture trapped between the panes of a dual pane skylight indicates a broken seal. This is unacceptable.

Builder Responsibility: If the broken seal occurs within the manufacturer's warranty period, Builder should replace the skylight glazing.

Homeowner Responsibility: None. However do not tint the inside surface of a skylight, as the warranty may be voided.

Condition #4: SKYLIGHT ADMITS TOO MUCH HEAT

Can Affect:

- Occupant comfort

Performance Guideline: A House with skylights must conform to California energy conservation standards. Assuming energy calculations have been done correctly, heat gain through a skylight is considered acceptable.

Comments: If a particular skylight warms the room too much and the Homeowner feels uncomfortable with the performance of the skylight, there are several screening and shading techniques and products available to provide additional protection.

Builder Responsibility: Builder installed skylights should conform to California energy requirements, and the energy calculations for the House.

Homeowner Responsibility: Install heat reflecting or absorbing systems according to their own taste and in accordance with the manufacturer's recommendations.

Paint and Stain

General Subject Information: Simply defined, stains are liquids that penetrate into the surface (usually wood) to allow the ***grain*** to be visible, while paints cover the surface of the material thus making the material not visible. Correct preparation of surfaces to receive paints and stains, and the selection of an appropriate product for the use intended are essential in achieving a satisfactory finish. Adequate Homeowner maintenance and refinishing at suitable intervals are equally important. The durability of painted and stained surfaces is also directly related to the exposure to which it is subjected. Surfaces that receive direct sun or the full force of storms can be expected to require more frequent refinishing. The first coat of paint, the one applied during construction, is the coat that will last the shortest time, as the material beneath the paint absorbs a much greater percentage of the first coat of paint than successive coats.

Condition #1: STAINS FROM UNDERLYING SURFACES BLEED THROUGH

Can Affect:

- Appearance

Performance Guideline: Colors, markings, wood sap, ***tannins***, etc., which are on the surface of or are within the composition of underlying materials should not bleed through to the surface of the paint.

Builder Responsibility: The Builder should ensure that surfaces to which paints and stains are applied are properly prepared and cleaned. If components of an underlying material have an inherent tendency to bleed through, the Builder should apply stain-blocking coatings or primers before proceeding with painting or staining.

Homeowner Responsibility: None.

Condition #2: PAINT BECOMES CHALKY OR FADES

Can Affect:

- Paint life
- Appearance
- Water resistance of surfaces

Performance Guideline: Paint should not chalk or fade within the period of time that the manufacturer warrants its performance from such deterioration.

Comments: Some types and colors of paints are more susceptible to fading and chalking when exposed to direct sunlight than other types and colors. For example, dark colors are more prone to fading than lighter colors. Manufacturers can provide useful guidance for selection of paints that will perform effectively under particular climactic conditions.

Builder Responsibility: The Builder should select paints and stains that are suitable for the exposure and climate zone for the House.

Homeowner Responsibility: ***Maintenance Alert!*** It is important to observe the condition of painted surfaces on a periodic basis. An annual inspection is recommended. Paints first begin to show signs of wear in limited areas. Maintenance and touch up should be undertaken before paint degradation proceeds too far. This can significantly extend the life of the overall paint job.

Condition #3: PAINT FLAKING OR PEELING

Can Affect:

- Moisture resistance of surfaces
- Appearance

Performance Guideline: Paint should not flake or peel during the manufacturer's warranted life of the product.

Comments: Paints that flake or peel prematurely tend do so because the surfaces to which they were applied were not adequately prepared. Sometimes primers are omitted, and surfaces may be too damp, or dirty. Paints sometimes flake off of metal surfaces because metal surfaces are very smooth and non-absorbent. Surface preparation with dilute acids or chemical bonding agents is usually required. Factory prime coats often need to be supplemented with a coat of primer applied at the construction site.

Builder Responsibility: The Builder should ensure that appropriate paint selections are made, and that surfaces are properly prepared to receive paints. In the case of premature flaking or peeling, the Builder should take appropriate action to remediate the non-performing condition, up to and including stripping and repainting affected surfaces, as may be required to provide a durable finish.

Homeowner Responsibility: Maintain paint surfaces in a clean and well-ventilated condition. Inspect painted surfaces periodically and touch up any initial onset of premature aging or deterioration that may be observed.

Condition #4: PAINTS APPLIED TOO THIN, TOO THICK, OR IN A SPOTTY MANNER

Can Affect:

- Paint life
- Appearance
- Water resistance of surfaces

Performance Guideline: All surfaces to receive paint should be uniformly coated without any unpainted or too lightly painted spots (called "***holidays***" in the painting trade). Paint coatings should be applied to at least the minimum thickness recommended by the manufacturer. Paint should not be applied too thick, which usually results in spots that are more reflective than surrounding surfaces (painters call these spots "shiners"). Paint should be applied smoothly and evenly, without any runs or drips.

Builder Responsibility: The Builder should conform to the Performance Guideline. Any areas that are not painted in conformance to the Guideline should be repainted properly.

Homeowner Responsibility: None.

Condition #5: PAINT OR STAIN OVERSPRAY ON ADJACENT SURFACES

Can Affect:
- Appearance

Performance Guideline: Overspray of paints or stains on surfaces that are not intended to receive paint or stain coatings is not acceptable. However, overspray must be clearly visible at a distance of five feet under normal natural lighting conditions to be non-performing.

Builder Responsibility: The Builder should take measures to protect surfaces that are not to be painted and which may be subject to overspray damage. If overspray occurs despite protective measures, the Builder should clean the affected areas in a manner that does not damage the affected surfaces.

Homeowner Responsibility: None.

Condition #6: MILDEW OR FUNGI GROWTH / STAINS ON PAINTED SURFACES

Can Affect:
- Appearance
- Paint life

Performance Guideline: Mildew and fungi that affect exterior surfaces may be difficult or impossible to avoid in some particularly moist and cool locations and therefore are not considered a condition of non-performance. Molds and mildews that appear on interior surfaces, and are the result of leaks, are considered unacceptable. Interior surfaces similarly affected by condensation may either be considered unacceptable or a Homeowner maintenance item, depending upon circumstances.

Comments: Mold and mildew on exterior paint surfaces generally have a different cause and affect than those on interior paint surfaces. Growths and stains on exterior surfaces are generally the result of constant exposure to cool, damp and shady conditions, whereas interior manifestations are often the result of leaks or condensation. Refer to the **Chapter 9, "Mold and Mildew"** for more information.

Builder Responsibility: The Builder is responsible for selection of paints that are reasonably resistant to the establishment and spread of mildews and fungi on exterior walls. Paints are now formulated with mildewcide and fungicide additives that inhibit the growth of mildew and fungi. The Builder should use these types of products on exterior walls when the orientation and climate at the homesite indicates their use is necessary. At interior walls, if mildews and molds become established as a consequence of leaks in the exterior walls, roof above, or any other building component, it should be the Builder's responsibility to correct the leaks, and to clean up and restore any affected areas (if leaks are a result of improper construction).

Homeowner Responsibility: ***Maintenance Alert!*** The Homeowner should periodically inspect exterior surfaces to determine if mildew or fungus growth is occurring. Any growth of these organisms should be addressed by the proper cleaning and application of products that will kill the organisms and retard their return. This should be done promptly upon observation of mildews or fungi, because once established, these organisms are progressively more difficult to control and eradicate. At interior locations, the Homeowner should always use the mechanical ventilation in bathrooms, laundry rooms, and kitchens while these rooms are in use, and regulary air out rooms that have windows. If the Homeowner observes significant condensation on exterior surfaces (usually at windows and cool exterior walls), an effort should be made to find the right balance of natural and mechanical ventilation to minimize the problem.

Condition #7: LACQUERS AND VARNISHES PEEL AND FLAKE RAPIDLY

Can Affect:
- Appearance

Performance Guideline: Clear exterior lacquer and varnish coatings are not recommended for use on exterior surfaces. They usually deteriorate rapidly and require substantial maintenance. Deteriorated exterior varnishes and lacquers are considered acceptable. Interior varnished and lacquered surfaces may be appropriate, provided they are not applied in locations subject to extensive direct sunlight or excessive moisture.

Builder Responsibility: Interior lacquers and varnishes that are not subject to Homeowner abuse or excessive moisture and that nevertheless peel or flake off, should be corrected by the Builder.

Homeowner Responsibility: The Homeowner should keep all varnished and lacquered surfaces reasonably free of excessive moisture, heat, dust and from other damaging conditions. Relatively frequent maintenance and recoating with a high quality marine spar varnish should be anticipated and performed by the Homeowner.

Condition #8: STAINED EXTERIOR SURFACES ARE BLOTCHY OR HAVE UNEVEN COLOR

Can Affect:
- Appearance

Performance Guideline: Stains are absorbed by wood to different degrees, depending on the prevalence of sapwood, knots, and the character of the tree from which the wood product was made. Stains on synthetic surfaces may be more regular, but some variation is still inevitable. Stained surfaces, however, should not be excessively blotchy, or vary markedly in color.

Builder Responsibility: The Builder should prepare surfaces and apply stains in strict accordance with the manufacturer's directions and recommendations, and in a manner that minimizes extreme variations in color or blotchiness. Surfaces that are not in conformance to the above Performance Guideline should be cleaned and re-coated in a manner that achieves a reasonable degree of regularity.

Homeowner Responsibility: The Homeowner is responsible for maintaining the stained surfaces clean and free of debris. Adequate ventilation of exposed surfaces should be provided. Homeowner should recoat stained surfaces at an interval no longer than that which is recommended by the manufacturer.

Condition #9: PAINTED STUCCO SURFACES DO NOT PERMIT MOISTURE TO ESCAPE

Can Affect:
- Structural integrity / framing
- Interior humidity

Performance Guideline: Stucco surfaces that are designed to receive paint should be painted with materials that allow water vapor to pass from the inner surface to the outer surface. The use of ***impermeable*** membrane paints is considered unacceptable for this application.

Comments: Some ***elastomeric*** paints used to coat the exterior surfaces of stucco are completely waterproof. When such paints are used, there is a risk of trapping moisture within wall cavities. This can result in deterioration of lumber, and the onset of molds because incidental leak water or condensation moisture cannot readily dry out. Therefore, it is important to use cement plaster-compatible paints on stucco. Fortunately, this condition has become well known, and paint manufacturers are very conscious of the need to specify the correct type of paint for use on cement plaster (stucco) surfaces.

Builder Responsibility: Apply only breathable surface coatings to stucco exteriors. Apply according to the methods and thickness recommended by the manufacturer.

Homeowner Responsibility: None.

Condition #10: BRUSH MARKS OR LAP MARKS SHOW

Can Affect:
- Appearance

Performance Guideline: When viewed in normal daylight at a distance of 6 feet, brush marks or lap marks should not be visible. Artificial light is not acceptable as a light source when measuring this Guideline.

Comments: Many paints manufactured today are difficult to brush without leaving brush marks or lap marks. Consequently, most paint applicators prefer the use of an airless sprayer to provide a uniform application. Problems arise when trying to touch up with a brush.

Builder Responsibility: If the Performance Guideline is not met, the Builder should take corrective measures to meet the Guideline.

Homeowner Responsibility: None.

Chapter Six

INTERIOR COMPONENTS

includes:

Fireplaces

Insulation

Doors and Door Hardware

Finish Flooring:
Tile, Marble, Granite and Stone
Carpet
Hardwood Floors
Vinyl Floors

Plaster and Drywall

Countertops

Appliances

Cabinets and Vanities

Moldings & Trim

Mirrors, Shower and Tub Enclosures

References for this chapter:

- *The Complete Idiot's Guide to Trouble Free Home Repair*, by David Tenenbaum
- *500 Terrific Ideas for Home Maintenance and Repair*, by Jack Maguire
- *Handbook of Construction Tolerances*, by David Kent Ballast
- *Problems, Causes, and Cures*, National Wood Flooring Association
- *Residential Construction Performance Standards*, NAHB
- *Residential & Light Commercial Construction Standards*, by Don Reynolds
- *Troubleshooting Guide to Residential Construction*, Builderburg Group
- *Uniform Building Code*, 1997 ed.
- *Workmanship Guidelines*, CA Contractors State License Board

A comprehensive list of references by author and publisher is found in the Bibliography section.

nterior Components

Fireplaces

General Subject Information: Fireplaces that are installed in houses today function more as decorative items than as sources of heat. Many fireplaces are considered gas appliances and are not equipped to burn anything other than the gas supplied to them. A wood burning fireplace operating without its glass doors closed will actually draw more heat from the room than heat it gives back to the room. Refer to Chapter Five "Chimneys and Flues" for additional information.

Condition #1: WATER DRIPS INTO FIREPLACE DURING RAINSTORMS

Can Affect:

- Ability to keep fire going
- Fireplace performance
- Interior finishes and furnishings

Performance Guideline: Water should not drip into the fireplace during normal rainstorms. However, rainwater may pass down the ***chimney*** into the fireplace during extreme wind driven storms.

Comments: A typical chimney built today will be capped with a code-approved ***spark arrestor*** usually underneath a metal bonnet. A few fireplaces are still being constructed with a masonry ***flue***. These chimneys will have a spark arrestor, but they may not have a metal, stucco or concrete cap. Because all chimneys must be open to the outside in order to perform, they may pass some rainwater during periods of extreme wind-driven rain.

Builder Responsibility: If water drips into the fireplace during normal or light rainstorms, it is most likely due to a seam leak at the ***chase*** cover or the rain cap. The Builder should repair the leak.

Homeowner Responsibility: Keep the ***damper*** closed when the fireplace is not in use. Note: If the fireplace is used for burning wood, be certain there are no live coals or embers before closing the damper. Otherwise, poisonous gases could enter the room. ***Maintenance Alert!*** The flue must be cleaned (swept) periodically from the top, going downward, in accordance with the manufacturer's instructions and according to the amount of use of the fireplace. This is a dirty job that is best left to professional chimney sweeps. Failure to keep the chimney clean can result in dangerous flue fires high up in the chimney. Special chimney cleaning logs are now available, and their manufacturer claims they accomplish the same task as a chimney sweep.

Condition #2: FIREPLACE WON'T DRAW (room becomes smoky)

Can Affect:

- Occupant health and safety related to air quality

Performance Guideline: Fireplaces should be constructed so that all gases from combustion are carried out the chimney or flue.

Builder Responsibility: Construct the fireplace assembly including firebox, flue, external combustion air vents, chimney, and termination cap in accordance with the Code and the fireplace manufacturer's installation instructions.

Homeowner Responsibility: Always be sure the damper is open before starting a fire. Do not overload the firebox with too much fuel or improper fuel (such as holiday gift wrappings). Use only the fuel that is approved by the manufacturer (a gas log fireplace is typically not suited to burn wood or paper). If installed, glass doors should be closed during fireplace operation.

Condition #3: REFRACTORY PANELS CRACK

Can Affect:

- Fireplace safety
- Appearance

Performance Guideline: ***Refractory*** panels that crack during the warranty period are considered unacceptable. ***Important! Refer to Homeowner Responsibility below.***

Builder Responsibility: Builder should replace cracked refractory panels if damage is not a result of improper use by Homeowner.

Homeowner Responsibility: ***Maintenance Alert!*** Homeowner should "cure" new refractory panels by building a series of small, low-heat fires before fully using the entire fireplace. It is important to read the owner's instruction manual and avoid creating high heat fires with items such as wrapping paper, composition logs, or lumber. Always place logs into the firebox using metal tongs; logs thrown into the firebox may hit the refractory and crack it. Avoid burning any composite wood material such as particle board or glulam beam scraps.

USE THE CORRECT FUEL FOR THE FIRE PLACE IN YOUR HOUSE

Condition # 4: DAMPER BECOMES RUSTY

Can Affect:

- Fireplace operation

Performance Guideline: The damper should be free of rust and operate smoothly at the time of the ***Walkthrough***.

Builder Responsibility: Meet the above Performance Guideline.

Homeowner Responsibility: ***Maintenance Alert!*** Dampers will become rusty because water is formed when any type of fuel is burned. It is normal to expect some rust on the damper and its hinges. If the damper becomes difficult to operate, the hinges can be sprayed with a rust removing lubricant. Do not spray when there is a fire or hot coals present. The spray may be flammable.

Condition #5: GLASS DOORS DO NOT OPERATE FREELY

Can Affect:
- Fireplace operation

Performance Guideline: At the time of delivery, glass fireplace doors should open and close freely without sticking, and should close with a gap of no more than ¼ inch when closed.

Builder Responsibility: Builder should make necessary repairs or adjustments so that the glass doors operate in conformance with the above Guideline.

Homeowner Responsibility: None. However, Homeowner should keep the glass doors closed during fireplace operation.

Insulation

General Subject Information: Insulation is important for house comfort and decreased dependency on energy usage. In a new house, insulation is required as part of California Energy Code compliance, also known as Title 24. The building department that issues the building permit requires the Builder to submit a series of calculations showing the house will meet the minimum requirements of the Energy Code. Because the Energy Code deals with energy consumption, it is important to note that insulation is just one of the components of proper energy conservation. Other components include efficient furnaces, water heaters, window glazing, air conditioning and ***weatherstripping***. For example, it is possible to have more insulation and a less efficient furnace as long as the energy value calculation of the entire house meets the Code. Also, Code requirements vary depending upon designated climate zones in the State. Therefore, a house in Lake Tahoe that looks identical to one in San Diego may have a significantly different insulation package.

Typically insulation comes in two forms: (1) batts, which are often fiberglass, pink or yellow in color and 15 or 23 inches wide by 8 or 10 feet long, and (2) loose fill, which looks like packing material, and is generally blown through a large hose into the attic space. Because insulation is only one component in the total energy saving package, it can be very difficult for a Homeowner to determine if the insulation package is unacceptable, but the following are some common examples of insulation problems.

Condition #1: THERE IS NO INSULATION IN THE ATTIC

Can Affect:
- Occupant comfort
- Energy consumption

Performance Guideline: Some insulation should be present in every attic that is built over habitable space, unless another package approved by the building department exists instead. Occasionally, on desert style homes with "flat" roofs and no attic, part of the roof assembly is made of insulating foam, and this qualifies as ceiling/roof insulation.

Builder Responsibility: All insulation should meet the ***R-Values*** as specified in the Title 24 compliance section of the building permit.

Homeowner Responsibility: None.

Condition #2: INSULATION IS PLACED AGAINST THE EAVE VENTS OR THE FOUNDATION VENTS

Can Affect:

- Attic and crawl space ventilation
- Occupant comfort

Performance Guideline: Insulation should not be placed against the eave (attic) or foundation vents. Clear space (between one to two feet) should be left between the end of the insulation and the vent screen to allow for proper air circulation.

Builder Responsibility: The Builder should remove any originally installed insulation that blocks the airflow of eave and foundation vents.

Homeowner Responsibility: None.

Condition #3: HOUSE IS TOO HOT IN SUMMER, TOO COLD IN WINTER

Can Affect:

- Occupant comfort
- Energy consumption

Performance Guideline: Each new House must be built in compliance with Title 24 section of the Energy Code. There is no guarantee that an individual level of comfort will be met.

Builder Responsibility: None, provided the House has been built in compliance with the Title 24 section of the Energy Code used in California.

Homeowner Responsibility: Much of the comfort a House provides depends on the lifestyle of the occupants. For example, it is unrealistic to expect that an air conditioner turned on at 5 pm on a hot summer day could effectively and entirely cool the House by bedtime. Refer to **Chapter Seven, "Cooling"**. In wintertime furnaces should be programmed to come on in the morning at least 30 minutes before the time occupants wake. Constant adjustments to the thermostat will result in uneven temperatures and periods of discomfort. Also, installation of insulating drapes and shades is an important way to increase House comfort and decrease energy consumption.

Additional Information

→ Insulation is probably the least expensive way to provide year-round comfort in a house. If a Homeowner wants to decrease energy consumption, adding insulation to the attic is most effective to achieve energy savings. If additional insulation is installed, care should be taken not to block the eave vents or allow the material to touch vents from gas fired appliances. Refer to Condition #2 above.

→ The contractor who insulates the House must sign a certificate stating that the House is insulated in compliance with the California Title 24 building permit documents. The Builder either keeps the certificate on file or gives it to the Homeowner at the time of delivery.

→ Do all new homes require dual pane windows and under-floor insulation? No. As stated under **General Subject Information**, the Builder is entitled to make substitutions, such as a more efficient furnace and air conditioner, as long as the entire House meets the requirements of the Energy Code.

Interior Doors

Condition #1: DOOR IS WARPED

Can Affect:
- Door operation
- Appearance

Performance Guideline: Doors that are warped more than ¼ inch in a 6 foot 8 inch height are considered unacceptable.

Builder Responsibility: Builder should replace doors that are warped in excess of the above Performance Guideline.

Homeowner Responsibility: None.

Condition #2: DOOR PANELS HAVE SPLIT

Can Affect:
- Appearance
- Privacy

Performance Guideline: Door panels that have split entirely through and allow light to pass through are considered unacceptable (this Performance Guideline applies to exterior doors also).

Builder Responsibility: Make necessary repairs to meet the above Performance Guideline.

Homeowner Responsibility: None.

Condition #3: DOOR HANGS CROOKED IN JAMB

Can Affect:
- Door performance
- Appearance

Performance Guideline: Doors that vary more than ¼ inch in measurement from the closest distance to the jamb to the furthest distance to the jamb or head are considered unacceptable.

Builder Responsibility: Builder should make the necessary adjustments to the door or jamb to meet the Performance Guideline, if condition is a result if improper or inadequate installation.

Homeowner Responsibility: Do not hang anything heavy on doors or doorknobs. This can pull the top hinges out of adjustment and negatively affect the door swing.

Condition #4: DOOR *LATCH* DOES NOT ENGAGE IN THE *STRIKE*

Can Affect:

- Door operation
- Privacy

Performance Guideline: Door latches should engage firmly in the strike.

Builder Responsibility: Builder should make the necessary adjustments to meet the Performance Guideline, if condition is a result if improper or inadequate installation.

Homeowner Responsibility: Do not hang anything heavy on doors or doorknobs. This can pull the top hinges out of adjustment and negatively affect the latch to engage.

Condition #5: DOOR OPENS OR CLOSES BY ITSELF

Can Affect:

- Door performance

Performance Guideline: Doors should stay open when opened, and stay closed when closed. "Phantom" openings and closings are considered unacceptable.

Builder Responsibility: Builder should make the necessary adjustments to conform to the Guideline, if condition is a result if improper or inadequate installation.

Homeowner Responsibility: Do not hang anything heavy on the door or doorknob. This can pull the top hinges out of adjustment and negatively affect the door swing. Seasonal humidity changes can result in impaired door swing performance; this is acceptable.

Condition #6: BOTTOM EDGE OF DOOR IS CUT TOO HIGH OR TOO LOW

Can Affect:

- Appearance
- Privacy
- Door performance

Performance Guideline: A door that swings over carpeted areas should not drag on the carpet. Doors should be cut to leave a gap of no larger than 1 inch above the uppermost tufts of the carpet. A door that swings over a non-carpeted surface should be cut to leave a gap of no larger than ½ inch above the floor surface. Exception: Doors opening to utility areas, such as laundry rooms and pantries, may have a gap up to 1 3/8 inches from the finish floor. This condition arises when vinyl flooring is glued to a concrete slab, and it is considered acceptable (see Comments below).

Comments: With the exception of a small number of custom homes, most doors are manufactured as completed assemblies, consisting of the door hung with hinges in the *jamb*. Door manufacturers routinely hold the bottom of the door up to 1 3/8 inches from the bottom of the jamb when building the door assembly. This allows for a variety of finish floor coverings of different thickness, such as wood, carpet, tile and vinyl.

Builder Responsibility: Builder should make necessary repairs to meet the above Performance Guideline, if condition is a result if improper or inadequate installation.

Homeowner Responsibility: If the Homeowner changes the type or texture of finish flooring or provides his or her own finish flooring, the Builder is not responsible.

Condition #7: *POCKET* DOOR BINDS BETWEEN THE POCKETS

Can Affect:
- Door performance

Performance Guideline: Door should not rub and/or bind in their pockets during normal operation.

Comments: ***Pocket doors*** should not be warped to the point that they rub on the sides of the pockets.

Builder Responsibility: The Builder should furnish and install all pocket doors to meet the Performance Guideline. If the door does not operate within the Guideline, the Builder should repair as necessary and refinish any work damaged by the subject repairs.

Homeowner Responsibility: Operate the doors in a normal fashion and do not negligently slam the doors back and forth.

Door Hardware

Condition #1: DOORKNOB MECHANISM OPERATES STIFFLY

Can Affect:
- Door latch performance

Performance Guideline: Door latch mechanisms should operate smoothly without requiring a great deal of effort to disengage the strike or deadbolt.

Builder Responsibility: Repair or replace any unacceptable door latch mechanisms whose improper performance is not a result of lack of Homeowner maintenance or misuse.

Homeowner Responsibility: ***Maintenance Alert!*** Door latch mechanisms should be lubricated annually with a dry lubricant made for door latch mechanisms.

Condition #2: DOORKNOB FINISH TARNISHES

Can Affect:
- Appearance

Performance Guideline: Doorknobs may tarnish over time. This is a Homeowner maintenance item.

Comments: Finish life of doorknobs and levers depends on finish type, location, and amount of use. Bright brass finishes are most susceptible to tarnishing. Oil from palms of hands and finger rings will contribute to the tarnishing process. Air pollution also contributes to the tarnishing process.

Builder Responsibility: Replace only those doorknobs that are tarnished at the time of the ***Walkthrough***.

Homeowner Responsibility: Learn about the proper care of metal finishes, especially bright brass, and conduct appropriate maintenance for the particular metal finish. If the House is located in a marine environment, expect pitting and tarnishing of the hardware finishes unless the hardware is labeled "lifetime finished". In all cases, refer to the manufacturer's warranty and maintenance requirements.

Closets

Condition: POLES PULL OUT OF ROSETTES

Can Affect:
- Function of closet

Performance Guideline: Closet poles should fit firmly into rosettes, and should not be held away from the inside end of the ***rosette*** by more than 1/8 inch. Poles should have an intermediate support for every four feet of length.

Builder Responsibility: Builder should make necessary repairs to meet the above Performance Guideline.

Homeowner Responsibility: Do not overload closet poles with heavy clothing or too much clothing. This will cause the pole to deflect and pull out of the ***rosette***.

Finish Flooring

General Subject Information: ***Subfloors*** for each of the flooring types (hardwood, ceramic tile, granite, marble, resilient flooring, and carpet) must be level, well supported, securely fastened and stiff enough to prevent unacceptable deflection (bending). Refer to Chapter Two, Floors and Ceilings for more information on subfloors. The following are typical conditions that can affect all types of floors:

Conditions: FLOOR NOT LEVEL, FLOOR SQUEAKS, EXCESSIVE DEFLECTION (sagging), EXCESSIVE FLEXIBILITY (bounce)

Can Affect:

- Occupant comfort

Performance Guideline: Finish floors should not deviate more than ¼ inch from true level in a horizontal distance of 8 feet. No point in the surface of a floor should be more than 1/8 inch above or below the plane of the floor. Squeaks are usually the result of separate parts of the floor moving relative to each other and rubbing against nails. Floors should be designed to accommodate Building Code required live loads.

Builder Responsibility: Repair or replace finish flooring that deviates from the above Performance Guideline, if condition is a result of improper or inadequate installation and not a result of Homeowner misuse.

Homeowner Responsibility: Maintain flooring using products and methods approved by the manufacturer and/or trade association whose products have been installed. Avoid overloading floors. Consult with the Builder or a qualified engineer prior to placing exceptionally heavy objects on a floor to ensure the floor load capacity will not be exceeded. If the Homeowner installs a finish floor, the Homeowner assumes complete responsibility for the condition of the subfloor or slab at the time of installation and thereafter.

Hardwood Floors

Condition #1: CUPPING OR CROWNING OF INDIVIDUAL FLOOR BOARDS

Can Affect:

- Appearance
- Life of finish floor
- Safety issue related to tripping hazard

Performance Guideline: Hardwood flooring should be installed in a manner that will prevent ***cupping*** and ***crowning***. This includes, among other measures, proper acclimatization of floor material prior to installation and the use of suitable moisture barriers under the flooring. Cupping or crowning should not exceed 1/16 inch in a 3-inch span as measured across the individual board.

Builder Responsibility: If cupping or crowning exceeds the Guideline, the Builder should replace or repair the floor as necessary to meet the Guideline. The Builder should provide the Homeowner with a book on hardwood floor care at the time of the Walkthrough.

Homeowner Responsibility: Always maintain hardwood floor in accordance with the manufacturer's recommendations, do not allow any spills or liquids to remain on floors, and do not clean floors with detergents. Use only those cleaning products recommended by the manufacturer or installer. Some minor random cupping or crowning can be expected over the years due to changes in humidity, and this condition is acceptable.

Condition #2: SCALLOPED AND ABRADED SURFACE

Can Affect:

- Appearance

Performance Guideline: Wood floors should be finished without gouges, abrasions or ***scalloping.*** Some unevenness can be expected because portions of the grain of wood are softer than others.

Builder Responsibility: Builder should repair or replace any non-performing boards noticed at the Walkthrough. The Builder should give the Homeowner a book on hardwood floor care at the time of the Walkthrough.

Homeowner Responsibility: Any surface gouges and abrasions should be brought to the attention of the Builder at the Walkthrough and prior to the move-in. The Builder is not responsible for gouges and abrasions noticed after the Walkthrough. Always maintain hardwood floor in accordance with the manufacturer's recommendations, do not allow any spills or liquids to remain on floors, and do not clean floors with detergents. Use only those cleaning products recommended by the manufacturer or installer.

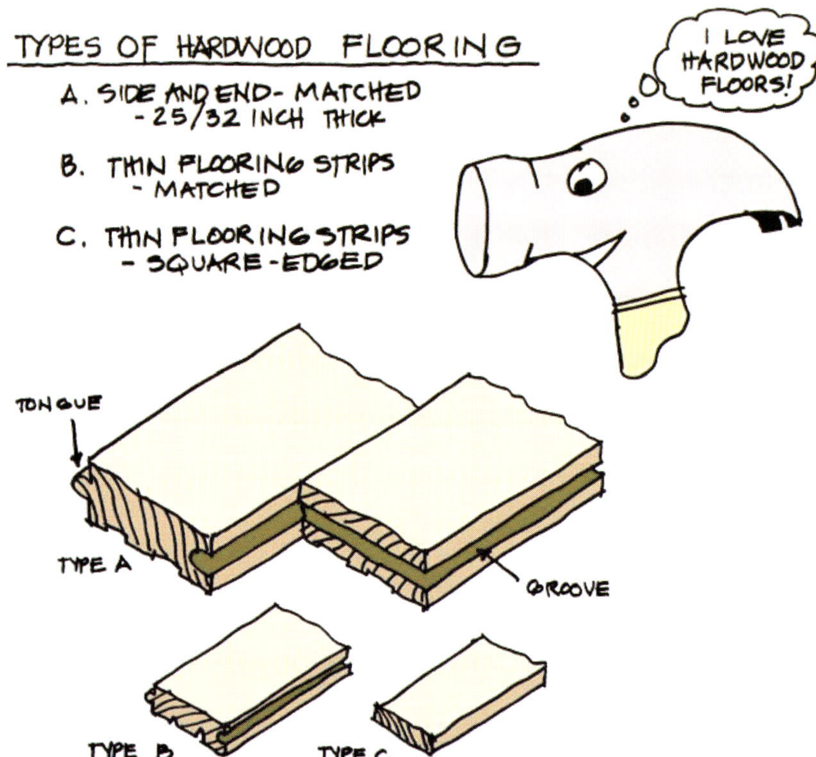

Condition #3: GAPS BETWEEN ADJACENT FLOOR BOARDS

Can Affect:

- Appearance
- Life of finish floor
- Ability to / ease of cleaning

Performance Guideline: Floor joints should be tight and without gaps. Gaps between boards are the result of shrinkage. Although wood flooring materials are dried by the manufacturer, they still contain moisture. New wood floors should not be subjected to extreme variations in temperature or humidity. Gaps should not occur in more than 5% of the total length of joints in a floor, and no gap should exceed 1/32 inch in width for boards in excess of 2 ¼ inches in width.

Builder Responsibility: If gaps between boards exceed the Guideline, the Builder should replace or repair the floor as necessary to meet the Guideline. The Builder should give the Homeowner a book on hardwood floor care at the time of the Walkthrough.

Homeowner Responsibility: Always maintain hardwood floor in accordance with the manufacturer's recommendations, do not allow any spills or liquids to remain on floors, and do not clean floors with detergents. Use only those cleaning products recommended by the manufacturer or installer.

Condition # 4: DIFFERENCES IN COLOR BETWEEN INDIVIDUAL FLOOR BOARDS

Can Affect:

- Appearance

Performance Guideline: Wood floors naturally have color variation. The same species of wood may come in many different colors, floor boards may vary accordingly.

Builder Responsibility: None.

Homeowner Responsibility: If uniformity of color is important to the Homeowner, advance arrangement should be made with the Builder at the time the flooring section is completed, so that the Homeowner is present when the floor is being installed. Homeowner should be aware that direct sunlight could cause wood floors to become darker; the Builder is not responsible for this condition.

Condition # 5: FLOOR BOARDS ON PRE-FINISHED FLOORS ARE NOT LEVEL WITH ONE ANOTHER AT SIDES OR ENDS

Can Affect:

- Appearance
- Life of finish floor
- Safety issue related to tripping hazard

Performance Guideline: Finish floor boards should not be higher or lower than the immediately adjoining board by more than .012 inch measured with a feeler gauge.

Builder Responsibility: Make necessary repairs to meet the above Performance Guideline, unless condition is a result of Homeowner misuse or improper maintenance.

Homeowner Responsibility: Floor care is important. If a water based liquid is spilled on the floor, or if areas of high humidity exist in poorly vented rooms, the floor boards may swell and become uneven. The Builder is not responsible for this condition.

Condition #6: SPLINTERS OR CHIPS ARE PRESENT AT THE EDGES OF FLOOR BOARDS AFTER INSTALLATION

Can Affect:
- Appearance
- Safety issue related to splinters

Performance Guideline: Whether the floor is pre-finished or sanded and finished in place, there should be no splinters or chips that could be caught in flesh or clothing after installation is complete.

Builder Responsibility: Repair or replace boards that do not meet the above Performance Guideline.

Homeowner Responsibility*:* Floor care is important. Always maintain hardwood floor in accordance with the manufacturer's recommendations, do not allow any spills or liquids to remain on floors, and do not clean floors with detergents. Use only those cleaning products recommended by the manufacturer or installer.

Condition #7: DARK LINES APPEAR PERPENDICULAR TO THE FLOOR BOARD

Can Affect:
- Appearance

Performance Guideline: Sticker lines across floor boards that cannot be removed during the sanding process are considered unacceptable. To be considered unacceptable, the dark line should be clearly visible to the untrained eye at a distance of 6 feet under normal daylight conditions.

Comments*:* Wood floor boards that are to be sanded and finished in place are shipped in bundles. The boards in the bundle are separated by small rectangular pieces of wood called "stickers". Under moist conditions, the stickers will "bleed" into the floor boards and impart a dark color across the board. If the bleed is not severe, it can be removed when the rough floor is being sanded.

Builder Responsibility: Replace or floor boards that do not meet the above Performance Guideline.

Homeowner Responsibility: Always maintain hardwood floor in accordance with the manufacturer's recommendations, do not allow any spills or liquids to remain on floors, and do not clean floors with detergents. Use only those cleaning products recommended by the manufacturer or installer.

Condition # 8: FLOOR BOARDS DISCOLOR AND ROT, PARTICULARLY UNDER AREA RUGS

Can Affect:
- Appearance
- Air quality

Performance Guideline: Floor boards should not discolor (turn very dark) and rot, or become brittle and crumble.

Comments: This condition can occur when pre-finished flooring is applied over a concrete slab. This condition worsens when the Homeowner places a rubber pad or rubber backed area rug over the floor. Although the concrete slab is likely to have a plastic ***vapor barrier*** under it, water vapor can pass through the slab in small amounts into the living area. The pre-finished floor boards are sealed very tightly at the factory and water vapor from the slab has difficulty passing through the wood. The addition of a rubber backed rug or tightly woven rug traps the moisture even more. While it is possible to successfully install pre-finished hardwood flooring over a concrete slab, it should be performed only by a specialty contractor who is very experienced at this trade. There are several manufacturers of pre-finished hardwood floors, and each manufacturer has its own set of installation instructions that should be strictly adhered to.

Builder Responsibility: The Builder should make repairs to bring the floor into conformance with the Performance Guideline, unless the damage is caused by Homeowner misuse or negligence.

Homeowner Responsibility: If the Homeowner covers a pre-finished hardwood floor with an area rug, he or she takes on the responsibility to monitor the condition of the wood on a quarterly basis (every three months). Alternatively, the Homeowner can obtain a separate warranty from the manufacturer of the floor; or place the area rug on the concrete slab and install the wood floor around it. Homeowner should also be aware that direct sunlight will cause wood floors to become darker; the Builder is not responsible for this condition.

Ceramic and Clay Tile Flooring

Condition #1: CRACKS AND / OR LOOSE TILES

Can Affect:
- Appearance
- Safety issue related to loose flooring
- Life of finish floor

Performance Guideline: Tiles having cracks that are visible to the untrained eye at a distance of 4 feet, and any loose tiles that can be moved by hand, are not acceptable.

Builder Responsibility: Builder should replace cracked tiles and reset loose tiles that do not meet the above Performance Guideline.

Homeowner Responsibility: The Homeowner should be aware that ceramic and clay tiles are brittle and they can be cracked, chipped or broken by placing or dropping heavy objects on them; the Builder is not responsible for the resulting conditions.

Condition #2: GROUT IS CRACKED

Can Affect:
- Appearance
- Floor deflection

Performance Guideline: Hairline cracks can occur in grout and are considered acceptable. Cracks larger than 1/32 inch should be regrouted as part of the Builder's Responsibility. If continual cracking occurs, the underlying floor may be deflecting. If this condition exists, it should be repaired as set forth in **Chapter Two "Floors and Ceilings" Condition #4**.

Builder Responsibility: Builder should meet the Performance Guideline by repairing or replacing the non-performing condition.

Homeowner Responsibility: Homeowners should familiarize themselves with proper procedures for cleaning and caring for their tile floors. Grout is very porous and should be sealed by the Homeowner within 30 days of occupancy.

Condition #3: INDIVIDUAL TILES ARE OUT OF PLANE

Can Affect:
- Appearance

Performance Guideline: This Guideline will vary depending upon the type of tile that is installed. Tiles can vary from flat ceramic, to raised, to uneven terra cotta. For tile that is flat, adjoining tiles should be no more than 1/16 inch higher or lower than the surrounding tiles. For tile that is handmade with uneven surfaces, the butts at the grout joints should not exceed ¼ inch in elevation from surrounding tiles.

Builder Responsibility: Builder should meet the Performance Guideline by repairing or replacing the non-performing condition.

Homeowner Responsibility: Homeowners should familiarize themselves with proper procedures for cleaning and caring for their tile floors.

Granite, Marble and Other Stone Flooring

General Subject Information: Granite, marble, and other stone flooring are natural products. There are many other stone products available today such as limestone, slate and travertine. Because they are natural products, the color and veining of granite and marble are never exactly alike. The Homeowner should expect variations from any installations in other similar homes.

Condition #1: CRACKS

Can Affect:

- Appearance
- Life of finish floor

Performance Guideline: Granite, marble, and other stone are susceptible to hairline cracking. This is a normal condition. Cracks in excess of 3/64 inch are unacceptable.

Comments: Granite, marble, and other stone flooring are vulnerable to impact damage (dropping heavy items on their surfaces). Floors should be designed to a very high level of stiffness. Unusually heavy items should not be placed onto a stone floor. It would be wise for the Homeowner intending to place a very heavy item (such as a grand piano) onto a stone tile floor to advise the Builder of this fact. The Builder may elect to add support at those locations.

Builder Responsibility: Builder should meet the Performance Guideline by repairing or replacing the non-conforming condition.

Homeowner Responsibility: Examine floors carefully at time of the Walkthrough. Homeowner should not place unusually heavy items onto stone flooring, unless Builder was notified and has provided appropriate support. Refer to "Additional Information About Stone Flooring" below.

Condition #2: STAINS

Can Affect:

- Appearance

Performance Guideline: The Builder should deliver a marble, granite, or other stone floor free of stains, with a consistent surface sheen or texture. The Homeowner should carefully examine the surface of the marble, granite, or other stone floor prior to taking possession of the House. The Builder will not accept responsibility for stained conditions if they are not noted at the time of the Walkthrough. Many times what may appear to be discolorations are actually natural variations in the stone.

Builder Responsibility: Builder should meet the Performance Guideline and repair or replace the non-conforming condition if noted at the time of the Walkthrough.

Homeowner Responsibility: None, other than careful examination of the floor during the Walkthrough. Refer to the following section "Additional Information About Stone Flooring".

Condition #3: SCRATCHES AND ABRASIONS

Can Affect:

- Appearance

Performance Guideline: Homeowner should note any scratches and abrasions during the Walkthrough. The Builder should deliver a marble, granite, or other stone floor free of scratches and abrasions, with a consistent surface sheen or texture.

Comments: Marble, granite, and tumbled stone will naturally have numerous pits and voids. Small pits are considered part of the "achieved look" of the surface and should not be deemed as non-performing. The manufacturer or installer usually fills voids in excess of 3/8 inch in diameter.

Builder Responsibility: Builder should meet the Performance Guideline and repair or replace the non-conforming condition if noted at the time of the Walkthrough.

Homeowner Responsibility: None, other than careful examination of the floor during the Walkthrough. Refer to "Additional Information About Stone Flooring" below.

Additional Information About Stone Flooring

- → Granite and marble, particularly marble, are susceptible to staining and etching by ordinary household products and fluids. Take caution with items such as vinegar, tomato paste, toilet-bowl cleaner, and cleaners containing ammonia, as they can easily stain and etch marble and granite.
- → While granite and marble, particularly granite, appear to be smooth and hard, the surfaces can actually contain small pits. The surface can appropriately be filled by the manufacturer with a clear epoxy filler or a colored filler.

Vinyl Flooring

Condition #1: WIDE SEAMS OR JOINTS

Can Affect:

- Appearance

Performance Guideline: Sheet and tile resilient floors should be laid with tight joints. Any separation in excess of 1/64 inch is non-performing.

Builder Responsibility: The Builder should meet the above Performance Guideline by making necessary repairs or replacements.

Homeowner Responsibility: Homeowners should follow the flooring manufacturer's cleaning and care instructions for vinyl flooring.

Condition #2: DELAMINATION

Can Affect:

- Appearance
- Life of finish floor

Performance Guideline: Occasionally resilient floors will separate from the ***underlayment***, particularly at edges. Such ***delamination*** is unacceptable and should be corrected by re-gluing.

Builder Responsibility: The Builder should meet the above Performance Guideline by making necessary repairs or replacements.

Homeowner Responsibility: Homeowners should follow the flooring manufacturer's cleaning and care instructions for vinyl flooring. To extend the life of vinyl flooring, use area rugs or mats at workstations and use dirt-trapping mats at exterior doors. Do not allow water or other liquids to remain on vinyl flooring for long periods of time. Spills or splashes should be promptly and properly removed. Vinyl flooring is water resistant and not totally waterproof.

Condition #3: DISCOLORATION

Can Affect:

- Appearance
- Life of finish floor

Performance Guideline: Floors should not become discolored as a result of moisture underneath the finish floor. If discoloration is a result of chemical and natural products with staining properties being allowed to remain on the surface of the resilient material without prompt cleaning, Builder is not responsible.

Builder Responsibility: The Builder should meet the above Performance Guideline by making necessary repairs or replacements if condition is a result of moisture underneath the finish floor and not a result of Homeowner misuse or negligence.

Homeowner Responsibility: Do not allow chemical or natural products with staining properties to remain on the finish floor. Homeowners should follow the flooring manufacturer's cleaning and care instructions for vinyl flooring. Do not allow water or other liquids to remain on vinyl flooring for long periods of time. Spills or splashes should be promptly and properly removed.

Condition #4: ADHESIVE APPEARS ON THE SURFACE THROUGH JOINTS

Can Affect:

- Appearance

Performance Guideline: Adhesives should not appear through the surface around joints or seams.

Comments: Various adhesives are used to attach ***resilient*** floors. Sometimes these adhesives do not set up properly. Under the pressure of foot traffic, they may be forced up through the seams and joints in the floor.

Builder Responsibility: The Builder should meet the above Performance Guideline by making necessary repairs or replacements. If after thorough cleaning with a manufacturer-approved cleaning agent the non-performing condition recurs, the floor should be removed along with the existing adhesive, and the floor re-laid by the Builder.

Homeowner Responsibility: None. However, Homeowners should follow the flooring manufacturer's cleaning and care instructions for vinyl flooring.

Condition #5: "TELEGRAPHING" OF IRREGULAR SURFACE BENEATH VINYL FLOORING

Can Affect:

- Appearance

Performance Guideline: Various types of irregularities, such as cracks in concrete floors, separations or unevenness in subfloors, or trapped debris, may show through the resilient flooring, appearing as unsightly bumps and lines. These conditions are non-performing.

Builder Responsibility: The Builder should meet the above Performance Guideline by making necessary repairs or replacements.

Homeowner Responsibility: None. However, Homeowners should follow the flooring manufacturer's cleaning and care instructions for vinyl flooring.

Condition #6: PATTERN DOES NOT MATCH OR ALIGN

Can Affect:

- Appearance

Performance Guideline: Patterns should match or align within 1/8 inch in a six-foot length of flooring.

Builder Responsibility: The Builder should meet the above Performance Guideline by making necessary repairs or replacements, assuming no damage or misuse by Homeowner.

Homeowner Responsibility: None. However, Homeowners should follow the flooring manufacturer's cleaning and care instructions for vinyl flooring.

Carpet Flooring

Condition #1: VISIBLE SEAMS

Can Affect:

- Appearance

Performance Guideline: Visibility of carpet seams is acceptable unless the seam is not butted tightly, and the seaming tape shows.

Comments: The visibility of seams depends on the type of carpet installed, and more importantly, on the height of the pile. Carpets with short nap, or pile, or with Berber type weaves will show seams. Higher pile carpets including plushes and shags can be installed where seams tend not to show. Carpet is a textile product that is manufactured in 12-foot widths. If the room is wider than 12 feet, it will have a seam.

Builder Responsibility: Builder should make the necessary repairs to meet the above Performance Guideline.

Homeowner Responsibility: None. However, follow the manufacturer's care and cleaning instructions.

Condition #2: CARPET IS LOOSE

Can Affect:

- Appearance

Performance Guideline: Carpets should be stretched tightly, without areas of looseness. If the carpet is loose, the Builder should have it re-stretched.

Builder Responsibility: Builder should make the necessary repairs to meet the above Performance Guideline.

Homeowner Responsibility: None. However, follow the manufacturer's care and cleaning instructions.

Condition #3: CARPET FIBERS SEPARATE FROM BACKING

Can Affect:

- Appearance

Performance Guideline: Carpet fibers usually do not separate from backing unless the carpet has been cleaned with improper products or has been allowed to remain wet for an extended period of time. Proper carpet maintenance is a Homeowner Responsibility.

Builder Responsibility: Deliver the finish floor in conformance to the Performance Guideline.

Homeowner Responsibility: Do not clean carpet with improper products or allow it to remain wet for extended periods of time. Promptly clean any spills in accordance with the material manufacturer's recommendations.

Condition #4: FADING AND DISCOLORATION

Can Affect:

- Appearance

Performance Guideline: Proper carpet maintenance is a Homeowner responsibility. Some amount of fading is unavoidable in areas that are exposed to sunlight. Spots are usually the result of spills or pet accidents. The Homeowner should promptly neutralize and remove any spills in a manner consistent with the manufacturer's recommendations.

Builder Responsibility: There should be no fades or discolorations at the time of the Walkthrough.

Homeowner Responsibility: Choose carpet colors and types that will provide the longest life at sun-exposed locations. Do not let sunlight continuously beam onto carpet, as it may cause fading. Promptly clean any spills in accordance with the material manufacturer's recommendations.

Condition #5: PADDING MISSING UNDER PORTIONS OF THE CARPET

Can Affect:

- Occupant comfort

Performance Guideline: Carpet padding that is missing is unacceptable and should be added by the Builder. The exception to this is that some Builders choose to eliminate padding from closets that are not walk-in closets. This condition is acceptable in those areas.

Builder Responsibility: Builder should make the necessary repairs to meet the above Performance Guideline.

Homeowner Responsibility: None. However, follow the manufacturer's care and cleaning instructions.

Condition #6: CARPET TEXTURE DOES NOT ALIGN AT SEAMS

Can Affect:

- Appearance

Performance Guideline: Texture at seams should run in the same direction. Quarter turns are not acceptable.

Builder Responsibility: Builder should make the necessary repairs to meet the above Performance Guideline.

Homeowner Responsibility: None. However, follow the manufacturer's care and cleaning instructions.

Condition # 7: CARPETS HAVE A DARK SOIL LINE AT STAIR AND BASEBOARD EDGES

Can Affect:

- Appearance

Performance Guideline: Soil staining of carpets due to air infiltration can be reduced, but not eliminated at stair and baseboard edges. Builder should seal the plate behind the baseboard and stair edges with foam, caulk, or by making the joints tight.

Builder Responsibility: There should be no soil lines visible at time of the Walkthrough.

Homeowner Responsibility: Homeowner can expect some soiling to occur at baseboard and stair edges, even if the Builder has made a good faith effort to seal the edges. Homeowner should consider this when selecting carpet colors. Light colors can show edge marks in a short period of time.

Condition # 8: THERE IS A BUMP AT THE TRANSITION BETWEEN CARPET AND HARD SURFACE FLOORING

Can Affect:

- Appearance
- Safety issue related to tripping hazard

Performance Guideline: There should be no more than a ¼ inch vertical displacement between different finish flooring surfaces. Ramping or floating the subfloor is an acceptable method to meet the Performance Guideline. Ramps should extend under the carpet at the rate of one foot horizontal for every ¼ inch of vertical. Specifically designed transition strips, such as metal or wood, may be placed at the transition threshold to alert persons that they are stepping onto a different surface at a different level.

Builder Responsibility: If the Performance Guideline is not met, perform appropriate repairs to satisfy the Guideline.

Homeowner Responsibility: None.

Plaster and Drywall

General Subject Information: Plaster and drywall are materials used to surface most of the inside walls of a house. Drywall, also known as Sheetrock®, gypsum board, or wallboard, is the predominant inside face covering. Plaster, while used exclusively 50 years ago, is used only in custom applications today. Both products have the same basic ingredients: ***gypsum*** and bonding or strengthening agents. While plaster is mixed and applied on the job-site, drywall is made in a factory in sheets that are typically 4 feet x 8 feet x ½ inch thick. Drywall is nailed or screwed to the wall studs, and the joints are covered with a paper tape and a gypsum based compound. Special corner pieces, known as ***beads***, are nailed on at wall corners. When the walls are smooth, they are textured with more gypsum compound. The texturing process may be accomplished by hand troweling or by spraying with a machine. Spray texturing, which is the method of choice today, can be made with a number of different patterns such as knock down, eggshell, fog and dash. Some patterns are intentionally rough and irregular while others are supposed to be uniform throughout.

Condition #1: DRYWALL / PLASTER IS CRACKED

Can Affect:

- Appearance

Performance Guideline: Cracks in excess of 3/32 inch in width are considered unacceptable.

Comments: As the wood frame of the House dries, cracks can be expected to appear in the plaster or drywall. Common places for cracks to appear are at the heads of windows and where walls and ceiling planes intersect. By and large, drywall and plaster cracks are a Homeowner maintenance item.

Builder Responsibility: Unless frame or foundation movement is causing significant cracking, the Builder should make necessary repairs to meet the above Performance Guideline. If frame or foundation movement is causing the cracking, this condition must first be remedied before attempting drywall or plaster repairs.

Homeowner Responsibility: Cracks less than 3/32 inch in drywall and plaster are Homeowner maintenance items and may be patched with spackle or caulk.

Condition #2: DRYWALL HAS NAIL POPS

Can Affect:

- Appearance

Performance Guideline: Nail pops that are visible from a distance of 6 feet under normal light conditions are unacceptable. Nail pops that have cracked the surface or with exposed heads are unacceptable. This Performance Guideline also applies to drywall screws.

Builder Responsibility: Make repairs as necessary to meet the above Performance Guideline.

Homeowner Responsibility: None.

Condition #3: *CORNER BEAD* OR TAPE SEAM POPS

Can Affect:
- Appearance

Performance Guideline: Cracked or pulled away corner beads, or tape seams that have pulled away and are visible by the untrained eye from any angle at a distance of 6 feet under normal lighting conditions, are considered unacceptable.

Builder Responsibility: Make repairs as necessary to meet the above Performance Guideline.

Homeowner Responsibility: None.

Condition #4: DRYWALL CROWNS IN CEILING, DRYWALL BOWS ON WALLS

Can Affect:
- Appearance

Performance Guideline: Drywall crowns in ceilings should not exceed ¼ inch in a 32 inch distance across. Drywall bows in walls should not exceed 3/16 inches in a 32 inch distance across.

Builder Responsibility: Builder should repair drywall crowns or bows in excess of the above Performance Guideline. Floating and retexturing is considered an acceptable repair method.

Homeowner Responsibility: None.

Condition #5: SURFACE TEXTURE IS UNEVEN OR IRREGULAR

Can Affect:
- Appearance

Performance Guideline: Textured surfaces should be consistent with the applicator's intent; that is to say that texture that is designed to be ***knocked down*** should be reasonably uniform, and texture that is designed to be sprayed on without further treatment should be reasonably uniform throughout, when viewed by the untrained eye from a distance of 6 feet under normal lighting conditions. Garages and other utility areas, which may be drywalled and textured, do not apply to this Performance Guideline for texture workmanship.

Comments: Surface texture is more art than science, and determining unacceptable texture is quite subjective. Hand textured walls and ceilings clearly bear the "signature" of the applicator, can be irregular, and may be nearly impossible to match by another applicator. Spray textured walls that are knocked down may have patches of texture that run together when compared to other areas. Unless these patches dominate the appearance of the wall, this would be considered normal application. Areas that are not knocked down, or areas that contain numerous tool marks, are likely to be unacceptable. Texture that is fogged (light coating) and texture that is egg-shell (medium coating) is intended to have a uniform, but bumpy, appearance. The best measure of texture evaluation is consistency from wall-to-wall and from room-to-room.

Builder Responsibility: If more than 10% of the wall surface contains dimples, blotches, tool marks or other irregularities when viewed at a distance of 6 feet under normal lighting conditions, the Builder should make repairs as necessary to provide a more uniform appearance.

Homeowner Responsibility: The Homeowner should realize that wall and ceiling texturing is an art and not a precise science. Expect some irregularities. These irregularities are often more prominent at night when single light sources, such as light fixtures, cast shadows. Determining wall texture performance by feeling it is not an acceptable measure.

Countertops

General Subject Information: The following types of countertop materials are commonly used in residential construction: ceramic tile, granite, marble, plastic laminate, solid surface, and cultured marble. These specific types of countertops are discussed individually in following sections. The Performance Guidelines below are for countertops in general.

Condition #1: COUNTERTOP IS NOT LEVEL

Can Affect:
- Appearance
- Functional

Performance Guideline: Countertops should not exceed ¼ inch of rise or drop in any 8-foot direction. Exception: certain tiles are made with an intentionally irregular, lumpy surface and these irregularities are acceptable (see below, Condition # 1: Uneven Surface, Ceramic Tile Countertops Section).

Builder Responsibility: Builder should take corrective measures to level the countertop, including leveling the cabinets, if necessary.

Homeowner Responsibility: None.

Condition #2: BACKSPLASH IS LOOSE

Can Affect:
- Function
- Appearance

Performance Guideline: Countertop backsplashes should be tightly adhered to the wall.

Builder Responsibility: Builder should make the corrections to repair the loose backsplash.

Homeowner Responsibility: Cabinets expand and shrink with room moisture. Cracks will occur between the top and the splash. Homeowner should maintain the cracks with caulk or grout.

Ceramic Tile Countertops

Condition #1: UNEVEN SURFACE

Can Affect:
- Appearance

Performance Guideline: Since there are a number of different types of ceramic tile, ranging from rough handmade varieties to the very precisely manufactured types, it is impractical to apply any one standard to all ceramic tiles. The general Performance Guideline for an entire countertop is no more than 1/8 inch of uneven surface (as measured between highest and lowest points) in any direction in eight feet horizontally. For handmade tiles, the condition is established by using a long straight-edge that rests on multiple high points along the countertop length. For very regular manufactured tiles, in addition to the level Guideline, no point should occur more than 1/16 inch above or below a line parallel to the surface, and adjacent tiles should not be more than 1/32 inch out of level with each other. Countertops can be totally level but should *never slope away* from drainage points such as sinks or basins.

Builder Responsibility: The Builder should make repairs as necessary to meet the above Performance Guideline for the specific ceramic tile.

Homeowner Responsibility: None. However, always follow the manufacturer's care and cleaning recommendations for the specific ceramic tile.

Condition #2: UNEQUAL GROUT JOINTS

Can Affect:
- Appearance

Performance Guideline: Different types of tiles call for grout joints of different widths. However, within any one area of tile (for precise and manufactured tiles), joints should not vary more than 1/32 inch from the widest to the narrowest.

Builder Responsibility: The Builder should make repairs as necessary to meet the above Performance Guideline for the specific ceramic tile.

Homeowner Responsibility: None. However, always follow the manufacturer's care and cleaning recommendations for the specific ceramic tile.

Condition #3: GROUT JOINT CRACKS

Can Affect:
- Appearance

Performance Guideline: Hairline cracks may appear in grout joints where there are changes in the plane of the tile surface and where tile abuts a dissimilar material, such as at a ***backsplash*** or at a sink or wall. Excluding joints at changes in plane, cracks exceeding 5% of the total length of grout joint in any one tile installation are considered non-performing.

Builder Responsibility: The Builder should make repairs as necessary to meet the above Performance Guideline, provided the condition is not a result of inadequate Homeowner maintenance or misuse.

Homeowner Responsibility: ***Maintenance Alert!*** Homeowner should maintain caulking and repair incidental grout cracking, especially at backsplash and sink openings.

Condition #4: CRACKED TILE

Can Affect:

- Appearance

Performance Guideline: Where cracks align across a number of consecutive tiles, the usual cause is movement of underlying building components. Isolated cracks in individual tiles may indicate Homeowner abuse of the countertop.

Builder Responsibility: If an underlying problem is identified after investigation, the Builder should make repairs as necessary to meet the above Performance Guideline.

Homeowner Responsibility: Do not place unusually heavy objects on the tile surface, avoid dropping things on the tiles. Always follow the manufacturer's care and cleaning recommendations for the specific ceramic tile.

Condition #5: COLOR AND TEXTURE VARIATIONS

Can Affect:

- Appearance

Performance Guideline: Tile used in any one area should be from the same batch, or lot, providing consistent appearance throughout. This does not apply to certain types of handmade tile in which variations are a desirable characteristic. Obvious changes in color and texture within a field of tile are not acceptable where the tile is intended to be of consistent appearance*.

*For the purpose of this Manual, "unacceptable color variation" is defined as an obvious difference in color apparent to the untrained eye, in the opinion of one or more independent observers who are qualified experts in the subject of tile manufacturing and/or installation. A similar general definition applies to "unacceptable texture variation."

Comments: Homeowner should note that trim tiles (the tile that caps the top or edge of a wall or countertop) are not manufactured in the same batch as the flat, or field, tiles. Consequently, there may be variations in color between trim and field tiles.

Builder Responsibility: Builder should make repairs as necessary to meet the above Performance Guideline.

Homeowner Responsibility: None. However, always follow the manufacturer's care and cleaning recommendations for the specific ceramic tile.

Condition #6: LOOSE TILE

Can Affect:
- Appearance

Performance Guideline: Generally, tile should not come loose from the underlying surface to which it is applied. More specifically, tile can come loose as a result of improper original application of ***mortar***; excessive deflection of the underlying material to which tile is applied, or because of exposure to impact from heavy objects.

Builder Responsibility: If condition is a result of improper installation or construction and not a result of Homeowner misuse, Builder should make repairs as necessary to meet the above Performance Guideline for the specific ceramic tile.

Homeowner Responsibility: None. Avoid dropping heavy objects on the tile surface. Always follow the manufacturer's care and cleaning recommendations for the specific ceramic tile.

Condition #7: WATER PENETRATION THROUGH TOP

Can Affect:
- Appearance
- Integrity underlying materials

Performance Guideline: Properly installed, countertops intended for use that involves exposure to significant amounts of water (food preparation areas, countertops adjacent to sinks and basins, etc.) should include a water resisting system adequate to prevent leaks through the countertop assembly.

Builder Responsibility: Builder should make repairs as necessary to meet the above Performance Guideline for the specific ceramic tile.

Homeowner Responsibility: None. However, always follow the manufacturer's care and cleaning recommendations for the specific ceramic tile.

Granite, Marble, and Stone Countertops

Also refer to "Granite, Marble, and Other Stone Flooring" Section of this Chapter.

General Subject Information: Granite, marble, and other stone countertops are natural products. There are many other stone products available today such as limestone, slate and travertine. Because they are natural products, the color and veining of granite and marble are never exactly alike. The Homeowner should expect variations from any installations in other similar homes. Granite, marble, and other stone surfaces are vulnerable to impact damage (dropping heavy items on their surfaces).

Condition #1: CRACKS

Can Affect:

- Appearance
- Life of countertop

Performance Guideline: Cracks in excess of 1/32 inch are considered non-performing. Cracks may be related to improper or inadequate installation, or a result of inadequate support. Improper use may also be a cause (see **Homeowner Responsibility**).

Builder Responsibility: After investigation, Builder should repair or replace as necessary non-performing countertops if the condition was not a result of improper use. Specialists in stone restoration should repair cracked marble, but before undertaking such repairs, the Builder should correct any underlying causes.

Homeowner Responsibility: Maintain countertop in accordance with the recommendations of the material manufacturer and supplier. Maintain caulking and repair incidental grout cracking, especially at backsplash and sink openings. Do not drop heavy objects on countertops. Do not stand on countertop without a protective separation.

Condition #2: TEXTURE AND COLOR VARIATIONS

Can Affect:

- Appearance

Performance Guideline: Countertops made up of multiple pieces should be assembled with reasonably well-matched colors. Severe variations* in surface texture and color are unacceptable.

Builder Responsibility: Meet the Performance Guideline at the time of delivery of House.

Homeowner Responsibility: While both texture and color are truly subjective in nature, a good rule of thumb is: If the Homeowner buys the House before the finish surfaces are set, the Homeowner should approve their placement. If the Homeowner buys the House after the finish surfaces are installed, the Homeowner accepts the finishes as installed. * Refer to Color and Texture Variations definition on page 135.

Condition #3: STAINS

Can Affect:

- Appearance

Performance Guideline: Granite, marble, and stone can be stained by a variety of products and natural materials, juices, etc. Protection of the surface is a Homeowner Responsibility. Any pre-existing stains should be noted at the time of the Homeowner ***Walkthrough***.

Builder Responsibility: Builder should correct any pre-existing stains noted at the Walkthrough. If pre-existing stains cannot be corrected, Builder should replace countertop.

Homeowner Responsibility: Examine countertops carefully at the Walkthrough. Builders cannot be held responsible for this type of damage unless it is identified and disclosed at the time of the ***Walkthrough***. Maintain countertop in accordance with the recommendations of the material manufacturer and supplier. Use only cleaning products approved by the manufacturer or the applicable trade association for the material (for instance, the Marble Institute of America for granite and marble countertops). Do not use abrasives to clean any type of countertop. Avoid placing hot pots, pans, Crockpots®, etc., in direct contact with the countertop.

Condition #4: CHIPS

Can Affect:
- Appearance
- Maintenance

Performance Guideline: Granite, marble, and stone countertops should not be delivered to the Homeowner scratched or chipped. Repairs of chips and scratches prior to the ***Walkthrough*** are acceptable provided the repair is indistinguishable. Chips on a top of any material should not penetrate more than 1/16 inch from the edge of the seam or grout joint, unless the manufacturing process (as with tumbled stone) intentionally created edge chips.

Builder Responsibility: Repair or replace countertops as necessary to meet the above Performance Guideline, provided that condition was not caused by Homeowner misuse or negligence.

Homeowner Responsibility: Examine countertops carefully at the Walkthrough. Maintain countertop in accordance with the recommendations of the material manufacturer and supplier. Do not drop heavy objects on countertop.

Plastic Laminate Countertops

Condition #1: OPEN JOINTS

Can Affect:
- Appearance
- Water tightness

Performance Guideline: A properly assembled plastic laminate countertop should have tight hairline joints without any openings where adjoining pieces meet. Joints that are separated by more than 1/32 inch are considered unacceptable and should be corrected by the Builder.

Builder Responsibility: Repair or replace countertops as necessary to meet the above Performance Guideline, provided that condition was not caused by Homeowner misuse or negligence.

Homeowner Responsibility: Examine countertops carefully at the Walkthrough. Maintain countertop in accordance with the recommendations of the material manufacturer and supplier.

Condition #2: DELAMINATION

Can Affect:
- Appearance
- Life of countertop

Performance Guideline: Delamination occurs when the plastic laminate does not adhere to the ***underlayment.*** This is usually an adhesive application problem or curing problem. Edge strips are most commonly affected by this type of problem. Delamination is unacceptable and should be corrected by the Builder unless there is evidence of abusive use by the Homeowner.

Builder Responsibility: Repair or replace countertops as necessary to meet the above Performance Guideline, provided that condition was not caused by Homeowner misuse or negligence.

Homeowner Responsibility: Maintain countertop in accordance with the recommendations of the material manufacturer and supplier. Maintain caulking, especially at backsplash and sink openings.

Condition #3: UNACCEPTABLE TRIMMING

Can Affect:
- Appearance

Performance Guideline: Unacceptable trimming can include edges that are not straight and edges that are burned because of overheating of trimming cutters. Trimmed edges should be very straight and neat. The edge exposure area should be of a constant width throughout the countertop.

Builder Responsibility: Repair or replace countertops as necessary to meet the above Performance Guideline.

Homeowner Responsibility: None. However, maintain countertop in accordance with the recommendations of the material manufacturer and supplier.

Condition #4: STAINS AND BURNS

Can Affect:
- Appearance

Performance Guideline: The countertop should be delivered to the Homeowner without stains, scratches or burns.

Builder Responsibility: Repair or replace any non-performing conditions noted at the time of the Walkthrough.

Homeowner Responsibility: Examine countertops carefully at the Walkthrough. Builders cannot be held responsible for this type of damage unless it is identified and disclosed at the time of the ***Walkthrough***. Maintain countertop in accordance with the recommendations of the material manufacturer and supplier. Use only cleaning products approved by the material manufacturer; never use abrasives. Avoid placing hot objects on countertops.

Solid Surface Countertops

"Solid surface countertops" refers to the class of plastics, called acrylic or polyester, or to a blend of plastics and fiberglass. This includes products such as Avonite™, Cerata™, Corian™, Corinthian™, Fountainhead™, Gibralter™, Hi-macs™, Staron™, Surrell™, Swanstone™, and many other synthetic surfaces.

Condition #1: OPEN SEAMS

Can Affect:

- Appearance
- Water tightness

Performance Guideline: Depending on the selected color and veining, there should be no conspicuous seams in the finished countertop. Proficient solid surface countertop installers are able to bond adjacent pieces so that the joint is virtually inconspicuous, but not necessarily invisible. Some solid surface pieces may be "softseamed" with a flexible silicone (such as the narrow solid surface strip behind slide-in ranges).

Builder Responsibility: Repair or replace countertops as necessary to meet the above Performance Guideline.

Homeowner Responsibility: None. However, examine countertops carefully at the Walkthrough. Maintain countertop in accordance with the recommendations of the material manufacturer and supplier.

Condition #2: ROUGHENED SURFACE

Can Affect:

- Appearance
- Cleanliness

Performance Guideline: To finish solid surface countertops, it is necessary to sand the surface smooth. The resulting final surface should be smooth and consistent throughout. Surface texture variations that are clearly rough to the touch are considered unacceptable.

Builder Responsibility: Repair or replace countertops as necessary to meet the above Performance Guideline, provided that condition was not caused by Homeowner misuse or negligence.

Homeowner Responsibility: None. However, examine countertops carefully at the Walkthrough. Maintain countertop in accordance with the recommendations of the material manufacturer and supplier.

Condition #3: STAINS AND BURNS

Can Affect:
- Appearance

Performance Guideline: There should be no stains or burns on any portion of the countertop at the time of the Homeowner Walkthrough.

Builder Responsibility: Repair or replace any non-performing conditions noted at the Walkthrough.

Homeowner Responsibility: Examine countertops carefully at the Walkthrough. Maintain countertop in accordance with the recommendations of the material manufacturer and supplier. Builders cannot be held responsible for this type of damage unless it is identified and disclosed at the time of the ***Walkthrough***.

Condition #4: BLEMISHES

Can Affect:
- Appearance

Performance Guideline: A solid surface countertop is a product that is manufactured under closely controlled conditions. Therefore the countertop should be delivered to the Homeowner free of blemishes.

Builder Responsibility: Repair or replace countertops as necessary to meet the above Performance Guideline.

Homeowner Responsibility: None. However, examine countertops carefully at the Walkthrough. Maintain countertop in accordance with the recommendations of the material manufacturer and supplier. Builders cannot be held responsible for this type of damage unless it is identified and disclosed at the time of the ***Walkthrough***.

Cultured Marble Countertops

General Comments: A cultured marble countertop is also a synthetic countertop. Unlike the other solid surface countertops discussed in previous Sections (which are considered the "new generation" of solid surface countertops), cultured marble has been around for at least 40 years. The Performance Guidelines of cultured marble are less rigorous than the new solid surface countertops. There is an upgraded version of cultured marble known as "onyx". Onyx has a smoother top and more uniform color spread than basic cultured marble. Performance Guidelines for cultured marble countertops also apply to Onyx countertops.

Condition #1: IMPROPER FIT

Can Affect:
- Appearance
- Water tightness

Performance Guideline: The top and backsplash pieces should fit together without gaps. The installer is likely to caulk these joints with a compatible caulk. If there is a gap between the backsplash and the wall, this gap should also be caulked so that no gap is visible. No gap should be more than ¼ inch wide, whether caulked or not.

Builder Responsibility: Repair or replace countertops as necessary to meet the above Performance Guideline.

Homeowner Responsibility: None. However, examine countertops carefully at the Walkthrough. Maintain countertop in accordance with the recommendations of the material manufacturer and supplier.

Condition #2: BLEMISHES AND INCONSISTENT COLOR

Can Affect:
- Appearance

Performance Guideline: Color swirls can vary significantly in cultured marble due to the fact that each batch is made like a marble cake. In general, the color swirls should be consistent throughout the top, and should not be concentrated in any one spot. The same Performance Guideline applies to metal sparkles, if added to the mix.

Builder Responsibility: Repair or replace countertops as necessary to meet the above Performance Guideline.

Homeowner Responsibility: None. However, examine countertops carefully at the Walkthrough. Maintain countertop in accordance with the recommendations of the material manufacturer and supplier.

Condition #3: VOIDS AT SURFACE

Can Affect:
- Appearance

Performance Guideline: There should be no voids (depressions) in the surface more than 1/32 inch in depth and no larger than 1 inch in diameter. There should be no more than four such voids in 8 square feet of surface.

Builder Responsibility: Repair or replace countertops as necessary to meet the above Performance Guideline, provided that condition was not caused by Homeowner misuse or negligence.

Homeowner Responsibility: Examine countertops carefully at the Walkthrough. Maintain countertop in accordance with the recommendations of the material manufacturer and supplier. Do not drop heavy objects on countertop surfaces.

Condition #4: LEAKS AT JOINTS AND FITTINGS

Can Affect:

- Appearance
- Cabinet contents / integrity

Performance Guideline: All penetrations at the faucets, sink rims and back splashes should be watertight.

Builder Responsibility: Repair unacceptable conditions to meet the Performance Guideline.

Homeowner Responsibility: Always maintain the countertop in accordance with the manufacturer's recommendations. If at any time the Homeowner discovers product or installation problems, the Homeowner should notify the Builder promptly.

Appliances

General Subject Information: In a house there are two broad categories of appliances: (1) kitchen type appliances such as the dishwasher, oven, range, etc. and (2) system appliances such as the furnace, air conditioner, water heater, and gas burning fireplace. Smoke detectors are often considered appliances. With respect to warranty responsibility, the Builder may treat each category differently. It is important that the Homeowner understand his or her responsibility in dealing with appliance warranty claims.

Generally, it is the custom and practice of Builders to exclude the kitchen appliances from the house warranty. Kitchen appliances are warranted by their manufacturer and warranty registration cards are provided for the Homeowner to complete. If the appliance is not performing as intended, a service technician from the appliance manufacturer is the source for repair.

System appliances also often have a registration and warranty card for the Homeowner to return. These manufacturers have a specific warranty of their product that does not necessarily tie to the Builder. For system appliance claims, the subcontractor who made the original installation also normally performs the repair.

Condition: APPLIANCES DO NOT PERFORM AS INTENDED

Performance Guideline: All appliances should function in the manner that the manufacturer intended.

Comments:

- → When does a non-performing appliance become a Builder Responsibility versus a manufacturer's responsibility? The rule of thumb is: if the problem is contained within the appliance itself, it is the appliance manufacturer's responsibility. If the problem is outside the appliance, it is the Builder's Responsibility. For example, if the dishwasher does not operate properly because the door latch won't close, it is the manufacturer's responsibility. However, if a water supply hose to the dishwasher is leaking, it is the Builder's Responsibility.
- → What if it is not easy to tell who is responsible for the non-performing condition? For example, if the furnace does not come on, is it a faulty thermostat or is the furnace not performing as intended? If the air conditioner does not start (after remaining idle all winter) is it a faulty compressor or a blown fuse? Depending upon the warranty, the Builder might contact the appliance manufacturer for you, or the Builder may expect you to make the contact directly. Assuming the Homeowner has not abused the appliance, and the non-performing condition occurs within the manufacturer's warranty period, the manufacturer is the likely source of repair.
- → It is very important that the Homeowner register the appliances with the manufacturer within the first 10 days of taking delivery of the House.

Manufacturer's Responsibility: Repair the appliance in a prompt manner in accordance with the manufacturer's warranty.

Builder Responsibility: Install the appliances in strict accordance with the installation instructions furnished by the manufacturer. Repair any faulty installation.

Homeowner Responsibility: Register all appliances with the manufacturer. Read and follow the manufacturer's operating instructions. Before making a service call, follow the Trouble Shooting Guide found at the back of most appliance owners manuals.

Cabinets and Vanities

General Subject Information: There are two conditions common to cabinet or vanities: (1) the finish is wearing prematurely, or (2) the drawer slide brackets fail. Cabinet finishes tend to age more in hot, humid rooms and in areas that surround sinks due to water that is splashed on the finish. Other problems are gaps that appear between cabinet cases or doors that do not align.

Condition #1: CABINETS DESIGNED TO SET FLUSH WITH THE CEILING HAVE A VISIBLE GAP, SPACE, OR SEPARATION

Can Affect:

- ♦ Appearance
- ♦ Safety issue

Performance Guideline: Any space or gap along the top or sides of the cabinet frame that exceeds 3/16 inch is considered unacceptable.

Comments: As the new House acclimates to the rough framing materials, the structure will have a tendency to contract when the rough lumber dries out. This has the potential to affect interior finishes and is considered normal. However if the condition worsens, this may indicate a lack of fastening or the lack of adequate backing for proper cabinet support.

Builder Responsibility: All cabinets should have the proper backing in the wall to support whatever product is being applied to that particular wall. If the cabinet or vanity does not meet the Performance Guideline and was not the result of negligence by the Homeowner, then the Builder should repair as necessary to meet the above Performance Guideline.

Homeowner Responsibility: The Homeowner should use caution when loading upper cabinets so as to not overload them. Heavy plates and dishes and canned goods do not belong in upper cabinets. Refer to "**Ten Most Common Mistakes Made By New Homeowners**" in the Preface.

Condition #2: CABINETS ARE NOT SET *FLUSH* WITH ONE ANOTHER

Can Affect:
- Appearance

Performance Guideline: The face (*front*) of a cabinet should not be more than 1/8 inch out of flat plane with connecting portions of other cabinet pieces. Corners should not be out of line more than 3/16 inch.

Comments: Cabinets are to set flush (in the same plane) and even with one another.

Builder Responsibility: If the cabinets do not meet the above Performance Guideline, then the Builder should repair or replace any non-performing cabinetry in order to satisfy the Guideline. When finishing or refinishing, Builder should attempt to match the original cabinetry.

Homeowner Responsibility: The Homeowner should properly maintain all cabinets, particularly any cabinetry that is located in areas that are subject to moisture, i.e. kitchens, bathrooms or laundry rooms. Water should not be allowed to remain on any wood products, whether sealed or not. If it is determined that the Homeowner was negligent with maintenance, the Builder will not be held responsible.

Condition #3: CABINETS ARE WARPED

Can Affect:
- Appearance
- Function / performance

Performance Guideline: Cabinet doors should not warp more than ¼ inch from the face of the frame. If the door is flat, but the frame is warped, the same Performance Guideline applies.

Comments: Cabinets in contact with water and lack of proper maintenance are major contributing factors to warping. Cabinetry that is in the proximity of water, i.e. in front of a sink, also may need to be refinished more often than other cabinets in the House when not properly cared for.

Builder Responsibility: Any cabinet or cabinetry, including doors and drawer fronts, that do not meet the above Performance Guideline should be replaced either in part or in whole (assuming condition was not cause by Homeowner negligence). When finishing or refinishing, Builder should attempt to match the original cabinetry.

Homeowner Responsibility: Cabinets, drawer fronts and doors need to be periodically inspected for excessive wear and/or deterioration of the finish.

Condition #4: CABINET DRAWER GUIDE HAS BROKEN

Can Affect:

- Operation

Performance Guideline: All doors and drawers should function smoothly and properly for their intended purpose.

Comments: Drawer guides that support the drawer opening commonly fail. Drawer guides are often made of plastic and may break over time. This is a very inexpensive replacement item that can be purchased at a hardware store.

Builder Responsibility: If a drawer or door does not meet the above Performance Guideline, then the Builder should repair or replace the portion of the cabinet that does not meet the Guideline

Homeowner Responsibility: Homeowners should be careful not to overload the drawers. This puts additional stress on the guides, which could cause them to prematurely fail.

Condition #5: CABINET DRAWER IS BINDING DURING OPENING

Can Affect:

- Operation

Performance Guideline: Cabinet doors and drawers should open and close smoothly without tugging or pulling.

Comments: Drawers should not be overloaded, and should be operated in a smooth fashion. Both doors and drawers should be operated without slamming the drawers shut.

Builder Responsibility: If a drawer does not meet the above Performance Guideline, then the Builder should repair or replace the drawer or door that does not meet the Guideline.

Homeowner Responsibility: Homeowner should operate doors and drawers smoothly and easily. Do not overload the drawers. ***Maintenance Alert!*** Metal drawer guides should be lubricated with a light lubricating oil every two years.

Condition #6: CABINET DOOR SWINGS OPEN AND / OR WILL NOT STAY CLOSED

Can Affect:
- Appearance
- Function / performance

Performance Guideline: All door hinge mechanisms and catches should operate and function as intended. Whether closing or opening, the door should operate smoothly with reasonable ease or effort.

Comments: Cabinets should be installed level and ***plumb*** to ensure proper operation. Hinges can become loose and occasionally may need to be retightened or adjusted, a relatively simple Homeowner maintenance item.

Builder Responsibility: If the door or doors do not meet the above Performance Guideline, then the Builder should repair or replace as necessary to meet the Guideline

Homeowner Responsibility: Doors can go out of adjustment, depending upon the care and use that they have been put through. Do not slam, hang objects from, or pull on the door, as this will cause hinge mechanisms to weaken not only at their fastening points but also within the mechanisms themselves. Periodically inspect hinges and retighten if necessary.

Condition #7: DOORS OR DRAWERS HAVE CRACKS IN THE PANELS

Can Affect:
- Appearance

Performance Guideline: Panel inserts in drawers and doors should not crack.

Builder Responsibility: Builder should replace cracked panels. An exact match of the wood grain or color cannot be expected.

Homeowner Responsibility: Consider stained cabinets as furniture and treat the wood faces with furniture polish.

Condition #8: PLASTIC LAMINATE SURFACES ARE PEELING AWAY

Can Affect:
- Life of cabinet
- Structural integrity of the cabinet

Performance Guideline: Cabinets that are covered with high-pressure plastic laminate should not delaminate.

Comments: Over time and without proper care, plastic laminate cabinets can delaminate at joints and corners. This usually occurs as a result of Homeowner negligence such as getting water into the core of the cabinet door.

Builder Responsibility: If the cabinet delaminates and is not a result of negligence by Homeowner, the Builder should make the repairs as necessary to meet the Performance Guideline.

Homeowner Responsibility: Proper care by the Homeowner is essential. Liquids should be cleaned up immediately and not left on a surface, particularly at joints or corners. This creates the potential for the breakdown of the glues used to laminate the surface to the substrate.

Condition #9: CABINETS DO NOT SIT LEVEL

Can Affect:
- Appearance

Performance Guideline: Cabinets should not have a deviation of more than 3/8 inch out of level.

Builder Responsibility: If the Performance Guideline is not met, the Builder should make the repairs necessary to meet the Guideline. When finishing or refinishing, Builder should attempt to match the original cabinetry.

Homeowner Responsibility: None.

Condition #10: CABINET DOORS DO NOT ALIGN WHEN CLOSED

Can Affect:
- Appearance

Performance Guideline: Gaps between abutting doors should not exceed 1/8 inch.

Builder Responsibility: Builder should adjust doors to meet the Performance Guideline.

Homeowner Responsibility: None.

Condition #11: CABINET FINISH (paint or stain) IS IRREGULAR, MISMATCHED, OR BLOTCHY

Can Affect:
- Appearance

Performance Guideline: Irregularities of wood color in stained cabinets are considered acceptable, unless two or more different stains were used. Painted cabinets should be uniform in color when viewed under normal lighting conditions at a distance of 6 feet.

Comments: Cabinet finishes are created two ways: (1) as a completely finished module that is either painted or stained in a factory, or (2) as a larger component that is made in a cabinet shop and painted or stained after it is installed in the House. Cabinets that are stained to show the *grain* of the wood will have irregularities in the finish color. This is due to the fact that no two pieces of wood have exactly the same characteristics. Stain absorbs differently through flat surfaces, soft grains, and ends. Painted cabinets are expected to be reasonably uniform in color because there is no intention to show the grain. Painted cabinets may be made of materials other than wood.

Builder Responsibility: Take corrective action to meet the above Performance Guideline.

Homeowner Responsibility: None.

Condition #12: GAPS APPEAR BETWEEN SECTIONS WHERE CABINETS ARE JOINED

Can Affect:
- Appearance

Performance Guideline: Gaps at the section where cabinet cases are joined that are in excess of 1/32 inch for painted cabinets and 1/16 inch for stained cabinets are considered unacceptable.

Builder Responsibility: Make repairs as necessary to meet the Performance Guideline.

Homeowner Responsibility: Be aware that painted cabinets will separate at the ***stiles*** due to normal drying out of the House frame. Bathroom and laundry fans should always be operating when those rooms are in use.

Moldings and Trim

General Subject Information: Interior trim, also called finish trim, is divided into two categories: standing trim and running trim. Standing trim is used for window and door casings. Running trim is used for baseboards, crown, or chair molding. The application of trim or moldings is not structural in nature. However the trim is a finished product of the house and it should meet the Performance Guidelines for manufacture and workmanship.

Condition #1: GAPS APPEAR AT JOINTS

Can Affect:
- Appearance

Performance Guideline: No separation should exceed 1/16 inch in width at the time the House is delivered to the new Homeowner.

Comments: Minor separation at the joints may occur as a result of expansion and contraction of the House. This occurs as the lumber in the House starts to dry out and stabilize. Expansion and contraction may also occur during seasonal changes with regards to humidity.

Builder Responsibility: If the gaps or splits are greater than the Performance Guideline at time of delivery, the Builder should make the necessary repairs to meet the Guideline. When finishing or refinishing, Builder should attempt to match the original material.

Homeowner Responsibility: ***Maintenance Alert!*** During the first year of the life of the House, the framing lumber will shrink. This action is likely to cause some gaps in trim and molding. If the gaps are less than the Performance Guideline, the Homeowner should putty and/or caulk, sand and refinish in order to prevent any further splitting or separation to the molding or trim.

Condition #2: NAIL HEADS ARE VISIBLE IN THE FINISHED WOODWORK

Can Affect:

- Appearance

Performance Guideline: Finish nails or staples should be set below the surface; holes should be filled and finished. If finish nail holes are visible from a distance of 6 feet under normal light (daylight), this is unacceptable.

Builder Responsibility: If the trim and molding does not meet the Performance Guideline, then the Builder should make the necessary repairs. When finishing or refinishing, Builder should attempt to match the original materials.

Homeowner Responsibility: None.

Condition #3: GAPS OCCUR WHERE MOLDING ABUTS ONE ANOTHER OR ABUTS ANOTHER MATERIAL

Can Affect:

- Appearance

Performance Guideline: No separation should exceed 1/16 inch in width at the time the House is delivered to the Homeowner.

Comments: Minor separations at the joints may occur as a result of expansion and contraction of the House. Contraction may occur as the rough framing lumber in the House starts to dry out and stabilize.

Builder Responsibility: If the gaps exceed the Performance Guideline, then the Builder should make the necessary repairs to meet the Guideline. When finishing or refinishing, Builder should attempt to match the original materials.

Homeowner Responsibility: If the gaps are within the Performance Guideline, Homeowner should putty and/or caulk, sand and refinish in order to prevent any further splitting or separation to the molding or trim.

APPLY SPACKLE TO INTERIOR TRIM. THEN, PAINT OVER THE SPACKLE

Condition #4: MOLDING OR TRIM IS SPLIT OR CHECKED

Can Affect:
- Appearance

Performance Guideline: All finished woodwork should be smooth and without any surface marks at the time of the Walkthrough. Caulking or filling gaps is acceptable, as long as the filled area blends in with the surrounding surface when viewed from a distance of 6 feet under normal light (daylight).

Comments: Wood has an inherent characteristic of hairline cracking, which is an acceptable condition. However, at the time of Walkthrough all trim and molding should be free of any splitting or checking.

Builder Responsibility: The Builder should meet the Performance Guideline at the time of the Walkthrough. If the subject woodwork does not meet the Guideline, then the Builder should correct by replacing and/or filling, puttying, sanding and refinishing as necessary to meet the Performance Guideline. When finishing or refinishing, Builder should attempt to match the original materials.

Homeowner Responsibility: ***Maintenance Alert!*** Depending on the climate/environment, wood products, even interior woods, may need more than normal maintenance. If cracks occur, it is important to seal these cracks by either caulking or puttying, then sanding and refinishing. This is very important in order to prevent any moisture from migrating to the unprotected back side of the wood, potentially causing twisting and warping.

Condition #5: HAMMER MARKS OR OTHER MARRS ARE VISIBLE

Can Affect:
- Appearance

Performance Guideline: Hammer head marks or other marrs should not be visible from a distance of 6 feet under normal light (daylight).

Builder Responsibility: The Builder should make all repairs necessary to meet the Performance Guideline. When finishing or refinishing, Builder should attempt to match the original materials and colors.

Homeowner Responsibility: None. However, the Homeowner should inspect all trim and molding work during the ***Walkthrough***.

Mirrors

General Subject Information: A mirror is a combination of high quality glass and a thin layer of silver or aluminum applied to the back side. The glass supports the metallic layer and will protect its shiny surface. Silvering quality glass is specially selected glass, which is exceptionally free of imperfections and other irregularities and is used in mirror and optical applications. A second grade is mirror glazing, which is also a superior glass for mirrors. Both silvering glass and mirror quality glass have very low distortion levels and must be smooth to within 1/25,000 inch.

Condition #1: SCRATCHES ON GLASS SURFACE

Can Affect:

- Appearance

Performance Guideline: If scratches or imperfections are visible under normal lighting conditions and are noticeable from a distance of 3 feet or more, the mirror is considered non-performing (providing the glass was not damaged as a result of any Homeowner negligence).

Comments: A scratch, or scratches, do not constitute a safety concern, but tends to be more of a visual distraction. Cracked glass may present a safety issue and should be replaced by a professional glazing company as soon as possible.

Builder Responsibility: Mirrors should meet the above Performance Guideline. If the mirror does not meet the Guideline, then the Builder should replace the mirror.

Homeowner Responsibility: The Homeowner at the time of the ***Walkthrough*** should thoroughly inspect all mirrors for any irregularities within the glazing. It is much harder to have the Builder respond to a complaint months after the Homeowner has taken possession of the House.

Condition #2: MIRROR BACKING IS DETERIORATING

Can Affect:

- Appearance
- Function

Performance Guideline: When viewing the mirror from the front, there should be no visible imperfections, peeling, flaking and/or discoloration within the metallic backing material of the mirror.

Builder Responsibility: If the mirror does not meet the above Performance Guideline, then the Builder should replace the mirror to meet the Guideline.

Homeowner Responsibility: The Homeowner at the time of the Walkthrough should thoroughly inspect all mirrors for any irregularities within the glazing and its metallic backing. It is much harder to have the Builder respond to a complaint months after the Homeowner has taken possession of the House. ***Maintenance Alert!*** When cleaning a mirror, use caution when using cleansers that contain ammonia or vinegar. Ammonia and vinegar are excellent glass cleaners, however they can be extremely damaging to the metallic backing of the mirror. Also, do not allow cleaners to go over the top, sides or to get into the track at the bottom of the mirror. Manufacturers often recommend applying cleaning agents to a cloth, and then wiping down the mirror.

Condition #3: MIRROR WARDROBE DOORS DO NOT HAVE SAFETY BACKING (Walk-in Closets)

Can Affect:

- Occupant safety

Performance Guideline: Mirror wardrobe doors used as the entry to walk-in closets should have safety backing with labels stating that they have met the following standards: ANSI Z97 and UBC 5406.

Comments: When a person can walk in or out of a closet that has mirror wardrobe doors, there is a potential to hit the door and shatter it. Mirror wardrobe doors on walk-in closets must have a backing such as fiberglass or wood that will resist a 400-pound impact test.

Builder Responsibility: Meet the Performance Guideline for all mirror doors used on walk-in closets.

Homeowner Responsibility: None.

Shower and Tub Enclosures

Condition #1: GLASS / PLASTIC IS SCRATCHED

Can Affect:

- Appearance

Performance Guideline: At the time of delivery of the House, shower and tub enclosure glass or plastic panels should not be scratched.

Builder Responsibility: Replace any glass or plastic panels that are scratched at the Walkthrough.

Homeowner Responsibility: None, but be aware that any claims for scratched shower and tub enclosure panels may not be honored by the Builder after the ***Walkthrough***.

Condition #2: SHOWER OR TUB ENCLOSURE LEAKS AT THE DOOR(S)

Can Affect:

- Flooring surface life
- ***Underlayment*** and frame integrity

Performance Guideline: Shower doors should not leak if used properly. This is a Homeowner use and maintenance item, unless watershield parts were omitted from original installation.

Comments: Except under unusual cases where the plastic or rubber parts used to keep water inside the tub or shower are missing, leaks at the door or sliding panel are due to two causes: (1) the bather has directed the shower head at the joint between the door and the fixed panel, or (2) the sliding panels at the tub have had their direction reversed by the bather. The inside panel must be the one closest to the shower head for proper use.

Builder Responsibility: None, unless watershield parts were omitted from the original installation.

Homeowner Responsibility: Become aware of the proper use of a tub and shower enclosure. Keep shower water directed away from the door and panels. Continuous leaking may result in rot of the ***underlayment*** and ***subfloor***. Continuous leaking also creates an environment for mold and mildew growth and for termites. Refer to **Homeowner Maintenance Summary** for proper care and additional details.

Condition #3: SHOWER / TUB ENCLOSURE LEAKS THROUGH THE FRAME

Can Affect:

- Flooring surface life
- ***Underlayment*** and frame integrity

Performance Guideline: Shower and tub enclosures should not leak at the frame. This Guideline includes any surface to which the frame is attached.

Builder Responsibility: The Builder should take corrective measures to eliminate leaking of shower and tub frame.

Homeowner Responsibility: Once Guideline is met, enclosure caulking becomes a maintenance item for the Homeowner.

Condition #4: SHOWER / TUB ENCLOSURES ARE NOT TEMPERED GLASS

Can Affect:

- Occupant safety

Performance Guideline: If glass is used in shower and tub enclosures, it must be tempered. If plastic panels are used, they must be approved by the local ***Building Official***.

Comments: Tempered glass has a small tempering "logo" or mark permanently placed on the panel by the glass maker. Before tempering glass and use of clear glass panels became prominent, many enclosures were made of glass with a wire grid in the glass.

Builder Responsibility: Unless approved plastic is used in shower and tub enclosures, all glass panels should be tempered.

Homeowner Responsibility: None.

USE A JUMBO PAPER CLIP TO CLEAN SHOWER DOOR TRACK WEEP HOLES

Condition #5: TOP RAIL OF SHOWER / TUB ENCLOSURE IS NOT SCREWED TO THE FRAME

Can Affect:

- Occupant safety

Performance Guideline: The top rail of a tub or shower enclosure should be screwed to the frame or mechanically connected in a manner approved by the local ***Building Official***.

Comments: Many shower and tub enclosures are sold as a "snap together" kit. While the side pieces screw to the tub or shower wall, the top piece (known as a rail) snaps into the top end of the side pieces. This is not a tight connection, and the bather could dislodge the entire top rail while getting in or out of the shower or tub. This action could cause the door panels to fall out of their tracks and break.

Builder Responsibility: The Builder should take the necessary corrective measures to conform to the above Performance Guideline.

Homeowner Responsibility: None.

Condition #6: GROUT IS CRACKED BETWEEN THE TUB / SHOWER AND FIRST ROW OF TILE

Can Affect:

- Water tightness of the assembly
- Appearance

Performance Guideline: The grout should not be cracked at the bottom of the first course of tile at the time of ***Walkthrough*** (hairline cracks are excepted).

Comments: The first row of tile around the shower floor or the top of the tub is susceptible to cracking and is primarily a Homeowner maintenance item.

Builder Responsibility: Meet the Performance Guideline at the time of the Walkthrough; make repairs as necessary if grout cracks are noted at Walkthrough.

Homeowner Responsibility: ***Maintenance Alert!*** Tile grout should be sealed by the Homeowner prior to use, using a silicone-based sealer that can be purchased at any hardware store. Grout should be cleaned frequently and should be kept free of mold and mildew. When significant cracking first appears, the grout joint between the bottom row of tile and the top of the shower floor or tub should be caulked with a caulking compound made for bathroom use. Many grout manufacturers also make flexible sealants, both standard and smooth, to match their grouts. Old caulk or grout should be dug out and discarded; new caulk should not be applied over old caulk.

Condition #7: WATER RESISTANT BACKING IMPROPERLY INSTALLED AT TUB OR SHOWER SURROUNDS

Can Affect:

- Life of structure

Performance Guideline: If backing is to be used at tub and shower surrounds, it must be water-resistant. Materials such as cement board or special water resistant paper may be used. However, lath and mortar are preferred. Water-resistant gypsum board is a Code-permitted alternative.

Comments: Because water splashes on tub and tile surround surfaces (even though they may be tile or some other hard water resistant finish), water and water vapor can penetrate the surface. Over time, water penetration may cause underlying wood or ordinary drywall to fail and/or grow mold and mildew. Except in the case of fiberglass or plastic tub and shower surrounds, water-resistant materials, properly sealed, flashed and caulked, should be used as backing for surface finishes. Water resistant drywall, commonly used as tub and shower surround backing in the past, is no longer favored for this purpose. It may be used in other damp locations such as walls and ceilings above surrounds. Water resistant drywall is easy to identify: the paper surface is either green or blue. On fiberglass tub and shower assemblies, it is not necessary to place backing behind the fiberglass walls (unless required by local code).

Builder Responsibility: Use an appropriate water-resistant backing material at tub and shower surrounds and water-resistant drywall at other potentially damp locations.

Homeowner Responsibility: Make certain that a coat of premium enamel paint is maintained on the drywall surface. Maintain the caulking between the tub or shower pan and the first row of tile (**see Homeowner Maintenance Summary**).

Paint and Stain

*For interior paint and stain Performance Guidelines, refer to **Chapter 5, "Paint and Stain"***

Chapter Seven

UTILITY SYSTEMS

includes:

Heating:
Forced Air
Radiant

Cooling:
Air Conditioning
Evaporative Cooling

Electrical

Plumbing:
Piping
Faucets
Sinks
Tubs/Showers
Toilets
Water Heaters

Fire Sprinkler System

Telephone

Cable TV

References for this chapter:

- *ASHRAE Handbook: Fundamentals*
- *Residential Construction Performance Guidelines*, NAHB
- *Residential & Light Commercial Construction Standards*, by Don Reynolds
- *Troubleshooting Guide to Residential Construction*, Builderburg Group
- *Workmanship Guidelines*, CA Contractors State License Board

A comprehensive list of references by author and publisher is found in the Bibliography section.

Utility Systems

Heating

General Subject Information: While there are several systems available to heat a house, the focus of this chapter will be on the two most common systems: forced air systems and radiant systems. Forced air systems consist of a gas or electric furnace and a series of large pipes in the attic and crawl space known as ducts. Ducts supply warm air to the ceiling, floor, or walls of the house. The forced air system also has a return air component that circulates the air back to the heat source. Forced air furnaces may use natural gas, bottled gas, fuel oil, or coal as a source of heat. Natural gas is the most common fuel. Less frequently used systems are heat pumps and electric furnaces. Electric furnaces operate solely with electricity. Heat pumps are reverse air conditioners. Heat pumps take heat from the air outside a house and transfer it to inside the house. Even on very cold days there is a small amount of heat present in the outside air. In the summertime, the heat pump operates like a standard air conditioner.

Radiant heat systems use either tubing filled with warm fluid or electrical wires that are heated to transmit radiant energy into the living space of the house. The system that uses tubing circulates a warm fluid, usually water or a light oil, through the tubes, which may be located along the baseboard or embedded in a concrete floor. Like the forced air system, the heat source to heat the fluid comes from burning natural gas or fuel oil. The flame heats the fluid in a small boiler and a pump circulates the hot fluid throughout the tubing in the house.

Radiant systems using electricity rely upon electrical resistance (much like the wires inside an ordinary household toaster) to create heat. The electrical heat strips are found either in the floor or ceilings of houses. While the electrical resistance system is low cost to install, it is rarely used anymore because it has a high cost to operate.

Radiant systems provide a quiet operation of uniform warmth, but they do not circulate air through the house as a forced air system does. A device called a thermostat controls the temperature of both types of systems. There is at least one thermostat in the house, perhaps more depending upon how many zones are created for heating within the house.

Many factors control interior comfort for heating a house. Some factors include:

- → the orientation of rooms in the house
- → the amount of window area in a room
- → whether the windows are shaded with a drapery that could provide additional insulation
- → the amount of insulation installed
- → the type of windows and exterior doors installed
- → the ceiling height or "volume" of the rooms

Condition #1: SOME ROOMS ARE COMFORTABLE, WHILE OTHER ROOMS ARE COLD

Can Affect:

- Occupant comfort

Performance Guideline: The heating system should be designed so that every room that is supposed to be heated achieves a temperature of 70° F. All measurements should be made in the middle of the room, three feet up from the floor, according to ASHRAE and Code standards. A temperature variation of 4° from room-to-room is considered acceptable.

Comments: Many factors affect the performance of heating systems. The most important is system design. Other factors include placement of furniture, solar orientation of the room, and location of the room in the House. For example, a room that is located above the thermostat will be warmer in winter than a room located below the thermostat. The downstairs room will be cooler in both summer and winter; this is because warm air rises to the ceiling and cool air falls to the floor.

Builder Responsibility: Builder should design and balance the heating system so that the above referenced Performance Guideline is met. If Homeowner has failed to cover large window openings so as to minimize heat loss, or has blocked the system's airflow in any manner, Builder should not be responsible.

Homeowner Responsibility: Homeowner should be aware that it is not possible to achieve a uniform temperature throughout the House. A difference in temperature will also exist between the thermostat location and other rooms, particularly if those rooms are located above or below the thermostat location. Large window areas should be properly draped or otherwise protected from heat loss, and no furniture or other devices should be placed in rooms so as to impede the airflow. Most air supply grills (registers) have dampers that can be adjusted in rooms for the difference in the summer and winter temperature needs. ***Maintenance Alert!*** Homeowner should change or clean the furnace filter pursuant to the manufacturer's recommendations (usually no less than every six months). A dirty filter will reduce airflow and cause the system to use more energy.

FIRST, YOU DETERMINE WHETHER THE FILTER IS IN THE ATTIC OR THE CLOSET... -THEN, REPLACE IT WITH THE SAME SIZE

Condition #2: THERMOSTAT DOES NOT WORK

Can Affect:
- Occupant comfort

Performance Guideline: Thermostat should perform as designed throughout its useful life. The thermostat can vary 4° F from actual room temperature without being considered unacceptable.

Builder Responsibility: Builder should replace non-performing thermostat, assuming that the condition is not resulting from Homeowner negligence or failure to change the batteries.

Homeowner Responsibility: Check thermostat periodically and change the batteries when it is indicated that batteries are weak. Do not leave dead batteries in a thermostat, especially during months when the system is not being used. Dead batteries can leak and corrode the thermostat.

Condition #3: SYSTEM IS NOISY WHEN OPERATING

Can Affect:
- Occupant comfort

Performance Guideline: Noise levels in bedrooms should not exceed 25 dB (decibels) and noise levels in other rooms should not exceed 40 dB.

Comments: The ***air handler*** fan (blower) will make noise as it blows warm air throughout the House. Noise will also be heard as air flows back to the furnace through the return air system. The architectural design of the House often puts restrictions on the design of the heating system. As a result, the system may have a noise level that is irritating to some occupants.

Builder Responsibility: Builder should control noise levels in the cooling and heating system in conformance with the Performance Guideline. Further, if part of the system is loose internally and rattles as the system is operating, Builder should make adjustments to remove the rattling noise. Systems mounted in attics should be isolated from frame members.

Homeowner Responsibility: None.

Condition #4: HEATING SYSTEM MAKES BOOMING NOISE WHEN FIRST TURNED ON, OR WHEN COOLING DOWN (Effect No. 1)

Can Affect:
- Occupant comfort

Performance Guideline: It may not be possible to completely eliminate the noise from this effect.

Comments: The booming noise created in forced air heating systems in Effect No. 1 is known as the "oil canning" effect. This effect may occur when a large area of sheet metal is rapidly heated or cooled.

Builder Responsibility: Builder should make all attempts to minimize this effect.

Homeowner Responsibility: None.

Condition #5: HEATING SYSTEM MAKES BOOMING NOISE WHEN FIRST TURNED ON (Effect No. 2)

Can Affect:

- Safety of occupants
- Occupant comfort

Performance Guideline: All furnace burners should ignite quickly and smoothly as designed, without delay, and should not permit excessive accumulation of unburned fuel gases.

Comments: The booming noise in Effect No. 2 is likely to be caused by the delay created when the furnace burner ignites too late. A larger than designed volume of gas accumulates and is not ignited (burned) soon enough, creating a small explosive effect in the furnace.

Builder Responsibility: The burner ignition device should be adjusted to meet the above Performance Guideline.

Homeowner Responsibility: If a booming noise is heard when the furnace is turned on, the Homeowner has a duty to notify the Builder of this condition.

Condition #6: COLD SPOTS DEVELOP ON THE FLOOR (Radiant System)

Can Affect:

- Occupant comfort

Performance Guideline: Radiant heating systems should not leak or become clogged during their useful life.

Comments: The radiant heat system using oil or water to transfer heat from the boiler to the slab is known as a closed loop system. Fluid is heated in the boiler and pumped to the floor or baseboard. There, it gives off its heat, and then the cooler fluid is returned to the boiler to be reheated.

Builder Responsibility: Builder should make the necessary repairs to assure the system provides continuous and uniform heat. However, beyond the initial charging of the system, Builder should not be responsible when unapproved fluids are added (such as ***hard water*** that may be used to recharge to system).

Homeowner Responsibility: ***Maintenance Alert!*** A radiant heating system requires little maintenance, but if make-up fluid constantly needs to be added to the system, there may be a leak. Leaks should be reported to the Builder immediately, since they can cause the soil to swell and undermine the slab.

Condition #7: DUCT WORK HAS SEPARATED

Can Affect:

- Occupant comfort

Performance Guideline: Duct work should be continuous and should not have gaps, breaks, or holes.

Builder Responsibility: Builder should secure and repair all separated duct work and repair any holes, provided that the unacceptable condition was not caused by the Homeowner or by an after market contractor (such as cable installer, alarm installer, termite inspector, etc.).

Homeowner Responsibility: None. However, the Homeowner should be aware that after market contractors who install alarm systems or pest control companies have well-deserved reputations for tearing and squashing ductwork in attics and crawl spaces. If the Homeowner is having work done of this nature, he or she should inspect the crawl space or attic both prior to and after the work is done, to ensure that all ductwork remains intact.

Cooling

General Subject Information: Regional climates in California vary significantly: from communities near the ocean which have little or no need for central air conditioning, to communities in the central and southern valleys which experience many summer days in excess of 100° F. Typically, central air conditioning systems are installed as part of the indoor comfort package of the house. Most central air conditioning systems share the same ***air handler***, duct work, and return air systems as the heating system. Note: Homes that are built with air conditioning or "prepped" for future air conditioning will have larger ducts than homes that are built for heating only. Therefore, the Homeowner should not assume that air conditioning could be installed successfully at a later date, if the home was built as heat-only. The difference between a house that has central air conditioning and one that does not is the addition of a circular or box-like unit called the condenser that is outside the house (or sometimes on the roof). A cooling coil is also added inside the furnace. Almost all central air conditioning systems use electricity as their power source.

Another type of cooling system used less frequently in residential construction is the evaporative cooler, commonly known as the "swamp cooler". Like central air conditioning systems, evaporative coolers use some of the same components of the heating system such as the ductwork. The evaporative cooler is usually mounted on the roof, and the cooling effect is a result of air being drawn through wetted filterpads. While evaporative coolers are cheaper to operate than central air conditioning, they are less efficient in their cooling operation.

Homes that are heated with radiant heating typically do not have central air conditioning, as there is no ductwork system to deliver cool air into the rooms. Central air conditioning can be installed in homes with radiant heating using ductwork, air handlers, and condensers, but the system is totally separate from the heating system. Because of the expensive installation, homes that have central air conditioning and radiant heat are custom homes.

Condition #1: AIR CONDITIONER DOES NOT COOL THE HOUSE

Can Affect:

- Occupant comfort

Performance Guideline: Central air conditioning should be capable of producing a temperature of 78° F in the center of each room as measured 3 feet up from the floor. In all cases, the system must be operating 2 hours prior to measurement. A temperature variation of 4° F from room-to-room is considered acceptable.

Comments: Air conditioning systems are installed as part of a package that must qualify under Title 24 of the Energy Code. Factors such as the solar orientation of the House (facing south and west), and the amount of glass area within a room influence the effectiveness of air conditioning. Rooms whose windows face west and south should have window coverings on them capable of reducing 50% of the heat gain to the room. **CAUTION**: Do not tint the inside pane of dual pane glass; it may cause the seals to fail. Refer to ***Ten Most Common Mistakes Made by New Homeowners*** in the Preface.

Builder Responsibility: Make the necessary corrections and repairs to meet the above referenced Performance Guideline.

Homeowner Responsibility: In rooms that have the potential for high heat gain, such as sun porches, solariums, and other rooms with a large number of skylights and windows, the Homeowner must provide effective solar blockage in order for the above referenced Performance Guideline to apply.

Condition #2: REFRIGERANT LINES LEAK

Can Affect:

- System efficiency
- Occupant comfort

Performance Guideline: Refrigerant lines should not leak. They are part of a ***closed loop system.***

Builder Responsibility: Builder should repair the leak and recharge the system, assuming the Homeowner or after market contractor did not cause the leak.

Homeowner Responsibility: None. However, Homeowners should prevent children from playing around air conditioning condensers. They should also maintain the manufacturer's recommended clearance between the condenser and any landscaping, fencing, or other structures.

Condition #3: CONDENSATE LINE IS PLUGGED

Can Affect:
- System performance

Performance Guideline: This is a Homeowner maintenance item.

Comments: The ***condensate line*** is typically a white plastic or copper pipe that comes out of the air handler portion of the furnace and discharges through an outside wall. Because the water is cool and the discharge is slow, the condensate line provides a great environment for algae to grow. Systems are installed with a primary line and secondary condensate lines. The primary line goes through a trap and then discharges near the outside foundation (or in some locations into a sewer trap). The secondary condensate line discharges above a window or patio door (if the air conditioner coil is in the attic furnace) or in the garage or other prominent place (if the air conditioner is located in the furnace in that area). The reason why the secondary condensate line is located in a prominent location is that it should only discharge when the primary line is plugged.

Builder Responsibility: None.

Homeowner Responsibility: ***Maintenance Alert!*** Condensate lines should be inspected twice a year: at the beginning of the air conditioning season and at the end. If a trickle discharge is reduced to an occasional drip, it potentially means that the condensate line is in the process of becoming plugged. Another symptom of a plugged condensate line is cold water droplets blowing out of the air supply grills in the House. If water is observed dripping in front of a window or patio door, or onto a garage floor, it is likely that the primary condensate line is plugged. If this occurs, shut off the air conditioner and schedule the system for servicing.

Condition #4: *COMPRESSOR* FAILS

Can Affect:
- System performance
- Occupant comfort

Performance Guideline: Compressor should not fail within the manufacturer's warranty period.

Builder Responsibility: Replace the failed compressor if it fails within the warranty period.

Homeowner Responsibility: None.

Condition #5: SYSTEM FAILS TO TURN ON WHEN FIRST ACTIVATED IN SPRING / SUMMER

Can Affect:
- System performance
- Occupant comfort

Performance Guideline: Air conditioning systems should turn on as intended. This is a Homeowner maintenance item.

Comments: Homeowners often encounter a situation where a functioning air conditioning system shut off in the fall will not start when it comes time to turn it on in the spring. Typically, this condition can be traced to one or two blown fuses. When the compressor remains idle during the winter months, its internal parts become resistant to turning. This resistance often results in a blown fuse when first turned on in springtime.

Builder Responsibility: None.

Homeowner Responsibility: ***Maintenance Alert!*** Once every two months, on warm winter days, the air conditioner should be started and run for a few minutes to keep the internal parts clean and lubricated.

Condition #6: COMPRESSOR UNIT IS OUT OF LEVEL

Can Affect:
- ***Compressor*** useful life

Performance Guideline: ***Compressor*** units should be set level to a tolerance of 1 inch in any direction, unless otherwise stated by the manufacturer.

Builder Responsibility: Set the compressor unit to meet the above Performance Guideline.

Homeowner Responsibility: None.

Condition #7: EVAPORATIVE COOLER BLOWS WARM AIR

Can Affect:
- Occupant comfort

Performance Guideline: Evaporative coolers should not blow air that is the same temperature as the outside air. The cooler should provide cool air in accordance with the manufacturer's specifications.

Builder Responsibility: If the evaporative cooler does not meet the manufacturer's performance specifications, the Builder should repair or replace the non-performing cooler. The Builder is not responsible for service problems due to poor water quality.

Homeowner Responsibility: ***Maintenance Alert!*** Evaporative coolers need to be kept clean and free of mineral build-up in order to operate properly. Depending upon local water quality, evaporative coolers need to be treated and backwashed periodically.

Electrical

General Subject Information: The electrical system in new homes is installed in compliance with the National Electric Code (NEC). Most cities and counties in the United States have adopted this Code, and it is truly a national code. Among other things, the NEC deals with wire size, circuits, breakers, and placement of outlets.

Condition #1: LIGHTS FLICKER WHEN APPLIANCES ARE TURNED ON

Can Affect:

- System useful life

Performance Guideline: If the circuit is not overloaded by the Homeowner, and if lights flicker continuously and the breaker does not trip, the circuit is unacceptable.

Comments: Flickering lights can indicate a possible overload or poor connection somewhere in the branch circuit. If a heavy-duty motor driven appliance is plugged into a wall outlet, it is likely to cause momentary flickering of the lights when it is first turned on. The Builder is not responsible for this condition.

Builder Responsibility: The Builder should inspect the circuit, determine the problem, and make the necessary repairs. The Builder is not responsible for momentary flickering when high capacity appliances are plugged into wall outlets.

Homeowner Responsibility: Avoid overloading circuits with multiple appliances and add-on outlets. If wires feel warm to the touch, they should be unplugged and reinserted into a separate circuit. Note: Circuit breakers are found in the main panel where the meter is located or in the ***subpanel*** (the gray metal panel typically located in the hallway, laundry room, or bedroom of the House). The circuits are labeled inside the panels.

Condition #2: BREAKERS TRIP OR FUSES BLOW FREQUENTLY

Can Affect:

- Electrical system performance
- Occupant safety

Performance Guideline: Circuit breakers that trip frequently and fuses that blow frequently, under proper design usage, are indications of an unacceptable circuit or a malfunctioning appliance.

Comments: Fuses and circuit breakers are electricity's safety valves. When a fuse blows, it must be replaced. When a circuit breaker trips, it can be reset. Most houses today are equipped with circuit breakers in the main panel (outside) or in the ***subpanel*** (inside). Special appliances like furnaces and air conditioning condensers have their own fuse boxes or circuit breakers. Usually when frequent tripping occurs, it is a sign that the circuit is being overused. As circuit breakers get older, they tend to wear out and will trip more easily.

Builder Responsibility: Builder should test circuits to determine their capacity and make necessary corrections if the circuits are found to be inadequate for expected normal usage by the Homeowner.

Homeowner Responsibility: Homeowner should not overload circuits to the point where fuses blow or breakers trip. If frequent tripping occurs, the Homeowner has a duty to notify the Builder. **DO NOT replace a fuse or circuit breaker with one that has a higher rating or one made by a different manufacturer! This action could result in a fire.**

Condition #3: *GROUND FAULT INTERRUPTER* TRIPS FREQUENTLY

Can Affect:

- Appliance performance at ground fault interrupter locations

Performance Guideline: Ground fault interrupters should be installed in accordance with the National Electric Code or other applicable Code in effect at that time.

Comments: A ***ground fault interrupter (GFI)*** is an especially sensitive breaker that is located in or tied to the outlets in the kitchen, baths, outdoors, and the garage. Any locations that could be moist or damp must be protected with a GFI. Appliances manufactured outside of the United States (although they may carry a ***UL label***) are notorious for tripping GFIs. Hairdryers frequently trip GFIs. When a GFI trips it can be reset at the outlet that has the small black button, or inside the subpanel if it is wired that way.

TEST G.F.I. OUTLETS MONTHLY
-IT'S EASY TO DO:
"TEST" IS BLACK; "RESET" IS RED

Builder Responsibility: None, assuming the installation was done pursuant to the applicable Code and that the GFI device itself is acceptable.

Homeowner Responsibility: None. Test GFIs monthly by pressing the black test button. Do not plug a freezer or refrigerator into a GFI outlet.

Condition #4: ALUMINUM WIRE, NOT COPPER WIRE, WAS INSTALLED

Can Affect:

- Usage by Homeowner

Performance Guideline: House wiring should be installed per applicable Code.

Comments: Use of aluminum wiring is permitted in residential construction under the NEC. When copper shortages occurred in the past, aluminum was used in its place. Aluminum conducts electricity better than copper, but aluminum requires special installation procedures that copper does not. Most new houses are wired with a combination of copper and aluminum wire. Aluminum is likely to be the main wire from the street to the House and also the wiring for electric ovens and electric dryers. Copper wiring is used in lower rated circuits.

Builder Responsibility: Builder should install wiring per applicable Code.

Homeowner Responsibility: None.

Condition #5: LIGHT FIXTURES TARNISH

Can Affect:

- Appearance

Performance Guideline: Light fixtures should not be tarnished at time of delivery of House.

Comments: Light fixtures, especially ones with a bright brass finish, will tarnish. The rate of tarnish depends upon outdoor and indoor air pollution and the degree to which the finish was coated with a protective film. It is very important not to use a higher wattage bulb in a light fixture than the wattage recommended by the manufacturer.

Builder Responsibility: Meet the Performance Guideline at time of delivery of the House.

Homeowner Responsibility: Inspect fixtures during the Walkthrough. Check with fixture manufacturers regarding their warranty. ***Maintenance Alert!*** Fixtures, especially bright brass, will need to be cleaned and polished as routine maintenance.

Condition #6: LIGHT SWITCHES AND OUTLET PLATES PROTRUDE TOO FAR FROM WALL

Can Affect:

- Appearance

Performance Guideline: Switch and plug plates that protrude more than 1/8 inch from the finished wall are considered unacceptable.

Builder Responsibility: Builder should adjust switch and outlet plates to be flush and level in the wall. For minor protrusions less than 1/8 inch, caulking is an acceptable repair.

Homeowner Responsibility: None.

Condition #7: LIGHT SWITCHES STICK OR MUST BE JIGGLED TO TURN THE LIGHT ON

Can Affect:

- Appliance performance
- System useful life

Performance Guideline: Light switches that stick or require tapping or jiggling to turn on lights or appliances are unacceptable.

Builder Responsibility: Builder should replace all light switches that operate in a non-performing manner.

Homeowner Responsibility: None.

Condition #8: WALL OUTLET IN BEDROOM DOES NOT WORK

Can Affect:

- Use of lights or appliances

Performance Guideline: A bedroom must have an overhead light or a wall outlet that is turned on from a switch by the door.

Comments: If a bedroom does not have a ceiling light, the Builder is required by Code to connect at least one wall outlet (one plug only, not both) to a wall switch near the door. Unless the switch is on, any light or appliance plugged into the outlet will not operate. Homeowners often mistake this condition as non-performing outlet.

Builder Responsibility: None, assuming that the outlet is properly switched.

Homeowner Responsibility: None.

Condition #9: BATHROOM FANS / LAUNDRY FANS ARE NOISY

Can Affect:

- Occupant comfort

Performance Guideline: These fans can be noisy. This is not a condition of non-performance, unless the sound is a result of fan blades hitting part of the housing.

Comments: Amounts of noise from exhaust fans varies by manufacturer. Exhaust fans are required to change over a certain volume of air in the room per hour. As long as the plastic or metal fan blades are turning freely, they are likely to be operating as intended. If the fan blades are hitting something solid, like the fan housing, they will make a distinct battering noise.

Builder Responsibility: None, unless the fan blades are hitting the housing or other solid object. If this is the case, Builder should repair the non-performing condition.

Homeowner Responsibility: Do not disconnect the bath or laundry fans because they create an annoying noise. Moist air must be exhausted to the outside; otherwise mold and mildew can form on the walls and ceiling. Fans should be operated while these rooms are in use.

Plumbing

General Subject Information: The plumbing system in a house consists of three main components: water supply piping, wastewater piping, and fixtures. Gas piping is a separate system used to convey natural or LP gas to appliances such as furnaces, water heaters, stoves, cook tops, ovens, fireplaces, and barbeques.

Both copper and plastic are used for water supply piping in new homes, but copper is the most prominent material used. Older homes were piped with galvanized steel, but due to corrosion problems, galvanized steel piping is no longer used in residential construction. Waste piping, which carries wastewater from the fixtures in the house, is typically black plastic piping called ***ABS***. Alternatively, some municipalities require waste piping to be copper or cast iron, or a combination of both. Unless the house is connected to a septic tank, wastewater flows in a sewer to a local sewage treatment plant. Wastewater piping also has pipes that protrude through the roof of the house. These are called vents; the purpose of the vents is to allow the wastewater to flow through the pipes without becoming "air locked". The vents also help to dissipate odors. Fixtures are items like toilets, bathtubs, and sinks. Nearly all plumbing fixtures have ***traps***, which prevent sewer gases from backing into the house. Traps can be seen under the sink and are a U shaped part of the piping where wastewater sits and blocks the flow of sewer gases. Toilets have traps built into the bowls.

Some water purveyors do not recommend the installation of water softeners as they may make the water more aggressive and lead to early pipe deterioration. Check with your Builder or water purveyor prior to any water softener installation.

Depending upon local regulations, the house may be fitted with a fire sprinkler system. The system consists of water under pressure in pipes that, in the event of fire, will spray water through the sprinkler heads located in the ceilings and walls. Unless there is a fire or excessive source of heat, the fire sprinkler system remains passive. However, routine testing of the fire sprinkler system is very important.

Condition #1: WATER OR GAS PIPING LEAKS

Can Affect:

- Structural integrity
- Contents of house
- Health and safety of occupants

Performance Guideline: Water supply piping, gas piping, wastewater piping, and fire sprinkler plumbing should not leak. Piping must contain and convey 100% of the liquid or gas that it is intended to convey.

Builder Responsibility: The Builder should make corrective repairs to any leaking piping system. The Builder should not be responsible for piping leaks caused by earthquakes or shifts in the structure that were not caused by Builder.

Homeowner Responsibility: The Homeowner has a duty to notify the Builder upon noticing any gas or liquid leaks in piping, no matter how small. Failure to give timely notice can result in health hazards, personal injury, and structural damage. ***Maintenance Alert!*** Homeowner should have the fire sprinkler system professionally tested annually (or more frequently if required by the local fire authorities) to determine that the system will operate as designed in the event of a fire.

Condition #2: WATER PIPES FREEZE

Can Affect:

- Water supply
- Structural integrity
- Contents of house

Performance Guideline: In geographic areas where freezing weather is normal, water supply and waste piping should be protected from freezing. For geographic areas where freezing weather is rare (extreme), unprotected pipes are considered acceptable.

Comments: In most heavily populated areas of California, freezing weather is very infrequent. In geographic areas where freezing weather is common and part of the normal weather pattern, unprotected pipes may leak at valves and joints during subfreezing temperatures. In areas where temperatures normally drop below freezing, the water supply piping should be installed in a manner to safeguard against freeze damage. Some safeguards include: bringing the water supply line into the interior of the House (not an outside wall); using deep seat valves on hose bibbs; wrapping pipes in unheated areas with thermostatic controlled heat tape; and providing a drain down valve at the lowest accessible part of the water supply system.

Builder Responsibility: Protect all pipes from freezing weather if the House is constructed in an area where freezing weather is normal and customary. If the Homeowner does not maintain minimum heat, the Builder is not responsible for any leaking pipes due to freezing that occurs in any portion of the House that is intended to be heated.

Homeowner Responsibility: To protect against the nuisance of infrequent freezing (extreme) weather, the Homeowner can at his or her option purchase protective materials such as pipe insulation and electric resistant heat tape at any local hardware store. If the Homeowner is going to be gone for a period of time during possible freezing weather, the thermostat should be set on "Heat" at its minimum setting.

Condition #3: WATER TASTES FUNNY, SMELLS, OR IS DISCOLORED

Can Affect:

- Occupant health
- Occupant comfort

Performance Guideline: Water should be of good quality. However, the Builder may not have control over the quality of water supplied by the local district.

Comments: In many subdivisions, the Builder installs the water system subject to specifications and inspections by the local water authority. Upon final testing, the water authority takes over responsibility for the water supply, including pressure and quality.

Builder Responsibility: None, unless the Builder is responsible for creating the water supply to the House. This does not mean installing the water piping system that is to be taken over by a municipal authority. If the Builder is responsible for supplying the source of water, the Builder should provide water that meets minimum quality standards as set by the governing agency, such as the local County Department of Health or the State of California Department of Water Quality. The Builder should not be responsible for changes in water quality once the quality meets the local or State set standards. For example, a change in nearby agricultural uses, or mining activity subsequent to construction, may cause changes in water quality that are not the Builder's Responsibility.

Homeowner Responsibility: If water quality standards are met by the Builder and/or the local water supply agency, and are still unacceptable to the Homeowner, consider a house filtration system or use of a drinking water service company.

Condition #4: TOILET BACKS UP, DRAINS BACK UP

Can Affect:

- Interior finishes and furnishings
- Occupant health

Performance Guideline: At the time of the Walkthrough, all fixtures should operate as intended and all drains should flow freely.

Comments: Backed up drainage systems, particularly toilets, are a frequent complaint of new Homeowners. For the vast majority of incidents, the occupants of the House have caused this condition. In some infrequent cases, the main line has received construction debris during the construction process. This can usually be determined within the first week of occupancy. It is very important that each toilet is flushed and the water be turned on to each fixture during the ***Walkthrough*** process.

A federal law requires that all toilets installed in new construction flush with 1.6 gallons of water or less. Homeowners who are used to larger capacity toilets (3.5 or 7 gallon flush) sometimes have difficulty making the transition to low flush toilets.

Builder Responsibility: Meet the Performance Guideline at time of delivery. Builder is not responsible for post-Walkthrough conditions, unless it can be determined that the cause of the blockage was from construction related activity.

Homeowner Responsibility: ***Maintenance Alert!*** Sink, tub, and shower traps should be kept free and clear as routine maintenance items. Material such as hair, toothpaste, etc. may accumulate in the traps and could eventually cause a back up. Try to keep these materials from getting into the trap in the first place, and use a drain cleaner every 3-4 months to keep the traps scoured out and free from debris build-up. Learn the proper use of a low-flush toilet.

Condition #5: INADEQUATE WATER PRESSURE

Can Affect:

- Use of plumbing fixtures

Performance Guideline: For Houses that are connected to the municipal water system or mutual water system of 10 houses or more, the House piping system should be designed to operate between pressures of 15 psi and 80 psi. For Houses that are connected to a well or a mutual water system of 10 houses or fewer, the water pressure should be subject to the capacity of the well and the output of its equipment.

Comments: Water pressure problems arise from two sources: (1) inadequate pressure from the water supply agency in their piping system, or (2) the piping system in the House is undersized. Most plumbing systems are designed to operate within the range of 15 psi (pounds per square inch) and 80 psi, measured at the point where the water supply pipe enters the House. High water pressure can be a problem because it creates a condition known as "***water hammer***" and causes noise and banging of the pipes. High water pressure can be reduced with a special pressure-reducing valve. Low water pressure can be increased with the use of a booster pump. It should be noted that all showerheads and most sink faucets are required to have flow restrictors placed in them for water conservation. Reduced flows from flow restrictors may give a mistaken impression of low water pressure.

Builder Responsibility: None, provided that the Builder has met the local Code for water pipe system sizing.

Homeowner Responsibility: In areas where the water service is at the lower end of the allowable pressure range, water flows from fixtures will be less. This condition is beyond the control of the Builder and should be addressed with the agency that supplies the water. If the problem persists, consider installing a booster pump to increase pressure. Using several fixtures simultaneously may also result in low water flow and decrease in pressure.

Condition #6: SEWER GAS SMELL COMING FROM DRAIN

Can Affect:

- Air quality
- Occupant health

Performance Guideline: This is a Homeowner maintenance item unless the sewer gas is coming from a cracked pipe (see **Condition #1 in this Section**).

Builder Responsibility: None.

Homeowner Responsibility: Sewer gas smells coming from drains typically indicate a lack of water in the trap. This occurs when a drain is not used for long periods of time and the water evaporates from the trap. Pouring a large glass of water in the drain will fill the trap sufficiently.

Condition #7: COPPER WATER PIPES OR BLACK GAS PIPES ARE WET ON THE OUTSIDE

Can Affect:

- Appearance

Performance Guideline: Condensation on the outside of water lines is a normal condition.

Comments: In geographic areas where humidity is high, condensation may form on the outside of cold water lines, gas lines, and toilet tanks. Cold water inside the pipe or gas moving through the pipe creates a cooling effect. Water in the surrounding air then condenses around the pipe.

Builder Responsibility: The Builder should install pipe insulation on cold water pipes where there is a likelihood of condensation and mold growth.

Homeowner Responsibility: None.

Condition #8: FAUCETS DRIP

Can Affect:
- Water consumption
- Occupant comfort

Performance Guideline: At the time of the ***Walkthrough***, all washers and cartridges should seat tightly and faucets should not leak.

Comments: Faucets are manufactured with either a washer or cartridge to prevent leakage when the faucet is turned off. Cartridges have approximately 10 times the useful life of washers. The quality of the water supply affects the useful life of both cartridges and washers. Both municipal water and well water contain a certain amount of very small particles of solid material. Over time, this may affect the performance of washers and cartridges.

Builder Responsibility: Any faucets that leak at the time of the Walkthrough should be repaired.

Homeowner Responsibility: ***Maintenance Alert!*** Washers and cartridges should be replaced at the time when dripping is first noticed. Many cartridges have a 5 year to lifetime guarantee on parts. Most of the current bathroom and kitchen faucets are made with cartridges and require only infrequent replacement. Hose bibbs (the valves that a hose is connected to on the outside of the House) are made with washers. Depending upon the amount of use, hose bibb washers may need to be replaced as frequently as every six months or as infrequently as every 3 years. If leaking occurs at the "stem" or handle of the valve (often at the hose bibb or water heater), the nut at the base of the stem can be tightened or repacked to solve this problem.

Condition #9: SINK / TUB IS CHIPPED

Can Affect:
- Appearance

Performance Guideline: Fixtures should not be chipped at time of delivery. Chips, marrs, or discolorations 1/32 inch or less are considered acceptable.

Builder Responsibility: Repair any chips, marrs, or discolorations that exceed the Performance Guideline that are observed at the time of the ***Walkthrough.***

Homeowner Responsibility: None.

Condition #10: SHOWER HEAD PIPE / TUB SPOUT IS LOOSE

Can Affect:

- Water tightness of structure

Performance Guideline: At time of delivery, shower head pipes and tub spouts should be secured so they cannot move in or out more than ¼ inch.

Builder Responsibility: Take corrective measures to meet the above Performance Guideline if non-performing condition noted at time of the Walkthrough.

Homeowner Responsibility: Avoid hanging heavy objects such as shower caddies full of bathing shampoos and lotions on the shower head pipe.

Condition #11: SHOWER ENCLOSURE / TUB ENCLOSURE LEAKS

See Chapter Six, "Shower and Tub Enclosures"

Condition #12: FIBERGLASS TUB / SHOWER FLEXES WHEN OCCUPIED

Can Affect:

- Occupant comfort

Performance Guideline: Fiberglass and acrylic tub and shower units should be installed in accordance with the manufacturer's instructions.

Comments: Fiberglass and acrylic tubs and showers will have a certain degree of flex depending upon how the unit was manufactured and the weight of the occupant. Some flexing is to be expected and each manufacturer furnishes installation instructions regarding their products.

Builder Responsibility: If installation is not made in accordance with the manufacturer's instructions, Builder should correct the non-performing condition.

Homeowner Responsibility: None.

Condition #13: WATER DRAINS FROM SINK / TUB WHEN STOPPER IS ENGAGED

Can Affect:

- Use of sink / tub

Performance Guideline: Water should not drain past the stopper mechanism at a rate of which the depth of water in the sink or tub decreases by more than one inch per hour.

Comments: Sink and tub stoppers are not designed to create a perfect seal. A perfect seal is not necessary for customary and usual use. Sink and tub stoppers easily get out of adjustment through continuous use and can be affected by debris trapped in the drain.

Builder Responsibility: Sinks and tubs which drain more quickly than permitted under the Performance Guideline, and whose stoppers have been properly maintained, should be adjusted or replaced as necessary.

Homeowner Responsibility: Periodic cleaning and maintenance of mechanical sink and tub stoppers is a Homeowner responsibility. Stoppers should be checked monthly.

Condition #14: BRASS BATHROOM FAUCETS AND DRAINS TARNISH

Can Affect:

- Appearance

Performance Guideline: Brass fittings should be free from tarnish at the time of delivery; brass fittings that become tarnished subsequent to the Walkthrough are acceptable.

Comments: As concrete is certain to crack, brass bathroom fittings are certain to tarnish. Most brass fittings are coated with lacquer. Eventually the lacquer chips or is rubbed off, and the brass tarnishes. The degree of tarnish depends upon the amount of use, the water quality, and pollutants present in the air. Some manufacturers offer a lifetime finish on their brass fittings.

Builder Responsibility: Replace any brass fittings on bathroom fixtures that are tarnished at the time of the ***Walkthrough***.

Homeowner Responsibility: ***Maintenance Alert!*** Brass is a beautiful but "soft" metal. It is easily scratched and tarnished. Follow the manufacturer's instructions when cleaning brass. Cleansers with abrasives and cleansers with ammonia are likely to scratch and chemically attack brass finishes. Wipe brass finishes frequently.

Condition #15: TOILET RUNS CONTINUOUSLY

Can Affect:

- Water consumption

Performance Guideline: When a toilet tank fills, it should shut off. Water should not run continuously through the overflow pipe or flapper valve.

Builder Responsibility: Make corrections to toilet tank system so that the water shuts off when the tank is filled to the appropriate level.

Homeowner Responsibility: ***Maintenance Alert!*** Toilet tanks have mechanical parts inside them and these parts wear out over time. Depending upon the amount of use and water quality, replacing worn flappers, floats, and valves can occur as frequently as once a year or as infrequently as every 10 years. Water supplies with high concentrations of minerals (known as hard water) will leave deposits inside the toilet tank and its parts. This condition will cause more frequent replacement and rebuilding of toilet parts than those areas that do not have high mineral content in the water supply.

Condition #16: TOILET LEAKS AT FLOOR

Can Affect:

- Appearance
- Structural integrity
- Termite attraction
- Mold and mildew growth

Performance Guideline: Toilets should not leak at the floor.

Comments: The connection between the pipe and the floor and the toilet base is made with a wax ring. This wax is the same inside diameter as the flange pipe. A portion of the wax ring fits slightly into the pipe. Pressing the toilet onto the wax ring makes a complete seal. When a toilet leaks at the floor, the chances are that the seal of the wax ring has failed. Wax rings dry out and become brittle over a period of time.

Builder Responsibility: For leaking toilets, make necessary repairs to ensure a watertight flow between the toilet and the House waste plumbing.

Homeowner Responsibility: The Homeowner has the duty to notify the Builder of any leaking toilet before additional damage occurs. Toilets that are permitted to leak will cause structural damage if the toilet is located over a wood subfloor. A toilet that leaks creates a condition for termites to enter the House, regardless of whether it sits on a wooden subfloor or a slab. Termites are attracted to dark, damp conditions in the soil. It is important to note that a toilet that rocks back and forth or moves side-to-side may be leaking, even though no leak is visible. The Homeowner has a duty to notify the Builder of this condition.

Condition #17: LACK OF HOT WATER

Can Affect:

- Occupant comfort

Performance Guideline: Builder should provide a water heater, either gas or electric, that meets the Energy Code of the State of California and supplies hot water to all appropriate fixtures in the House. All hot water pipes that pass through unheated spaces (such as garages, crawl spaces, and attics) should be insulated.

Comments: In most houses, the source of hot water is a water heater. The source of heat for the water heater is likely to be gas, as required by the Energy Code. In areas where gas is not available, electric water heaters are permitted. Gas is a more efficient method of heating water than electricity. There are several factors that could contribute to a lack of hot water: a power failure that cuts off the supply of gas or electricity; the pilot light has gone out; a non-performing water heater; a temperature setting too low on the water heater; and heat loss through the piping system, particularly at far ends of the House. Typically the water heater installer will set the water temperature between a low of 120° F and a high of 140° F. Since kitchen dishwashers only operate with hot water, 140° F is considered hot enough to effectively kill bacteria that may be present on dirty dishes.

Builder Responsibility: If the above Performance Guideline is not met, Builder should take corrective measures so that the Guideline is met.

Homeowner Responsibility: Frequent demand over short time periods (such as morning showers by an entire family) can result in a lack of hot water until the water heater has had time to recover; this is not a Builder responsibility. If the Homeowner wishes to increase water temperature, he or she can adjust the control dial on most water heaters. Electric water heaters are often pre-set and cannot be adjusted. However, it is very important to recognize that the higher the temperature setting, the greater the danger of scalding. **CAUTION!** Before entering the tub or shower, always turn on water and adjust it to a safe and proper temperature. Children, elderly people (or any person), should never be placed in a tub or shower before the water is turned on and the temperature safely adjusted. Although many of the gas water heaters today have automatic ignition systems, the Homeowner should become familiar with how to manually light a water heater pilot.

Condition #18: WATER HEATER IS NOT EARTHQUAKE SECURED

Can Affect:

- Occupant safety

Performance Guideline: Water heater should be strapped or secured in Code approved manner to prevent tip-over during an earthquake.

Builder Responsibility: If the water heater is not strapped or secured to the frame of the House in a manner prescribed by Code, Builder should take the proper corrective measures.

Homeowner Responsibility: None.

Condition #19: ELECTRIC WATER HEATER CIRCUIT BREAKER TRIPS CONTINUOUSLY

Can Affect:

- Occupant safety
- Occupant comfort

Performance Guideline: Electric water heater breakers should not trip. Tripping is an indication of an electrical problem within the heater or the wiring to the heater.

Builder Responsibility: Builder should take corrective measures to eliminate electrical water heater breaker tripping.

Homeowner Responsibility: None. However, as electric water heaters age, their heating element can wear out and fall to the bottom of the tank. If this condition occurs, the circuit breaker cannot be reset, and the Homeowner needs to replace the water heater.

Fire Sprinkler System

General Subject Information: Many jurisdictions in California require automatic fire sprinklers to be installed in new homes. Usually the Homeowner does not have occasion to find out if and how the system works until it is needed. However, periodic testing of the system and alarms must be done, subject to local regulations.

Condition #1: FIRE SPRINKLER PIPES OR FITTINGS LEAK

Can Affect:

- Surrounding finishes
- Mold and mildew growth
- Alarm performance

Performance Guideline: Fire sprinkler systems should not leak.

Builder Responsibility: Repair leaking pipes, fittings, etc. as required to eliminate leaks. Notify pipe manufacturer if plastic piping is used.

Homeowner Responsibility: Do not paint any fire sprinkler heads or covers or hang any objects from the head. Be aware that if the drywall is removed from the ceiling, such as in repair or remodel, plastic sprinkler pipes could melt because they would be exposed directly to a fire.

Condition #2: SPRINKLER HEADS AND *ESCUTCHEONS* DO NOT FIT FLUSH TO WALL, OR ARE OUT OF LINE WITH DRYWALL OPENINGS

Can Affect:

- Appearance
- Function

Performance Guideline: All sprinkler heads and their ***escutcheons*** should fit neatly and tightly to wall and ceiling finishes. Escutcheons should not protrude more than 1/8 inch beyond the wall surface.

Comments: This condition can be the result of poor workmanship, or more infrequently because the frame of the building has shrunk or settled. If copper pipes are used in the sprinkler system, the pipes will be rigid and will not settle with the building. To some extent, a similar condition may occur with plastic piping, but plastic has some flexibility. Once the shrinkage has run its course, the building will be stable and this condition should not recur.

Builder Responsibility: Installation should conform to the Performance Guideline. Correct any sprinkler heads that are out of line or do not fit neatly to finish surfaces.

Homeowner Responsibility: None.

Telephone

General Subject Information: Telephone wiring in homes today can range from a simple two-pair wire system to a complex, high-tech fiber optic system for voice and data transmission. Unlike in years past, the wiring of the telephone system within the house is likely to be done by a specialty contractor hired by the Builder and not by the company providing the telephone service. The telephone service comes into the house in a box called the ***interface***, located on an outside wall. The company providing telephone service takes responsibility from the street to the interface, and the Builder or the Homeowner takes responsibility from the interface throughout the inside of the house. When telephone problems occur, it is often difficult to determine the area of responsibility.

Condition: NO DIAL TONE, OR STATIC SOUNDS ARE HEARD

Can Affect:

- Intended use of telephone

Performance Guideline: A clear signal (dial tone) should be provided from the interface to all ***jacks*** within the House. The maximum signal loss between the interface and any jack should not exceed 6 dB.

Builder Responsibility: If the telephone service provider identifies the problem as being on the House side of the interface, the Builder should take corrective measures to meet the above Performance Guideline.

Homeowner Responsibility: None, but the addition of after market alterations to the House telephone system. After market alterations may affect the performance of the original wiring.

Cable TV

General Subject Information: Cable TV, or CATV as it is commonly known, is the acronym for Community Antenna Television. Like the telephone system described in the previous section, there is an ***interface*** on the outside of the house. The cable service provider takes responsibility for the quality of the cable signal to the interface; from the interface throughout the house is the responsibility of the Builder or Homeowner. It is most likely that a specialty contractor, working for the Builder installed the cable wiring within the house. A simple system is run directly from the interface to the wall outlet. A more complex system involves a panel within the house and an amplifier that boosts the signal to the various rooms in the house.

Condition: TV RECEPTION IS SNOWY, WAVY, OR OTHERWISE UNCLEAR

Can Affect:

- Intended use of television

Performance Guideline: If the CATV wiring within the House is installed by the Builder, there should be a clear, uninterrupted signal to each outlet, with a maximum signal loss of 8 dB between the interface and any one outlet.

Builder Responsibility: Upon report of a problem by Homeowner and a statement by the CATV provider that the problem is on the House side of the interface, Builder should take corrective measures to meet the above referenced Performance Guideline.

Homeowner Responsibility: None. But with the addition of after market splitters, boosters, and other cable enhancing devices, the system may not perform as originally intended. The Builder should not be responsible for any conditions created by after market changes

Chapter Eight

GROUNDS

includes:

Drainage

Landscaping

Irrigation

Retaining Walls

Fencing

References for this chapter:

- *Operating Cost Manual for Homeowners Associations*, CA Department of Real Estate
- *Residential Construction Performance Guidelines*, NAHB
- *Residential Water Problems*, by Alvin Sacks
- *Troubleshooting Guide to Residential Construction*, Builderburg Group

A comprehensive list of references by author and publisher is found in the Bibliography section.

Grounds

General Subject Information: Water must be kept away from foundations in order to reduce the potential for structural and interior damage. Not only can seeping water cause interior damage, it can cause the foundation to move. There are several potential causes for these conditions: 1) lack of gutters and downspouts (downspouts should be piped either to the street or away from the foundation, see **Chapter 5 "Gutters and Downspouts"** section); 2) lack of required slope away from the foundation; and 3) overwatering landscaping near the foundation. Site drainage that may be the responsibility of a Homeowners Association is also subject to good irrigation practice and maintenance. The subject of soil movement is discussed in **Chapter 1 "Landslides and Other Soil Movement"** section.

Drainage

Condition #1: WATER DOES NOT DRAIN AWAY FROM FOUNDATION

Can Affect:

- Interior finishes and furnishings
- Foundation integrity

Performance Guideline: All soils that surround the ***foundation*** of a building should slope a minimum of ¼ inch fall per every foot of horizontal distance. This required slope must be maintained for a minimum of 5 feet away from the foundation, unless water is diverted from the foundation into an approved structure (such as concrete drainage ditch or graded swale). It is advisable to check slope requirements with the local building department, since several cities and counties in California require slopes to be more than 2%.

Comments: Keeping water away from the foundation is one of the most critical responsibilities of the Homeowner. When water has an opportunity to pond (stand), it can lead to severe interior damage to both finishes and furnishings. Water vapor can migrate through concrete as well as through cracks beneath the foundation. All "soils" must maintain a minimum vertical distance of 6 inches from finish floors / any portion of the wood floor that is subject to decay to top of finished soil. The 6 inch distance can be reduced to 4 inches if the surface that surrounds the foundation is a hard surface, i.e. concrete or asphalt. Any water that is standing or ponding within 6 feet of the foundation must dissipate within 24 hours after a rain.

Builder Responsibility: At the time of delivery, the Builder must meet the above Performance Guideline.

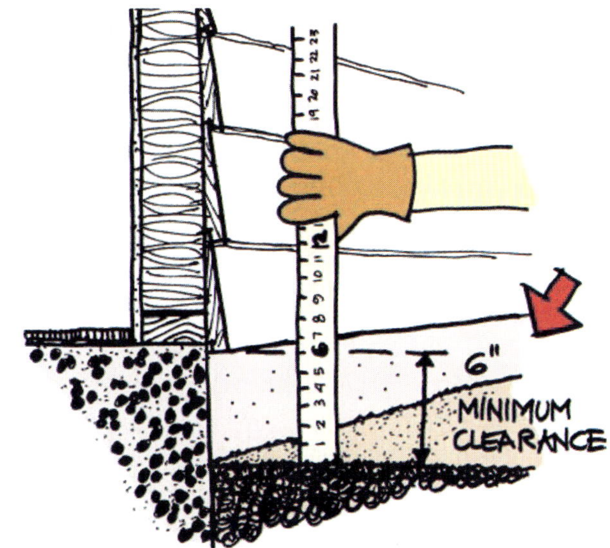

SEPARATION BETWEEN WOOD AND SOIL
(USE CARE WHEN INSTALLING PATIOS AND DECKS)

Homeowner Responsibility: ***Maintenance Alert!*** The Homeowner has a responsibility to always maintain the above Performance Guideline. Homeowners may violate this Guideline in one of two ways: (1) during the installation of landscape materials, they modify the existing grade by leveling it out, causing either a ***negative slope*** or a flat slope, or (2) they hire a landscape company that modifies the grade during soils preparation and planting, causing either flat or negative slope. It should also be noted that if gutters and downspouts are not installed, the Homeowner should take it upon themselves to either install them or have them installed. If downspouts are installed, the water should discharge on to approved splash blocks or into a pipe collector system.

Condition #2: IMPROPER SITE DRAINAGE (Areas beyond 5 feet of the perimeter of the foundation)

Can Affect:
- Adjoining properties
- Foundation integrity

Performance Guideline: Existing grades and ***swales*** are not allowed to drain onto adjoining properties. Water that is transferred via yard drains, ***swales***, or ***sump pumps*** may require 48 hours to drain.

Comments: Under extreme weather conditions, ponding or standing water may take longer to dissipate. Water that stands or ponds under extreme conditions is considered acceptable and is not the responsibility of the Builder.

Builder Responsibility: The Builder is responsible for establishing the proper ***grades*** prior to the Walkthrough.

Homeowner Responsibility: The Homeowner is responsible for keeping swales and drains free of silt and other debris.

Condition #3: SETTLING OF SOILS AROUND THE FOUNDATION

Can Affect:
- Site drainage
- Integrity of concrete walks and foundations
- Water tightness of structure

Performance Guideline: Soils that settle and cause water to stand or pond within 5 feet of the foundation perimeter and which does not dissipate within 24 hours after a rain, is considered unacceptable.

Comments: If soils that surround the foundation (within the 5 foot perimeter) settle more than 3 inches in depth in any one area larger than 3 feet in diameter, the Builder should be responsible to correct the settlement, providing that the soil settlement is not a direct result of any actions of the Homeowner.

Builder Responsibility: The Builder should be responsible to meet the above Performance Guideline. Soils that surround the foundation should be reasonably compacted in order to meet the above Guideline.

Homeowner Responsibility: ***Maintenance Alert!*** Any soils that are within the Performance Guideline should be considered a maintenance issue and corrected by the Homeowner. Erosion occurring during a rainstorm is the responsibility of the Homeowner to repair. **NOTE***: If the Homeowner modifies the existing grades that surround the foundation which cause the soils to subside in any manner, the Builder should not be held responsible.*

Condition #4: SETTLING OF SOILS AT UTILITY TRENCHES

Can Affect:
- Integrity / use of driveways, walkways, patios, streets
- Occupant safety related to tripping hazard
- Utilities

Performance Guideline: Trenches in landscaped areas should not settle more than 6 inches or cause water to pond within 5 feet of the foundation perimeter. Water that does not dissipate within 24 hours after a rain is considered an unacceptable condition. Trenches that are overlaid with concrete or asphalt are considered unacceptable if water ponds for more than 48 hours after a rain. If a paved-over trench subsides more than one inch from the surrounding pavement, it is unacceptable, whether it drains or not.

Builder Responsibility: The Builder should repair any utility trench condition that does not meet the Performance Guideline set forth above.

Homeowner Responsibility: None.

Landscaping

General Subject Information: The addition of landscaping is a significant positive amenity to any individual house or housing project. In the case of individual houses, the Builder either (1) does not provide the landscaping, (2) the Builder provides a minimum package in front to satisfy the requirements of a local planning agency, or (3) may install a more complete landscape package and irrigation system. Alternatively, in most condominium projects, the Builder provides the entire landscape installation. The care taken in the initial installation of landscaping and proper maintenance afterwards are essential in keeping the property looking well kept and attractive.

Condition #1: IMPROPER SOILS PREPARATION

Can Affect:
- Growth of planted materials
- Life expectancy or failure rate of planted materials

Performance Guideline: Soils should be prepared according to generally accepted local conditions, as specified by a landscape architect or as recommended by a soils test report.

Builder Responsibility: The Builder is responsible for reasonable and proper soil preparation in accordance with generally accepted local conditions prior to the planting of materials. This includes placing amendments into high clay soils.

Homeowner Responsibility: The Homeowner should maintain the soils by periodically adding the proper amount of nutrients, i.e. fertilizer, mulch, humus, and minerals required for the particular type of planting.

Condition #2: PLANTS DIE WITHIN THE WARRANTY PERIOD

Can Affect:

- Appearance
- Slope erosion

Performance Guideline: Any plants that die within the warranty period must be replaced, provided that replacement is not due to improper maintenance or irrigation by the Homeowner.

Comments: Each Builder should provide a written warranty agreement for any planted landscape materials. Typically, trees, shrubs, and ground cover have different warranty periods. Common grounds of large developments that have a Homeowners Association should have a start-up maintenance schedule with their independent maintenance company, followed by a standard yearly maintenance schedule thereafter.

Builder Responsibility: If the Builder furnishes and installs plants, shrubs, trees and/or sod, the Builder should then issue a warranty and maintenance schedule (usually provided by the actual landscape installer) regarding such planted vegetation. This should include the length of warranty and any inclusions and exclusions to said warranty. If any plants die within the warranty period, and is not a result of improper care and/or maintenance by the Homeowner and/or the Homeowners Association, then the Builder should replace any plants that die or appear unhealthy.

Homeowner Responsibility: The Homeowner or Homeowners Association should supply the required maintenance to ensure that the plants stay healthy. Do not overwater the plants. Any water that is standing (***ponding***) 30 minutes after watering is a sure sign of overwatering. If there are no specific instructions as to the proper maintenance of the subject plants, then the Homeowner should consult an expert, i.e. nursery, the Builder, or a licensed landscape maintenance contractor. All plants, shrubs, sod and trees should be maintained properly to ensure the healthy growth of the plants.

Condition #3: WEED GROWTH IN LANDSCAPED AREAS

Can Affect:

- Appearance
- Plant life

Performance Guideline: Minimal weed growth is to be expected; "minimal" defined as less than 25% of the planted area.

Comments: Even after applying ***pre-emergent*** weed control it is still virtually impossible to guarantee against some weed growth in planted areas.

Builder Responsibility: The Builder has the responsibility to ensure that proper weed control has been provided prior to planting and immediately after planting.

Homeowner Responsibility: Homeowners and Homeowners Associations should provide proper maintenance regarding weed control. This may include application of pre-emergent herbicides, spot spraying of contact weed killers and hand weeding.

Irrigation

Condition #1: IMPROPER DESIGN AND / OR INSTALLATION OF IRRIGATION SYSTEM

Can Affect:

- Exterior wall integrity
- Structural framing integrity
- Drainage
- Plant health

Performance Guideline: Water should not spray directly onto the building. Minor overspray and wind driven overspray is acceptable. Excessive watering that causes ponding or standing water for more than 24 hours is unacceptable.

Comments: Particular attention should be taken regarding sprinkler head location. Water should not spray directly onto building walls, masonry, metal and wood fencing. Some landscape professionals recommend drip irrigation at the foundation perimeter.

Builder Responsibility: The irrigation system should be designed to supply the proper amounts of water needed for all landscape (sod, shrubs and trees) that was installed by the Builder. All irrigation and planting should be according to generally accepted industry standards and local Building Codes. It should be suitable for the geographic region and microclimate, as well.

Homeowner Responsibility: ***Maintenance Alert!*** The Homeowner must pay particular attention not to overwater the landscape. Ponding or standing water that accumulates at and around foundations can cause serious structural damage, insect infestation, and plant root rot. Adjusting the watering times on the irrigation controller to avoid overwatering is an important maintenance item. In Homeowners Associations, where landscape maintenance is likely to be done by a professional service, overwatering may be commonplace.

Condition #2: CONTROLLER / CLOCK DOES NOT OPERATE

Can Affect:

- Landscape health

Performance Guideline: The landscape irrigation controller / clock should operate as intended by the manufacturer within the warranty period.

Builder Responsibility: Repair or replace the controller/clock if it fails within the warranty period.

Homeowner Responsibility: Change the backup battery (if the controller has one) once a year.

Retaining Walls

General Subject Information: Typically the most prominent material used in retaining wall construction is CMU (*Concrete Masonry Unit*) block. A proper masonry or concrete retaining wall properly engineered for the intended application will have steel reinforcement, a properly sized footing, in some cases a waterproofing or dampproofing membrane applied to the backside, as well as drainage design. Retaining walls more than 3 feet high are required in many localities to have a civil engineer's stamp on the plans and receive a building permit. When retaining walls fail, water is generally the biggest catalyst for failure. There are two ways that water attacks retaining walls: (1) surface water and (2) sub-surface water. Surface water should be directed into concrete ***swales*** or ***brow ditches*** to a proper drainage area. Subsurface water should be diverted through a sub-drainage system, i.e. trench drain, and directed to a proper drainage location.

Cement products can and often do crack. However, walls that are designed to retain soil or gravel may have some form of a ***waterproofing*** product applied to the side of the wall that is against the hillside. Along with a waterproofing membrane, a protection board is also often applied to protect the membrane from damage when soils are placed against it. A swale or berm is often utilized in order to transfer surface water away from the wall. In order to remove any sub-surface water from the hillside, a ***trench drain*** or weep holes are generally used as a vehicle for subsurface water removal and removed via a pipe to a designated location. Some walls, notably the loose block variety (blocks not held together with mortar), are designed to have ground water pass through the joints.

Condition #1: WALL LEAKS

Can Affect:

- Structural integrity
- Appearance

Performance Guideline: Water that leaks or migrates through the wall is unacceptable, except through ***weep holes*** that are intentionally designed for that purpose.

Comments: If the retaining wall leaks and is structurally sound, the cause can often be a result of several things: (1) a waterproofing/dampproofing membrane was never installed, (2) the membrane was improperly installed, or (3) the ***sub-drainage*** system has failed, i.e. trench drain.

Builder Responsibility: The Builder should meet the Performance Guideline mentioned above. If the wall does not meet the Guideline, then the Builder should make any and all repairs necessary to meet the Performance Guideline.

Homeowner Responsibility: It is important for the Homeowner to maintain the method for surface water to be diverted away from the wall either through a concrete ***swale*** or ***berm***. The Homeowner should also try and identify where the trench drain (providing that one has been installed) ***daylights*** (daylight refers to the end of the drain pipe that is visible) in order to determine whether or not the drain system is clogged during heavy rains.

Condition #2: CRACKS IN WALLS AND MORTAR JOINTS

Can Affect:

- Appearance
- Structural integrity

Performance Guideline: Cracks greater than ¼ inch are considered unacceptable.

Comments: Wall cracks are generally considered acceptable up to ¼ inch, as long as there is no dislocation of the plane of the wall and no vertical dislocation. Cracks should not be left open to the weather. They should be filled with an epoxy, have epoxy injected into them, or be filled with expansive set grout.

Builder Responsibility: The Builder should meet the above Performance Guideline providing that the Homeowner has not modified the slope above the retaining wall. If the wall exceeds the Guideline, the Builder should make the repairs as necessary.

Homeowner Responsibility: The Homeowner has a responsibility to repair any cracks that are within the Performance Guideline (anything up to ¼ inch) in a timely fashion. On long slopes that are relatively steep, surface water should also be diverted away from the top of the wall to prevent conditions that could lead to cracking.

Condition #3: WHITE CHALK-LIKE SUBSTANCE APPEARS ON THE FACE OF THE WALL

Can Affect:

- Appearance
- Integrity of the reinforcing steel

Performance Guideline: This is a normal condition and is considered acceptable.

Comments: ***Efflorescence*** is a white chalk-like powder that appears as a result of moisture migrating through the mortar, dissolving salts within, and leaching to the surface. Salts in the brick or block itself may also cause efflorescence. A high alkaline in the cement may be another cause. In geographic areas where high concentrations of sulfates are in the soil, there may also be a chemical attack on the concrete.

Builder Responsibility: The Builder is not responsible for common efflorescence. However if there is severe efflorescence (where the entire face of the wall has a coating of white powder), this condition should be investigated further. If there is a large recurring area, there is the possibility that the waterproofing membrane has been installed improperly, was deliberately not installed, or is possibly missing. It may also be possible that a subdrain is failing or missing.

Homeowner Responsibility: Common efflorescence is easily removed by brushing or by a high-pressure water spray.

Condition #4: WALL IS OUT OF PLUMB

Can Affect:
- Appearance
- Occupant safety
- Slope

Performance Guideline: Walls should not exceed ¾ inch out of plumb in a 6 foot vertical direction.

Comments: Brick or masonry type walls do not need to be perfectly plumb or level.

Builder Responsibility: If the wall does not meet the above Performance Guideline, the Builder should make the necessary repairs to meet the above Guideline. Builder should replace all landscape materials damaged in the repair process.

Homeowner Responsibility: None, providing that the Homeowner has not built something on top of the wall or altered the slope in a way that would compromise the design of the wall.

Fencing

Condition #1: WOOD POSTS, PICKETS OR PANELS ARE ROTTING

Can Affect:
- Useful life of fence
- Security
- Privacy

Performance Guideline: Posts should be made of ***pressure-treated*** wood, ***heartwood*** of cedar, or redwood. Bottom rails and pickets or side boards should maintain a minimum clearance of two inches to finished grade. Posts should be set in concrete above grade so that water does not accumulate against the post.

Comments: In regards to decay, the Building Code does not specify any requirements for fencing. However, by not maintaining adequate clearance between fence-to-finished grade, the useful life of the fence may be drastically reduced.

Builder Responsibility: The Builder should furnish a completed fence with the appropriate clearance between wood and finished grade. If the fence (railings, pickets or siding) is in contact with the finished grade, the Builder should make the repairs necessary to meet the above Performance Guideline.

Homeowner Responsibility: The Homeowner should not change the finished grade in any way that would affect the above Performance Guideline. If natural conditions (i.e., rains washed soils down onto the fence) cause the Guideline to be compromised, it is the Homeowner's Responsibility to make the appropriate corrections. Planting shrubs whose foliage is in constant contact with the fence may also potentially reduce the life of the fence boards.

Condition #2: FENCING IS PREMATURELY WEATHERED OR RUSTED

Can Affect:

- Appearance
- Useful life of fence

Performance Guideline: Wood fences are expected to weather unless they are painted at the time of installation. Thereafter they become a Homeowner maintenance item. For information on "wrought iron", see Comments below.

Comments: True wrought iron fences are seldom installed today. What is referred to as "wrought iron" is really square or round tubular steel. Because the tubes are hollow, they can be more susceptible to rust at the welds. Any fence will need regularly scheduled maintenance in order to maximize the full ***useful life*** of that fence. There are many different factors that play a part as to how often the Homeowner needs to maintain a fence, such as:

- → Site-specific location of the fence—is it located in an area of direct harsh sunlight or is it in a wet and shady area;
- → Type of material—metal, wood or masonry;
- → Is there a finish or not—stains, sealers, paint;
- → Geographic location—coastal, desert, inland, or mountain environments, etc.

Builder Responsibility: Wrought iron or ornamental iron fences should be completely painted upon installation. All weld joints must be painted.

Homeowner Responsibility: ***Maintenance Alert!*** Do not allow irrigation sprinklers to spray directly onto the fence. It is recommended to paint or seal a wood fence every three years. Wrought iron fences should be inspected semi-annually and painted whenever rust is evident.

Condition #3: WARPS, KNOTS AND CRACKS EXIST IN FENCE BOARDS

Can Affect:

- Appearance
- Security value of fence

Performance Guideline: Fence boards that have loose or dislodged knots covering more than 25% of the width of the board are considered unacceptable. Boards that are split top to bottom and where the split is 3/8 inch wide are considered unacceptable. Boards that warp more than one inch in 6 feet of length are considered unacceptable.

Builder Responsibility: Builder should replace boards that do not meet the above Performance Guideline.

Homeowner Responsibility: Homeowner should keep the fence in good repair by periodic renailing of loose boards. Painting and sealing wood fences will prolong their useful life.

Chapter Nine

includes:

Ice and Snow

Noise Transmission

Mold and Mildew

Septic Tanks

Smoke Detectors

References for this chapter:

- *500 Terrific Ideas for Home Maintenance and Repair*, by Jack Maguire
- *Fire Resistance Design Manual*, Gypsum Association
- *Mold in Residential Buildings*, NAHB
- *Residential Construction Performance Guidelines*, NAHB
- *Residential Water Problems*, by Alvin Sacks
- *Troubleshooting Guide to Residential Construction*, Builderburg Group
- *Uniform Building Code*, 1997 ed.

A comprehensive list of references by author and publisher is found in the Bibliography section.

Miscellaneous

Ice and Snow

General Subject Information: While ice and snow problems are common to a large portion of the United States, only a small number of houses built in California are affected by ice and snow. Nevertheless, in areas where ice and snow are common, good design and construction practices are important. In general, there are three areas of concern related to ice and snow, discussed in the following conditions.

Condition #1: ROOF SAGS OR FAILS UNDER SNOW LOAD

Can Affect:

- Structural integrity
- Occupant safety

Performance Guideline: Roofs should not fail under normal snow loads for the region; roofs may sag or deflect by only the amount permitted under the local Code.

Comments: Accumulations of snow will add substantial weight on the structure of a House, particularly to roofs and decks. Houses built in geographic areas subject to snow are required to accommodate these additional loads. However, storms may exceed normally predicted ranges, producing excessive snow accumulations. This can result in unacceptable deflection of beams and rafters, which may lead to cracking of interior finishes and in extreme circumstances, to structural collapse.

Builder Responsibility: Be certain before starting construction that snow load requirements for the local area are met. Make necessary repairs if the above Performance Guideline is not met.

Homeowner Responsibility: During periods of exceptionally heavy snowfall, it is likely that accumulations of snow will have to be removed from the roof. Except in isolated areas, there are companies that perform this service.

Condition #2: DOORS AND WINDOWS ARE BLOCKED WITH SNOW

Can Affect:

- Occupant comfort

Performance Guideline: This is a Homeowner maintenance issue.

Comments: During periods when heavy snow and icing occur, access doors, garage doors and even windows can be blocked. Proper "snow country" design should provide reasonable protection at essential openings such as exit doors and garage doors. Reasonable protection would include overhangs and orientation away from customary storm exposure. Snow and ice accumulations can also create hazards from, among other things, snow loads falling from roofs and heavy icicles from overhead projections.

Builder Responsibility: None.

Homeowner Responsibility: ***Maintenance Alert!*** When garage doors, access doors and windows become blocked, it is up to the Homeowner to take preventive measures to keep repetition of these problems to a minimum. The severity of this condition tends to depend upon local geographic location, House design and orientation to the weather conditions.

Condition #3: ICE DAMS CAUSE EAVES TO LEAK

Can Affect:

- Interior finishes
- Structure

Performance Guideline: Ice dams should not cause eaves to leak.

Comments: When snow melts and then re-freezes, ice may form dams at areas such as roof eaves and deck perimeters. Subsequent melting or rainfall can accumulate behind such dams, and the depth of resulting ponds can exceed the height of waterproofing systems. When this happens, water can enter the interior of roof and wall systems causing damage. In addition, ponded water on flat roofs and decks can exceed the design loads for these components of the House.

Builder Responsibility: Construct the House in conformance to the requirements of the Building Code and local Code amendments with respect to ice dam elimination. Make necessary corrections if ice dams persist under normal weather conditions. If a structural or other type of failure occurs because of extreme weather conditions, the Builder is not responsible.

Homeowner Responsibility: Become aware of the causes of ice dams and the preventive steps that can be taken. ***Maintenance Alert!*** Keep gutters, drains, deck openings and major catch basins free of debris and other obstructions. If there are publicly owned drainage facilities nearby that are subject to blockage, do not hesitate to contact authorities to request maintenance. Failure to do this could result in localized flooding during periods of rapid snow melt, with consequent property damage.

Noise Transmission

Condition: SOUNDS CAN BE HEARD THROUGH WALLS AND FLOORS

Can Affect:

- Occupant comfort

Performance Guideline:

1. Party walls (also referred to as common walls) and floors between units: Sound transmission must be limited by Code to meet a Sound Transmission Coefficient (STC) standard of 50. Measurement of sound transmission can only be made using specialized equipment.
2. Devices (fans, etc.) should be of the quiet operating type; water and plumbing waste lines should be installed in a manner that minimizes transmission of noise directly from pipes to the structure of the building.
3. At interior walls and ceilings: insulate vertical waste lines; use sound-absorbing underlayment at floors (particularly hard surfaces such as tile and uncovered hardwood floors) when units on different floors are not under control of the same owner.
4. The Performance Guideline regarding noise transmission between walls and floors of detached single-family homes is that the occupants of detached houses can control their own noise level.

Comments: To prevent sound transmission between adjoining units from exceeding Performance Guideline, walls must be assembled in accordance with industry accepted cross-sections (for example, those published by the Gypsum Association), or their established equivalents. Prior to granting a building permit, the Building Inspection Department checks the floor and wall design to see if it meets an approved design standard. If it does not, the Builder or architect is required to prove that their design will satisfy the requirements of the Code. Some common measures that should be used to diminish noise transmission include avoidance of plumbing lines within party walls, offsetting of electrical outlets so that none are back-to-back, and insulation of all necessary openings at such walls (for example, electrical outlets and switches). The structural frame of the building should not be continuous, but should be interrupted between adjacent units. Sprayed cellulose insulation is also an effective way to increase the STC.

Builder Responsibility: Correct any deviations from STC standards where identified. Inform the Homeowner that it is impossible to totally eliminate noise transmission in party walls and common floor housing.

Homeowner Responsibility: Avoid any changes that affect the assembly of sound-insulating party walls or ceilings; avoid making new openings in walls and floors. A common Homeowner error is to install a stereophonic speaker system in the party walls of a townhouse or condominium.

Mold and Mildew

General Subject Information: Mold and mildew (fungi) and the ***spores*** by which they reproduce are present everywhere in the environment, including indoor air and surfaces of buildings. Usually the small numbers of these tiny organisms do not cause any problems. However, high levels of moisture combined with organic materials provide conditions that can result in their rapid growth. In high concentrations, some of these fungi may consume wood and other building materials sufficiently to cause decay and rot. Others may produce stains and unattractive coatings on interior and exterior surfaces. Some people can develop allergy-like symptoms if exposed to mold. While it is quite difficult (if not impossible) to entirely eliminate these organisms in normal residential environments, control of interior humidity and preventions of leaks limits their growth and minimizes any resulting affects.

There are thousands of types of molds and mildews. A limited number of varieties are commonly associated with damage to buildings. Under conditions favorable to growth, these fungi can form dense colonies that may be visually unattractive. Of all the known varieties of mold and mildew, only a few are believed to pose health hazards. Among these few are "stachybotris chartarum" which can produce toxic mycotoxins. In the few varieties of mold and mildew that are believed to produce adverse health effects, concentrations must be relatively high to affect most healthy individuals. It is important to note that at the present time, there are no accepted federal, state, or local health-based standards for permissible exposure to mold and mildew. Nevertheless, whether it is believed that the potential for ill affects is little or large, it is universally accepted that houses should be kept free from mold.

Some common areas for mold and mildew growth in the typical residential environment are: 1) around window frames. Two major reasons for this are condensation and leaks. Condensation often occurs at window frames if the residence is tightly sealed and inadequately ventilated and if the temperature is colder outside than inside; 2) at and near toilets, sinks, and tubs (anywhere water splash and leaks are likely to occur); 3) in basements and other spaces which are below ground level, when drainage and/or waterproofing of walls is not adequate, or is failing due to age or lack of maintenance; 4) anywhere two or more pieces of wood are tightly fitted together, and water can get between them (typical examples are unflashed wood trim around windows and doors, wood railings and caps with open miter joints, and failure to maintain caulking in these areas); and 5) in poorly ventilated and damp enclosures.

Sometimes mold will grow in enclosed (not visible) locations, such as the cavities at exterior walls. If the building construction or lack of maintenance allows water to leak into wall cavities, mold can grow in the affected areas. Resulting damage can progress unseen for some time. Aside from gray or black stains and blotchy patches that are readily identifiable as mold, signs that should help identify some potential problems include softness in drywall, water stains at walls and ceilings, damp carpets, buckling or swelling of exterior surfaces, and a persistent musty odor. These are *possible* indications and do not prove that mold or mildew exist. The actual existence of mold and mildew must be established by visual observation and in some cases by appropriate testing and expert inspection.

General Homeowner Responsibility:
Homeowners should familiarize themselves with strategies to identify, minimize, and prevent mold growth. Watch for and eliminate condensation on walls, around windows, and other cool places. Indoor humidity should be kept low by proper use of ventilation devices. Generally, a relative humidity of 60% or less should limit condensation-caused mold. Here are eight Homeowner Guidelines:

1. Inspect and maintain air conditioning and heating systems on a periodic basis. Clear out or repair the condensate line if the air conditioner's drip pan overflows.

2. Promptly dry any damp or wet indoor areas. This includes shower stalls and tubs.

3. Always use vent fans in baths, kitchens, and laundries. Keep the vent fan running for 15 minutes after use of room, to assure condensation is adequately removed.

4. If mold or mildew begins to grow around the edges of window frames (where condensation is the cause), remove it promptly with a bleach/water mixture and a disposable rag.

5. Establish / maintain roof drainage into gutters and downspouts. Maintain the ground slope away from the House foundation.

6. Repair leaks as soon as they are discovered. Keep in mind that mold can grow within 24 hours after the start of a leak. Proper homeowner inspections and prompt maintenance are essential.

7. Do not store organic materials (such as paper, wood, cardboard, books, or clothes) in damp locations.

8. If the House experiences a flood or sewer overflow, make sure that all affected areas are cleaned up thoroughly and promptly.

Homeowners should seek help if they are concerned about possible indications of mold and mildew. Some sources for help include biology departments of major universities, city and county health departments, and the organizations to which health and hygiene specialists belong, such as the American Conference of Governmental Industrial Hygienists (ACGIH). This group can be contacted through their website:http://www.acgih.org. The California Department of Health Services also has a website: http://www.cal-iaq.org.

→ **IF MOLD AND MILDEW IS SUSPECTED TO EXIST, THE MOST IMPORTANT THING TO DO IS TO STOP THE SOURCE OF WATER, IF POSSIBLE, AND TO NOTIFY THE BUILDER IMMEDIATELY.**

Condition #1: MOLD AND MILDEW GROWTH WHERE LEAKS OCCUR

Can Affect:
- Appearance
- Life of building materials
- Air quality

Performance Guideline: No condition should be permitted to exist, such as a rainwater leak, plumbing leak, or use of excessively wet framing lumber, which fosters the growth of mold and mildew.

Comments: Prevention and elimination of leaks is discussed in other sections of this Manual (See Chapters on Walls, Roofs, Exterior Components and Utility Systems). Nevertheless, where leaks *do* occur, it is possible that mold and mildew may follow. If mold and mildew are present as a result of leaks, the repair of leaks should include removal of materials that are stained, coated or otherwise adversely affected by such organisms. Because removal of moisture can arrest the growth of these organisms and because surfaces that are not significantly damaged can be cleaned or treated, it may be possible to retain some or all affected building components during the repair process. In severe cases, removal or retention of building components is a technical matter that is best handled by a specialist in mold and mildew. The specialist will determine whether the types of molds and mildews present are a potential health hazard and if they are, the best way to remove them.

Builder Responsibility: Perform repairs of leaks caused by Builder as necessary to eliminate sources of water intrusion. Remove and arrest the growth of mold and mildew.

Homeowner Responsibility: The Homeowner is responsible for promptly addressing any instances of leakage, and if Builder caused, reporting to the Builder any instances of leakage, so that preventive repairs can be accomplished before significant damage occurs. If leaks are corrected quickly, mold and mildew may not flourish, and repairs and clean-ups are much easier to accomplish.

Condition #2: MOLD AND MILDEW GROWTH AROUND WINDOWS, DOORS, BASEBOARDS, BATHROOM SURFACES, ABSENT OF OBVIOUS LEAKS

Can Affect:
- Appearance
- Air quality
- Life of materials

Performance Guideline: No condition should be created, as a result of construction practices, so as to foster the growth of molds or mildews. Absent of leaks, this is a Homeowner maintenance item.

Comments: Most of the molds and mildews that appear around window frames and doors, in tile grout at tubs, showers and kitchens, as well as other interior items, are the result of the Homeowner's lifestyle. At times interior humidity may rise sufficiently so that moisture condenses on cool surfaces (such as windows, doors, and walls). These conditions provide a fertile environment for the growth of molds and mildews, which most frequently appear around window and door frames, and at the joint between frames and surrounding drywall and wood trim.

Because of their warm and moist conditions, shower stalls and tub surrounds are also ideal places for mold and mildew to grow. Most of these conditions are controllable through appropriate use and maintenance of the House.

Builder Responsibility: Repair any conditions that may result from improper construction that cause mold and mildew growth.

Homeowner Responsibility: ***Maintenance Alert!*** Showers and tubs should be routinely cleaned and dried after each use and window frames and joints should be periodically cleaned in order to prevent mold and mildew growth. If mildew or mold is observed, use a mildewcide (available at any cleaning supply or hardware store) to prevent and retard any regrowth. In addition, it is helpful to air out rooms on a frequent basis. Ensure that all exhaust fans and other air circulation devices are functioning properly and used routinely. Do not install air deflectors over heat supply grills. Open draperies often during rainy periods to allow air to circulate around windows. Limit the use of atomizers or humidifiers. Windows should be open or vent fans should be operating at all times while showering or bathing. Window tracks and ***weep holes*** should be cleaned at least twice yearly to prevent mold and mildew.

Condition # 3: MILDEW GROWTH ON SIDING, STUCCO, AND OTHER EXTERIOR SURFACES

Can Affect:
- Appearance
- Useful life of exterior surfaces

Performance Guideline: 1) The installation of siding should be made so that it prevents water from entering behind siding; 2) The design and location of buildings on the site that are clad in hardboard or ***OSB*** siding should provide for adequate exposure to sunlight and ventilation, and should avoid unusually damp surroundings; 3) Interior spaces should be adequately ventilated and protected by vapor barriers to avoid excessive condensation build-up that may result in the growth of mildew, mold and fungi.

Comments: The appearance of mildew or fungi on siding may result from three principal sources: 1) leaks that allow water to enter between the siding and the material behind the siding; 2) an environment that is excessively damp, shady and lacking in air circulation; and 3) condensation of moist air on interior surfaces.

Builder Responsibility: Install or construct exterior surfaces to meet the Performance Guideline. Once the Builder has met the above Guideline, there is little the Builder can do to prevent mold and mildew from occurring on outside walls. Variations in orientation, weather and the spore count in the air can all have an effect on the growth of mold and mildew on exterior walls.

Homeowner Responsibility: ***Maintenance Alert!*** Keep siding sealed and painted. Avoid spraying siding and stucco with landscape sprinklers. If mold and mildew grows on outside walls, take prompt action. Use of mildew-killing sprays and brushing with water and soap can arrest or reverse mildew conditions. The Homeowner should also avoid planting shrubbery that will block sunlight and ventilation from siding. Do not allow ivy or other vine plants to grow on siding and keep existing shrubbery pruned back from siding.

Condition #4: MILDEW OR MOLD GROWTH IN HEATING AND VENTILATING DUCT WORK

Can Affect:

- Indoor air quality

Performance Guideline: The design and installation of heating and ventilating ductwork should be accomplished in a manner that does not encourage the growth of organisms within the enclosed system.

Comments: Mildew or mold should not be allowed to remain in the heating and ventilating systems. The problem usually results from moisture getting into the ductwork, either from a leak or condensation. Improperly insulated ductwork can also be a cause. It may be difficult to identify the presence of mold or mildew in ductwork, although a musty odor can be an indicator.

Builder Responsibility: The Builder is responsible for installing a properly assembled and insulated heating and ventilating system and repairing conditions resulting from improper installation.

Homeowner Responsibility: Notify the Builder promptly of any suspected problem of this nature.

Condition #5: MOLD OR MILDEW GROWTH NEAR ENCLOSED PLUMBING PIPES

Can Affect:

- Indoor air quality
- Structural integrity

Performance Guidelines: Cold water pipes in wall cavities and other interior spaces subject to moist, warm air should be insulated.

Comments: This condition is caused by moisture when interior air condenses on cold water pipes.

Builder Responsibility: The Builder should install pipe insulation on cold water pipes where there is a likelihood of condensation and mold growth.

Homeowner Responsibility: None.

Septic Tanks

General Subject Information: A typical private waste system works in the following manner: waste is piped out of the house and into a watertight holding tank. There, bacteria break the waste down into solids, liquid and scum. The sludge settles into the bottom of the tank, the scum rises to the top, and the liquid flows into 1) a distribution box, which channels through perforated pipes that leach out into a field of loose gravel, known as the leach field, or 2) to a separate pit through solid pipes.

Condition #1: SEWER SYSTEM / DRAINS NOT OPERATING PROPERLY

Can Affect:

- Occupant health
- Interior finishes and furnishings

Performance Guideline: All septic or waste systems should be capable of operating as designed, under normal use without any stoppage or back up.

Comments: Under certain conditions sewer systems can fail or overflow as a result of saturated leach lines, freezing, change in water tables, or excessive use of plumbing fixtures. Use of high phosphate detergents and overuse of detergents can result in leach field failure.

Builder Responsibility: At time of delivery of the House, the Builder should demonstrate that the septic system is operating as designed. If a clogged sewer line/drain is the result of improper installation by the Builder, then the Builder should repair the non-performing condition so that it meets the above Performance Guideline. The Builder will not be held accountable for sewers and drains that are clogged because of Homeowner negligence or misuse.

Homeowner Responsibility: ***Maintenance Alert!*** The tank should be pumped out every 2-3 years, depending on the size of the system and the number of people that live in the household. The local health department may require more frequent pumping. The following items are examples of Homeowner negligence regarding septic tanks:

- ☒ Pouring paint thinners, pesticides, motor oils, or chemicals down drains or in toilets.
- ☒ Disposing of grease, fat, paper towels, or feminine sanitary products in toilets.
- ☒ Drain cleaners should be used with caution and sparingly (drain cleaners kill bacteria that break down sewage).
- ☒ Use of dyed toilet tissue (dyes are harmful to the bacteria in the tank).

Condition #2: SEPTIC TANK EMITS FOUL ODOR

Can Affect:

- Air quality

Performance Guideline: Septic tanks should not emit unreasonably foul odors, given proper Homeowner use and maintenance.

Comments: The odors that come from a septic tank are largely the result of use and maintenance. A septic tank that is overused (beyond its capacity) and a septic system that has not been regularly pumped out will become quite odorous.

Builder Responsibility: None.

Homeowner Responsibility: ***Maintenance Alert!*** Keep the tank pumped out on a regular basis. Periodically add a bacteria-enhancing agent (sold at any hardware store). If the number of persons using the system increases, consider expanding the system.

Smoke Detectors

General Subject Information: According to Code, smoke detectors are required to be installed in specific rooms in a residence, interconnected with each other, and maintained in an operating condition. New installations of smoke detectors must be wired to the house electrical system as well as having a battery operated back-up. If one smoke detector alarm sounds, all should sound.

Condition #1: DETECTORS SOUND DURING USE OF FIREPLACE / KITCHEN

Can Affect:

- Occupant comfort

Performance Guideline: Smoke detectors are designed to be smoke sensitive; this is for the protection of the occupants. In all likelihood when smoke detectors sound at the time of cooking, the room has been overloaded with cooking vapors. If the detector sounds each time a fire is built in the fireplace, there may be a ventilation problem (See Chapter 6 "Fireplaces" or Chapter 5 "Chimneys and Flues").

Builder Responsibility: The Builder is responsible for installing a Code-compliant detector system. If the detectors sound at inappropriate times, and the fault lies with poorly constructed ventilation systems, the Builder should correct the non-performing condition.

Homeowner Responsibility: The Homeowner should operate fireplaces and cook in a manner that does not cause undue quantities of smoke to be generated within the House.

Condition #2: DETECTORS DO NOT OPERATE WHEN TESTED

Can Affect:

- Occupant safety

Performance Guideline: All smoke detectors should operate as intended by Code, and in compliance with manufacturer's specifications. Smoke detectors that do not operate because the battery is dead are considered a Homeowner maintenance item.

Builder Responsibility: In the event of a malfunctioning detector, the Builder should conduct an investigation to determine the cause, and should take corrective action as appropriate to restore function.

Homeowner Responsibility: ***Maintenance Alert!*** Homeowners should test detectors once a month using the test button on the detector. All newly installed detector systems operate both off the House wiring and battery back-ups. The Homeowner must make sure the batteries are changed on a regular basis so the back-up system will function in the event of a power failure.

TEST SMOKE-DETECTORS MONTHLY

Homeowner Maintenance Summary

The following list summarizes minimum maintenance requirements that should be performed by the Homeowner (or Homeowners Association) along with the Schedule. For more specific details, each maintenance item is referenced to a section within the Manual. This work should be done either by the Homeowner or by a maintenance person who is experienced and insured. A maintenance person who holds a contractor's license is typically better qualified. A tear-out Maintenance Schedule is provided at the end of this Section. Failure to adequately maintain the following areas may eliminate or reduce the Builder's Responsibility if problem conditions arise.

→ **Bathroom Caulk.** The caulk joints in bathrooms need to be inspected and re-caulked (if necessary) every six months. This includes the joint at the bottom of the shower, the joint between the tub and the wall, the joint where the tub or shower pan meets the floor, and vertical inside corners and seats. It is very important that these joints do not pass any water; otherwise dryrot can accumulate progress unseen for years. Refer to **Chapter Seven, Plumbing** for additional details. Joints should be cleaned of old caulk before re-caulking. Any mold or mildew found growing in bathrooms (or other places in the House) should be removed immediately with a mildewcide, available at most hardware stores. The cause of the mold or mildew should be discovered (for example a leaky window or failure to use vent fan while bathing) and the cause subsequently eliminated.

→ **Ceramic Tile Grout.** Regrout or color caulk all cracks after the first year. Once the House frame reaches equilibrium (in less than two years), regrouting or caulking should not be required. Tile grout should initially be sealed with a silicone based sealer and thereafter every two years. Refer to **Chapter Six, Countertops** for additional details.

→ **Chimney Cleaning.** The chimney flue should be professionally cleaned every two years if there are more than 50 fires per year or if there are more than 25 fires per year using wax and sawdust logs; subject to any restrictions or requirements of the manufacturer. **Refer to Chapter Five, Chimneys and Flues** for additional details.

→ **Doors.** Patio sliding doors should have their tracks (bottom sill) swept and vacuumed monthly. The weep holes should also be inspected and cleaned as needed. Dust and dirt build-up in slider door tracks will interfere with the proper operation of the small wheels that the doors slide on. For swing doors, the hinges and latches should be lubricated annually with a dry lubricant specifically made for locks and latches. **Refer to Chapter Five, Windows and Patio Doors** for additional details.

→ **Drains**

- **Deck.** Deck drains should be flushed with a garden hose and should show evidence of free-flow prior to the start of each rainy season. **Refer to Chapter Five, Decks** for details.
- **Yard.** Yard drains should be flushed with a garden hose prior to the start of the rainy season and should show evidence of free flow at the curb or at the sump (if applicable). **Refer to Chapter Eight, Drainage** for additional details.
- **Subdrains**. If the House is equipped with a subterranean drainage system around the foundation or through the foundation, the cleanouts (if applicable) of this subdrain should be

flushed prior to the start of the rainy season. There should be evidence of free-flow through the curb or into the sump. **Refer to Chapter Eight, Drainage** for additional details.

→ **Drywall**
- **Cracks.** Minor cracks in drywall usually appear within the first 12 months of occupancy. These cracks typically occur around doorframes, cabinets, and window frames and can be easily caulked. **Refer to Chapter Six, Plaster and Drywall** for additional details on cracks and Performance Guidelines.
- **Nail Pops.** Nails will sometimes back out of the drywall as the frame of the House dries out. This is not a structural problem, but the nails should be redriven and the heads should be spackled and painted with touchup paint. **Refer to Chapter Six, Plaster and Drywall** for additional details.

→ **Electrical**
- **GFIs.** Ground Fault Interrupters should be tested monthly. When testing, pressing the black TEST button should cause the red or white RESET button to pop out. Push in the RESET button to restore the circuit. If the GFI will not reset, it may be faulty or there may be an open circuit. Contact a qualified, licensed electrical contractor to check the circuit. **Refer to Chapter Seven, Electrical** for additional details.
- **Closet Ceiling Lights.** Light bulbs in the closets must be covered with a lens or globe as part of the fixture. When changing bulbs in the closet light fixtures, do not exceed the manufacturer's recommended wattage for the bulb requirement, and do not leave the fixture cover off. Lights left on in closets can generate a significant amount of heat and become a fire hazard. **Refer to Chapter Seven, Electrical** for additional details.
- **Aluminum Wiring.** While most household wiring is copper, the larger wires (known as cables), are likely to be aluminum. All wires are covered with insulation. Aluminum cables are often used to provide power to air conditioners, heat pumps, electric clothes dryers, and electric ovens. Aluminum is a softer metal than copper. Over time it can deform, or "creep", where it is connected. When aluminum creep occurs, the connection is no longer tight and sparking jumps through the gap. Appliances will consume more power and breakers will trip. It is recommended that the terminal connections of aluminum cables be inspected and tightened if necessary by a qualified, licensed electrical contractor within the first two years after occupancy. **Refer to Chapter Seven, Electrical** for additional details.

→ **Fencing**
- **Wood.** The condition of wood fences should be inspected every spring. Look for nails that have backed out of boards, fence posts that are leaning and kick boards (at the bottom) that have rotted. All leaning posts should be straightened, all loose boards should be renailed and if the kick boards have rotted significantly, they should be replaced. **Refer to Chapter Eight, Fencing** for additional details.
- **Wrought Iron.** Wrought iron gates and fences should be inspected four times a year to check for rust, particularly at the base of all posts. If rust is discovered, it should be scraped away and the section should be painted with rust-resistant touchup paint. **Refer to Chapter Eight, Fencing** for additional details.
- **Stucco.** Stucco fencing (patio fencing), should be inspected annually, in the springtime. Cracks on the top of the fence should be caulked and repainted and fence post bases should be inspected for dryrot. All dirt should be removed from the fence post bases. **Refer to Chapter Eight, Fencing** for additional details.

→ **Furnace Filters.** If the House has heating and air conditioning, the furnace filters should be changed at least every six months or at the filter manufacturer's recommendation. If the House has heating only, the furnace filters should be changed prior to the winter season. If the Homeowner lives in an area that has considerable wind driven dust, the above filter change schedule should be doubled. **Refer to Chapter Seven, Heating** and **Chapter Seven, Cooling** for additional details.

→ **Garage Doors**

- **One Piece.** One-piece garage doors (doors that raise and lower as one single piece) with automatic openers or garage doors without automatic openers should be lubricated at the hinge points every six months with 30w oil. The keepers (the long threaded rods that run across the top and bottom) should be kept tight to prevent the door from sagging in the middle.
- **Sectional.** Sectional doors (doors that roll up into the garage ceiling on tracks) should have the track rollers lubricated with 30w oil annually.
- **Automatic Opener.** The automatic openers, whether they are chain drive or screw drive, should have the drive mechanism (chain or screw) lubricated with a light grease annually.
- **Bolts.** Garage doors vibrate while opening and closing. Therefore, it is important that an inspection be made every six months for the first year and annually thereafter for bolts that can be wiggled or moved by hand. For all of the above, refer to **Chapter Five, Garage Doors** for additional details.
- **Weatherstripping.** Check flexibility and contact with floor.

→ **Gutters and Downspouts**. Gutters and downspouts should be cleaned and flushed twice annually. The first task is performed just prior to the rainy season, and the second task is performed during the rainy season after the trees have shed their autumn leaves. Prune branches that overhang roofs and gutters. **Refer to Chapter Five, Gutters and Downspouts** for additional details.

→ **Insect Control**. Insects, particularly termites and carpenter ants, can be harmful to the structure of the House. An annual inspection should be made of the foundation (both on the outside and inside of the crawlspace). Look for brown termite tubes running up the foundation walls and bore holes of the carpenter ants on the exterior of the House. Builders typically do not warrant against any type of insect invasion. Homeowners should pay close attention to pest control maintenance and should not hesitate to call a pest control service if destructive insects are suspected to be present. Firewood should be stored away from the House in a structure or holder that is not in contact with the ground. Do not let vines grow on the House; they will attract insects.

→ **Irrigation Sprinklers.** Irrigation sprinklers should be checked annually at the beginning of the growing period (usually March or April) to be sure that the heads are clean and do not spray against the House and that the sprinkler lines have not broken during the winter. Spray patterns should also be checked during the growing season. **Refer to Chapter Eight, Irrigation** for additional details. During the rainy season, irrigation controller times should be changed frequently to avoid overwatering and flooding.

→ **Locks**. Once a year, or when they become stiff, apply a dry lubricant as directed into the lock. Use a lubricant specifically designed for locks and avoid use of popular oil synthetic sprays. The latter can form a gummy residue on lock parts.

→ **Sink Traps.** Depending upon frequency of use, sink traps should be cleaned with a cleanser approved for the type of plumbing pipes under the sink (plastic or metal). For a kitchen sink that receives daily use, a cleaning every 60 days should be sufficient. DO NOT put sink cleaner into a garbage disposal. It may corrode the cutting blade edges.

→ **Solid Surface Countertops**. Do not apply countertop surface enhancers or cleansers such as Pledge™ or 409™ to a new solid surface countertop. These products will only attract and hold discoloring items such as coffee, wine, catsup, etc. to the surface. The new nonporous, bacteria-free solid surface countertop will remain in its natural state if it is simply wiped off with a soft sponge or cloth, with an ammonia based product such as glass cleaner, or with a mild soap and water solution. For integral solid surface sinks, use a mild abrasive such as Softscrub™ to cut any grease or discoloring buildup that has accumulated on the surface of the sink. Clean off any harsh chemicals such as nail polish remover as soon as possible. Do not cut directly on the solid surface countertop or slide any rough edged objects across the countertop, since these items will create surface scratches in almost any type of countertop. To prevent shocking the surface of any type of sink, do not pour extremely hot grease or water into any sink without simultaneously running cool water. Do not place extremely hot items (such as sheet pans from a 450 degree oven) directly on the countertop or sink. **Refer to Chapter Six, Countertops** for additional details.

→ **Trim and Siding.** The term "trim" refers to the wooden trim either abutting the stucco or placed on the wooden siding around windows and doors. The trim should be inspected each year prior to the start of the rainy season; and if the trim is pulled away from the House or the caulking has deteriorated, these areas should be re-caulked. If warping or twisting is severe (more than ½ in.), the trim should be replaced. Refer to **Chapter Six, Moldings and Trim** for additional details. Do not caulk the bottom gap of the trim piece over a window or patio door. Also, the siding (exterior wall material such as panels, lap boards, shingles, or other non-stucco, non-brick, or non-stone material) should be inspected for warpage and protruding nails. Inspections should be annual and prior to the start of the rainy season. Warpage should be caulked and painted, and protruding nails should be pulled and replaced with a slightly larger nail. Use hot dipped galvanized box or common nails in exterior applications. Drive the nail head even with the siding; DO NOT drive the nail head into the siding. Driving the nail head into the siding may break the seal and cause the siding to swell and leak during precipitation. Touch up all work with caulk and paint.

→ **Vents.** This includes kitchen hood filters and bathroom laundry fans. The hood filters should be removed and washed with a grease removing cleanser at least 4 times a year (depending upon use). Bathroom and laundry fans should be vacuumed with a hose vacuum and crevice tool at least once a year.

→ **Water Heater.** To prolong the life of the water heater, accumulated sediment should be removed from the heater tank once a year. This task can be performed by attaching a thick wall garden hose to the drain spigot at the bottom of the tank and draining out no more than two gallons. **Since the water being drained is very hot, be very careful that the hot water does not come into contact with persons, animals, plants, or any material that could be damaged by scalding water (120 degrees F to 160 degrees F).**

→ **Windows (includes Patio doors)**

- **Seals.** Inspect for broken or breached window seals in dual pane windows at least annually. Windows with broken or breached seals are easily identified by having a moist, foggy, or filmy condition between the two panes of glass. When this condition exists, the insulating value of the window is greatly diminished. The only repair is to replace the window. **Refer to Chapter Five, Windows and Patio Doors** for additional details.
- **Weep Holes.** The weep holes at the bottom of windows and patio doors serve a purpose: to allow water to drain out from the track during rainstorms. Weep holes should be inspected at least annually to make sure that no debris has plugged the holes and that rainwater will drain freely from them. **Refer to Chapter Five, Windows and Patio Doors** for additional details.
- **Tracks.** The tracks of windows and patio doors should be swept and vacuumed frequently to prevent dust and debris buildup. Clean window and door tracks, allowing the sliding vent to move more freely, so that the drainage through the weep holes will not be impaired by any wet debris. In open areas where there is ongoing construction or agricultural operations that generate dust, track cleaning should be done weekly. **Refer to Chapter Five, Windows and Patio Doors** for additional details.

HANDY HAMMER

READY TO WORK

RECOMMENDED MAINTENANCE SCHEDULE

FOR HOMEOWNERS AND HOMEOWNER ASSOCIATIONS

Maintenance Item	Purpose	Frequency	Difficulty	Date Performed											
Air Conditioner	Start twice during winter months; keeps mechanical parts from sticking.	2 Y	●												
Bathroom Caulk	Seal joints that are subject to being wetted; prevent leaks, dry rot, mold and mildew.	2 Y	▲												
Ceramic Tile Grout	Seal grout with silicone based sealer; cracked grout should be caulked with a caulk specifically made for filling grout. Improves appearance, prevents leaks.	Y	■												
Chimney Cleaning	Removes build up of tar and creosote from flue; prevents flue fires.	Y 2	◆												
Doors	Vacuuming tracks and lubricating hinges and latches keeps operating parts smooth.	M/Y	●												
Drainage	Keep drains from backing up and flooding during the rainy season. Make sure debris is removed from ditches and swales. Maintain positive drainage away from buildings.	Y	●												
Drywall (cracks and nail pops)	Set nails, caulk and paint. Improves appearance of finished interior wall surfaces.	Y	■												
Electrical (GFI Test)	Safety of electrical circuits. Test GFI circuits (kitchen, bath, garage and outdoor) monthly.	M	●												
Electrical (Wiring)	Elimination of possible fire hazard and open circuits. Within first two years all connections should be checked for tightness.	2 Y	◆												
Fences (inspection and repair)	Retains privacy and security. Prolongs useful life of fence. Wrought iron schedule is 4Y.	Y	■												
Furnace Filter Change	Helps remove dust and pollen from interior air; improves furnace efficiency; less energy consumption.	2 Y	●												
Garage Door Systems	Lubrication promotes smoother, less noisy operation; extends system life. Tighten keepers to avoid sag on one piece doors.	2 Y	●												
Garbage Disposer	Fill with ice and operate. Cleans and sharpens blades.	M	●												
Grounds	Inspect for pavement breaks, heaving sidewalks from tree roots, dry rot at decks and blockage of drainage system. Avoids more expensive repair costs.	Y	■												
Gutters and Downspouts	Prevents overflow onto walls; prevents eave leaks; extends gutter life.	2 Y	●												
Insect Control	Detected and treated early will prevent structural damage; controls annoying pests. If found, treat monthly.	Y	▲ ◆												
Irrigation Sprinklers	Direct water spray properly. Eliminates excess watering, staining of exterior walls and dry rot of structures.	2 Y	■												
Roof Inspection/Maintenance	Detect and correct conditions that can lead to leaks and premature roof replacement. Be sure to read Chapter Four to learn the process for inspection and repair.	Y	■ ◆												
Sink Trap Cleaning	Avoids backups and plugged drains; promotes sanitation. Use only cleaners recommended by manufacturer.	4 Y	●												
Trim and Siding	Caulking and painting keeps system water tight; improves appearance, extends major maintenance periods; reduces chances of mold and mildew.	Y	▲												
Water Heater (partial drain)	Extends water heater life; provides more efficient operation; uses less energy.	Y	■												
Windows (tracks and weep holes)	Keeps windows sliding freely. Avoids water standing in tracks and potential leaks.	2 Y	■												
(seals-dual pane)	Appearance, broken seals reduce insulating ability. Replace when foggy.	Y	◆												

Key

Frequency:

Monthly = M

Yearly = Y

Twice a year = 2Y

Four times a year = 4Y

Every two years = Y2

Difficulty:

● Easy, no special skill required.

■ Some skill required.

▲ Good idea to get instruction on this item from a local home improvement store.

◆ This task should be performed only by a qualified professional.

Refer to Homeowner Maintenance Summary for additional details.

Glossary

A glossary of terms is an important tool for each Homeowner. Like almost every trade or profession, the homebuilding industry has, throughout time, developed a language all its own. Many of the industry used terms such as "heart, stud, cricket, jack, apron and chase" have completely different meanings in everyday life. While it is not possible to list all of the homebuilding terms and their meanings here, the ones most likely to needed by a Homeowner are defined below.

ABS-black plastic pipe used to carry waste water (sewage) from the various drains in the House to a pipe known as the soil pipe. The soil pipe is located just outside the foundation of the House. ABS pipe is also used as plumbing vents through the roof.

ANSI-the acronym for American National Standards Institute. This is an organization that tests building components and determines if the components meet certain prescribed standards.

ASHRAE-the acronym for American Society of Heating, Refrigerating, and Air-conditioning Engineers. This Association establishes standards for heating and cooling, among other things.

Aggregate-a mixture of small smooth rocks; an ingredient used in making concrete.

Air handler-the specialized fan inside the furnace or air conditioner that blows warm or cold air through ducts to the rooms.

Anchor bolts-bolts that hold the frame of the House to the foundation. Anchor bolts, also known as J-bolts, are cast in the wet concrete of the foundation during the concrete pouring process to secure the mudsill, which is the wood framing member bolted to the foundation using the anchor bolts.

Apron-the small strip of trim wood that is underneath the windowsill. The windowsill is known as a stool in the homebuilding industry.

Attic-the attic is the space in the House between the ceiling of the top floor and the underside of the roof. The attic needs to be insulated over living areas and vented to allow proper air circulation from the House in the summer and winter. Most houses have an interior attic access panel which can be located in the ceiling of a hallway, closet or bedroom, and allows access to the attic.

Backsplash-a part of the countertop in a bathroom and/or kitchen (and sometimes laundry room) that is a vertical piece of countertop material connected to the wall. A backsplash is typically 4 inches to 6 inches in height.

Baluster-the posts that support the handrails, located on the sides of stairs. The posts where the handrails start or stop are called the newell posts.

Barge board-a board attached to the edge of a roof that projects beyond the wall of the House (also referred to as varge board).

Batten-a strip of wood or plastic (usually 1 inch x 2 inches) that is applied to a roof to hold the concrete or clay tiles in place. Also, a batten is a strip of wood used to cover the joints of panels of exterior siding.

Beam-a horizontal piece of lumber that is used to carry part of the weight of the House. Beams are found at the roof, between floors, and between the basement or crawl space and the first floor.

Berm-a mound of dirt that is placed in landscaped areas to control the flow of storm water. Berms are also used in landscape beautification, to break up flat areas.

Bird stop-a metal, plastic, or wood insert found at the lowest point of a tile roof (typically the round or barrel shaped tiles). This is to keep birds and other creatures from nesting in the underpart of the roof.

Bleed through-a term that describes a material that passes through another material and generally discolors the second material. An example of bleed through is redwood and cedar wood sap (tannins) that bleed through paint. It can also apply to rust from nails and staples that bleed through stucco.

Blocks-blocks are pieces of wood installed at the ends (and sometimes at intermediate points) of floor joists, as to prevent the joists from twisting. By the use of blocks, the floor joists are tied together to create a more rigid component. Blocks are also found where floor joists lap one another (the joists cannot span the entire distance so a lap is created). Blocks are also used between studs to serve as a firestop. The blocks are typically made from the same material as the joists or the studs.

Breaker-a specialized switch found inside a panel (usually gray and known as a breaker panel) that will interrupt the flow of electricity in the event of a short circuit or an electrical surge. The act of interrupting is called "tripping". The small handle of a tripped breaker will be in the middle position between the markings OFF and ON. A tripped breaker will have to be turned off before it can be reset to the ON position. Breakers are usually found in groups in the panel and they are labeled as to which circuits they control.

Brow ditch-a ditch that sits on top of a retaining wall. It is designed to keep surface water from flowing behind and over the wall.

Building Official-the person who is the head of the local department that issues building permits. This is usually a county or city agency. Building Officials, through their deputies, perform inspections and enforce the various Building Codes.

Building paper-a specially made thick paper that is stapled to the outside of the frame of the House. Building paper is used prior to application of the exterior finish material (such as stucco, wood siding, shingles etc.). The paper is impregnated with a substance during its manufacturing process that makes it resistant to the flow of moisture. If the stucco or siding leaks, the building paper will serve as a secondary backup to prevent moisture from getting into the walls.

Bull nose-a piece of material that projects slightly past the supporting material and is rounded at its outer edge. Bull nose pieces can be found on roofing, interior trim, stair tread and countertops and "finish off" a flat surface.

Capillary action-the act of drawing a liquid, usually water, into another material. A good example of this is a sponge absorbing water. In the building industry, water can be drawn up into wood, stucco, or concrete by capillary action.

Casing-known as trim pieces that will finish off an opening. Most commonly found at door openings and mistakenly called frames, but casings can also be found around windows and shadowboxes.

Caulk-a gooey material that is used to seal joints for the purpose of keeping water out. Caulk is usually found around bathtubs and is applied with a tool known as a caulking gun. There are many different types of caulks for various uses. It is critical to use the correct variety of caulk product for each situation.

Cement-a term that has been mistakenly interchanged with the word concrete, but in fact is one of the ingredients of concrete. Cement is the "paste" that will bind sand and aggregate together. Because of its chemical composition and alkalinity, cement can burn the human skin.

Chain drive-the mechanism that opens and closes the garage door and is part of the automatic garage door opener. These automatic garage door openers operate with three types of drives, either chain drive, screw drive, or belt drive.

Chase-a chase is a horizontal or vertical box in which a flue pipe, generally a chimney flue, is located. The chase is built around the flue and it extends above the roofline by an amount specified in the Building Code. Chases can also contain plumbing pipes or wiring.

Cleanout-an opening in a plumbing waste line to allow access to the piping for the purpose of inspection and cleaning. Cleanouts are required by the plumbing codes and are typically found beneath kitchen sinks and just outside the foundation of the House.

Closed loop system-any system that uses the same fluid or gases over and over and is returned to the source for heating or cooling.

Coffered ceiling-a ceiling that is not flat but has a portion of it lifted up to create a more dramatic architectural effect. The lifted portion is usually found in the middle of the ceiling.

Common area- refers to areas that are owned in common by all members of a homeowners association. This term is associated with condominium projects and planned unit developments and may include such items as the exterior of buildings, landscape, driveways, recreation facilities and mailboxes. Common areas usually have their own legal description located in the deed to the condominium or individual lot, as applicable.

Compaction-an engineering term given to the degree of tightness of the soil around and under the House or behind a retaining wall. The soil under the foundation must achieve a certain degree of compaction before the foundation can be poured. Driveways, patios and walkways should be poured on compacted soil. Uncompacted soil is often referred to as native soil or loose soil.

Compressor-a motor driven pump that compresses a gas as part of the air conditioning process.

Concrete-a mixture of sand, gravel (sometimes called aggregate) and cement. This mixture becomes concrete when it is mixed with water and is allowed to cure.

Condensate line-the plastic or metal pipe that comes out of the air conditioning part of the furnace. Condensate lines conduct water from the air conditioner coil to the outside of the House or to a trap.

Condominium-buildings, parts of which are owned in common with other people. This is a legal term and is often confused with an architectural style. Condominiums can include townhouses, flats and even detached homes, so long as part of the project is owned in common by all of the owners of the project.

Control joint-a linear separation made during the pouring of concrete (or stucco in the case of the installation of an expansion joint) made by troweling with a v-shaped tool. Its purpose is to provide a slightly weaker spot in the concrete so it will crack along the joint. The joint can also be a groove made with a concrete saw at least one day after the concrete is finished.

Corbel-a bracket having at least two sides at right angles and often ornately carved. This bracket may support a shelf or an element that projects out from a House such as a bay window or a fireplace mantel.

Corner bead-a corner bead is a long strip of material that is applied vertically to “finish off” a corner. The corner may be a drywall corner or a stucco corner. Corner beads are usually made of metal, including wire, and sometimes are even made of stiff paper.

Counter-flashing-metal flashing that fits up under the visible flashing on roofs, around chimneys and windows.

Crawl space-this is the space between the soil and the underside the first floor joists. It is found in houses that have a pier and grade beam foundation, and do not have a basement. The Building Codes specify the minimum height of the crawl space.

Cricket-a section of the roof that is often found between the roof and a vertically projecting structure, such as a chase. The cricket is constructed to deflect water away from the chase, where the chase and the roof meet. This is so that water does not accumulate and leak into the House.

Crowning-a condition usually applied to wood, often hardwood floors, where the wood takes on moisture and the center portion of the board becomes higher than the edges. The opposite of cupping. This condition can also apply to floor joists, where the center of the joist becomes higher than the ends.

Crown molding-a decorative architectural trim piece made of wood, plastic, plaster, or foam that covers the intersection of walls and the ceilings.

Cupping-a condition that occurs when boards (including flooring) dry unevenly and the edges become higher than the center.

Cure-the act of a building material drying out and coming to equilibrium with its surroundings. A good example of curing is concrete. Concrete cures from the initial placement as it dries out. In the first three days concrete is very weak and after 28 days concrete, when properly mixed, is said to reach 90% of its maximum strength. Other materials that cure are stucco, paint, deck coatings and fireplace linings.

Damper-a hinged flap of metal found above the firebox in fireplaces to close off the flue to warm air escaping from the room when there is no fire. The damper must be open when using the fireplace. It also prevents wind from blowing down the chimney when it is not in use. Dampers are also found in the ducts of heaters and exhaust fans.

Daylight-a term given to a condition where a covered or buried object protrudes through its cover and becomes visible. An example is the visible end of a buried pipe—at the point where the pipe becomes visible, it is said to have "daylighted".

Displacement-refers to any horizontal or vertical movement of a building or the component within. More frequently it is used to describe the settlement or the heave of a foundation and the settlement of utility trenches that were once level with their surroundings.

Door-a movable structure used to close off an entrance to a room, building or covered enclosure, consisting of a panel of wood, glass or metal or other various building materials. An entire glossary could be written about doors, but here is a condensed version:

- **Exterior door-**any door that is on the outside wall of a House. The door has been manufactured to be weather resistant subject to proper maintenance.
- **Fire rated door-**a door that has been rated by an independent laboratory and has a label attached setting forth its rating. These doors can be made of many materials including wood, fiberglass, steel and composite wood material. A 20-minute fire-rated or 1 3/8 inch solid core door is generally required to be placed between the garage and House and sometimes the entrances to condominium homes. The rating usually states that the door will withstand a fire for a certain number of minutes.
- **Flush door-**a door that has a front and back panel (also known as the skin) that is perfectly smooth with an adjoining wall.
- **French door-**a door or series of doors that are hinge mounted (as opposed to a patio door that moves on tracks) and provides access to a courtyard, patio or garden. French doors are often found with divided lites (small panels of glass in individual frames as opposed to one large panel). May be used as interior doors between rooms.
- **Hollow core door-**refers to the method of construction of that door. These doors have an airspace between the front panel and the back panel of the door. The airspace between the front and back panel often contains a cardboard "honeycomb" inside.
- **Interior door-**any door that is found inside the House and may include doors from one room to the other as well as cabinet doors.
- **Overhead door-**also known as the garage door. May be constructed as a one-piece door or may be constructed in sections. A sectional door rides up into the garage ceiling on tracks whereas the one-piece door operates with springs and hinges.
- **Patio door-**an exterior door that is usually comprised of two panels, one sliding and one stationary. Patio doors are also known as sliding glass doors.
- **Pocket door-**a door that does not swing in or out, but slides across the opening from a "pocket" inside the wall.

- **Raised panel door-**a door that is manufactured with panels either individually inserted into the door or embossed into the face of the door as part of the manufacturing process. Raised panel doors can be solid core or hollow core.
- **Shower door-**the glass or plastic door that permits access to the shower.
- **Solid core door-**a door that has no airspace between the front and back panel, but is instead solid wood or some material that is glued or laminated to the front and back panels. Used in exterior applications and more custom interior applications.

Doorstop-the piece of trim that is put around three sides of a door jamb to stop the movement of the door when it is closed and sometimes to provide a rudimentary seal for light, noise and air.

Downspout-a specialized pipe usually made of aluminum, galvanized steel or plastic that runs from the roof gutter opening down the wall to the ground.

Draftstop-material that is inserted into a wall to limit the spread of fire and smoke. Frequently used materials are wood, drywall, insulation and masonry block. Draftstops are also found in chimney chases and between floors of multi-story condominium units. They are usually made of sheetmetal.

Drain:
- **Deck drain-**a drain located in a patio or elevated deck to control and direct rainwater in that area.
- **French drain-**similar to trench drain, but there is no pipe at the bottom of the trench.
- **Overflow drain-**an overflow drain protects the structure in the event that the main drain plugs up. The overflow drain is typically two inches higher than the main drain. Overflow drains are also found on bathtubs and lavatory sinks.
- **Plumbing drain-**any drain that is found at the low point of the plumbing fixture, such as a bathtub, shower, sink, etc.
- **Roof drain-**any drain that drains the roof area including the hole in the gutter. If the drain is at the edge of a flat roof, it is called a scupper.
- **Trench drain-**a drain often located in a yard or hillside area that consists of a trench with a perforated pipe at the bottom and gravel filled on the top. The term is incorrectly interchanged with french drain.
- **Yard drain-**also known as an area drain or a site drain. This drains rainwater and irrigation run-off from landscaped areas.

Draw-the ability of a flue, chimney, or vent to pass air, smoke, or other vapors from the bottom up and out the top. Unless impeded by some source, all vertical tubes have a natural draw due a difference in atmospheric pressure.

Drip irrigation-a method of irrigating plants, shrubs and trees with low pressure, low volume piping and tubing system. The advantage of drip irrigation is that it significantly conserves water compared to conventional methods of irrigation.

Driveway-see Flatwork

Dryrot-refers to a condition of rotting, usually wood but sometimes paper and drywall when the material is wetted repeatedly and dries between wettings. Wood that is dryrotted is internally infected by a fungus. The wood will often look almost in its original form, but it will have no structural value and can be easily pierced with a screwdriver.

Drywall-a gypsum based panel that is nailed or screwed to the studs that makes up the interior wall of the house. These panels are also known as Sheetrock®. Drywall derives its name from being a dry process as opposed to the wet lath and plaster process that was used years ago to finish off interior walls. Drywall is typically finished by placing tape over the panel joints and applying drywall compound, known as taper's mud, and finishing the process by spraying or troweling drywall texture onto the wall.

Dual pane-a term applying to the construction of a window, skylight or patio door. Dual pane means that there is an outside layer of glass and an inside layer of glass separated by a spacer up to 5/8 inch in thickness and a dead air space between the two panes of glass. This is sometimes called insulating glass.

Dutch gutter-a rainwater diverter found on roofs, often over doorways or where the placement of a conventional gutter is impractical. It is usually inserted between rows of shingles or tile, and it protrudes up above the roofline by about three or four inches.

EIFS-an acronym standing for Exterior Finish Insulating System. This component system, when applied to the exterior of a House, consists of building paper, foam insulation, wire mesh (lath) and a synthetic stucco product.

Eave-the underside of a section of the roof that extends past the walls of the House.

Efflorescence-white powdery material that appears on the surface of concrete and stucco as the drying out process occurs. Wet winter weather may cause concrete and stucco to effloresce.

Elastomeric-a term given to coatings that have "stretch" characteristics and are applied to many decks and low-pitched roofs. Elastomeric components are mixed together and applied with trowels or rollers. Several coats are applied and if the surface is to be walked upon, often sand, pebbles or crushed walnut shells are applied in the final coat. Some elastomeric paints are made to be applied to stucco.

Escutcheons-a piece of trim, chrome, brass, plastic or wood that is used to finish off the area of penetration of a pipe through a wall or ceiling. They are usually round and one inch to three inches in diameter.

Expansion joint-a cut that is made or a gap that is deliberately left between sections of building materials to allow for expansion and contraction of those materials. Examples of expansion joints are found in large expanses of stucco walls, in concrete driveways and garage slabs and in swimming pool decks and patio decks. Expansion joints that are trowelled into concrete when it is poured are also called control joints or cold joints. Since concrete frequently cracks, the cracks are supposed to occur at these joints to control the cracking from occurring elsewhere.

Exposure-a measure for roofing, usually in inches, of the amount the roof shake, tile, or shingle is exposed to the weather.

Fascia-the trim board that covers the edge of the rafters at a pitched roof. May also be incorporated with a gutter to collect rainwater from the roof.

Filter fabric-a textile made of synthetic threads that allows water to pass through but keeps particles of soil from passing through. Used to wrap underground drainage pipes and placed underneath roadways in unstable soil areas.

Finish coat-refers to the final coat of material to be applied to a House. Examples are stucco, paint, drywall texture, deck coatings and other materials that require more than one application before being complete.

Firebox-that portion of the fireplace where the fire is actually built.

Firestop-these are very similar to draft stops in their location and purpose. Firestops are placed between floors, between walls, in vent shafts, in soffit ceilings, and in chimney chases to retard the spread of fire.

Flapper valve-the rubber or plastic valve at the bottom of the toilet tank that keeps the water in the tank until the flush lever is pushed.

Flashing-strips of material, usually metal, that are used to direct water and wind from one surface to another. Flashing is placed where a roof and a wall intersect. It is also placed around the intersection of chimneys and roofs, as well as where roof planes come together and where trim pieces often protrude from walls. Walls that terminate without being under a roof, such as a parapet, are flashed with cap flashing. Sometimes two flashing components work together, when one piece of flashing slides underneath the other; this is called counter-flashing.

Flatwork-a broad-based term referring to concrete placement that is flat. Examples include driveways, patios and walkways.

Flue-the pipe protruding from the top of the firebox, furnace, water heater, or other gas fired appliance that carries the hot burned gases to the atmosphere and outside the House.

Flush-to be in the same plane or level with another object.

Foundation-the lower most structural element of the House that supports the weight of the House. There are two primary foundation types: the raised footing and the slab on grade. There are also several variations of the two primary foundation types:

- **Basement-**these foundations are a form of grade beam foundation, since the basement wall becomes the grade beam. Basement walls are founded on perimeter footing and a slab is poured between the footings to complete the basement floor.
- **Conventional slab-**this refers to the method of reinforcing a building slab. Steel bars, called rebar, are crisscrossed to form a mat over which concrete is poured. In some cases, the reinforcing may be welded wire mesh.
- **Footing-**a term given to the underside of the grade beam or the underside of the edge of a slab. To provide additional foundation stability, foundations are made wider than the grade beam itself, and deeper than the thickness of the slab.
- **Grade beam-**concrete is poured in a form to allow a first floor framing of the House to occur at least 6 inches higher than the surrounding ground. The grade beams comprise the exterior perimeter of the House and sometimes the interior grade beams are also poured to support bearing walls.
- **Piers-**piers are holes drilled into the ground typically between 6 and 18 feet deep, reinforced with steel rods known as rebars, and filled with concrete. Piers are typically connected to the underside of grade beams. Less frequently, piers independently support the underside of houses. Even less frequently, piers are connected to the underside of slabs where unstable soil conditions warrant. The purpose of a pier is to provide additional stability to a foundation against upward and downward pressure.
- **Post tension slab-**a method of reinforcing where cables are crisscrossed in the slab area prior to pouring concrete. After the concrete is cured, the cables are tightened under extreme tension to provide a tight and dense foundation.
- **Slab on grade-**where the concrete is poured on top of the finished and prepared lot that is ready to receive the concrete. Hence the concrete slab becomes the first floor of the House. Slab foundations can also have grade beams poured underneath them.

Frame-the frame is the skeleton of the house. It contains the elements to support the weight of the house as well as defining the shape of the house. The frame and the foundation are the most important structural components of the house.

Furnace–a mechanical device located in, around, or under the house, or sometimes in the attic, that is powered by either gas (natural or bottled), electricity, or fuel oil or a combination of sources of power. The furnace provides a source of heat for the house.

Garage door-see Doors, garage.

Grade-a term denoting the elevation of a particular lot above sea level and the degree of levelness of that lot. Finished grade is the elevation of the lot (sometimes known as the pad) after the grading operations have been completed. A slab on grade is a foundation that has been poured on the finished grade. Grade is also a term used to describe the type, quality, and strength of lumber that is used in the frame of a house.

Grain-the lines of harder and darker wood that run though the field of a piece of lumber.

Greenboard-a special type of drywall that has moisture resistant characteristics. Its common application is basically seen around tubs and showers. Typically, it is either green or blue in color.

Ground fault interrupter-a special electrical breaker that is more sensitive to electrical changes than standard circuit breakers. Areas that are subject to moist or wet conditions such as kitchens, baths, garages, and outdoor areas must have their electrical outlets connected to a ground fault interrupter.

Grout-material, usually containing cement, sand, or a plastic polymer material, and a coloring agent, that is placed between pieces of tile or marble. The joints between pieces of tile or marble are called grout joints. Stonework can also be grouted. Grout is also used to fill voids under foundation sills.

Gusset-a triangular piece of material often made of wood, plastic, or metal, which is used to strengthen intersecting corners. Gussets are used inside hollow core doors and inside cabinet frames.

Gutter-an open linear collector and distributor of water. Gutters may be found at the eaves of roofs, or can be associated with curbs and sidewalks in streets and parking areas. Another possible location for gutters is in the middle of driveways and streets.

Gypsum-a powdery mineral that is white in color, non-combustible, and is the primary ingredient in indoor plaster and drywall.

Gypsum board-see drywall.

HVAC-an acronym standing for Heating, Ventilating and Air Conditioning. Refers to the specialty work of contractors who install furnaces, fans, air conditioning systems and sometimes other sheet metal items such as flashing, gutters and downspouts.

Hardboard-a general term used to describe a variety of simulated wood products that are used primarily as exterior siding.

Hard water-water that is high in mineral content, mainly compounds of calcium and magnesium. Hard water restricts soap from lathering, and it can form deposits inside water lines and water heaters.

Header-a structural framing member made of wood or steel that spans the opening over a window or door.

Heart (Heartwood)-a term referring to the grade of lumber, usually redwood. Heart wood is from the inner core of the tree trunk. It is considered the best lumber because it is more uniform in appearance. The opposite of heart wood is sap wood. The term "sap wood" refers to the lumber that is milled from the outer-most portion of the tree. Sapwood is usually lighter in color than heartwood.

Hold-downs-structural metal straps that are embedded in the foundation at the time of pouring concrete and then are nailed to the framing members during construction. Hold-downs can also be comprised of anchor bolts, threaded rods, and metal gussets to tie the frame to the foundation in the event of an earthquake or loads (forces) caused by wind.

Holidays-a small area that the painter has missed or covered very lightly. Derived from the saying "it looks like the painter took a holiday".

Impermeable-the term given to the ability of a material to resist the passage of liquid through it. A plastic sheet or membrane that will not pass water is considered impermeable. Semi-permeable membranes allow for the passage of some moisture.

Insulation-a material used in the home building industry that keeps a house from either gaining or losing heat. Normally insulation is put into the walls, under the bottom floor, and into the attic space during construction. Sometimes insulation is placed on the outside of slab foundations and is attached to the outer face of the studs before applying the exterior finish.

Interface-a point where two or more functions interact. For example, the telephone service company wiring meets and interacts with the house telephone wiring at a box called the interface.

Jack-has three meanings in home building. The first refers to the metal assembly on the roof through which the plumbing vents and furnace flues run. The jack may be a combination of metal and a rubber gasket to ensure a watertight seal. The second use of the term jack refers to a screw device that can remedy certain out of level conditions on foundation and floor frame members. The third definition applies to a "phone jack", or the wall plate into which the phone cord is plugged.

Jamb-the stationary component of a door assembly to which the hinges are attached. The door assembly (excluding the door itself) is comprised of a jamb, stop, and casing.

Joist-the horizontal members of the house frame that are the most common elements of a floor or ceiling system. While joists are the most common element of the floor system, other horizontal members known as beams or girders can also make up the floor system. Common joists have one nominal dimension, typically at 2 inches and the other nominal dimension at 8 inches, 10 inches, 12 inches, or 14 inches, depending upon how far they span. It is common practice today to use a manufactured component as a joist. This is called a truss; it is comprised of wood, metal or a combination of both. If a truss is used, it has been manufactured in a factory and approved for use by a structural engineer.

Knocked down-a style of finished wall texture that is applied coarsely with a texture spray gun. The bumpy surface is then "knocked down" with a large metal straight edge known as a texture knife.

Latch-that portion of the doorknob assembly that protrudes out from the door and upon closing the door fits into the hole provided by the strike. The term can also generically refer to any part of a door, gate or opening mechanism that hooks into a receptacle designed to receive it.

Lath-a material to which plaster is applied. Lath is usually metal in the form of wire or mesh that is applied over building paper to the exterior of the house prior to plastering. The lath provides a surface for the plaster to hang onto during its wet application, and lath reinforces plaster much in the same way rebar reinforces concrete. Prior to the wide spread use of drywall, interior house walls were plastered with gypsum plaster. The lath used behind this type of plaster were long strips of wood.

Leaf-a term given to the section of a door that swings in or out with another companion door, and which does not close into a jamb on the strike side. Good examples are french doors that connect to one another when closed.

Ledger-a horizontal piece of lumber or steel used to support joists and rafters. The wood ledger, which is at least 2 inches nominal thickness, may support the joists by having them sit on top of the ledger or hang from the face of the ledger by metal brackets known as joists hangers. The most common application for the ledger is in the construction of a deck attached to the outside of the house.

Membrane-a thin sheet of material used to prevent the passage of water or water vapor into an area that would be damaged by water. Often used under deck surfaces.

Millwork-refers to house components that are generally part of the interior finish of the house, and which are manufactured in a mill or shop, rather than constructed at the site of the house. Examples of millwork are cabinets and doors.

Miter cut-a method of cutting wood (usually trim pieces) at an angle other than 90 degrees so as to conceal the joint when the pieces of wood are placed together. Corner pieces of trim such as door casings and baseboards are often miter cut so that the cut end is not visible.

Mortar-mortar is a mixture of sand and cement and may be used for setting brick, stonework, and preparing a bed upon which tile is set. Unlike concrete, mortar does not have aggregate (smooth rocks of various sizes, up to about ¾ inch). Grout is a form of mortar.

Mudsill-The 2x4 or 2x6 section of lumber that is bolted to the foundation as the very first framing member. It must be pressure treated or foundation grade redwood.

Mullion-a strip that divides, or appears to divide, the panes of glass in a window. With many dual pane windows, a faux mullion is placed in the dead air space between the panes of glass.

Negative slope-a slope or grade that runs in the wrong direction, causing water to flow opposite of the direction that is intended (see **Slope**).

OSB-the initials meaning oriented strand board. OSB is a manufactured wood product that comes in sheets that are 4 feet wide by 8, 9, or 10 feet in length. It can be part of the house frame on the subfloor, walls, or roofs. It is always covered by the finish flooring, siding, or roofing material.

Overhead door-see Doors, garage.

PVC-a plastic pipe made from polyvinyl chloride. The most extensive use of this pipe is for irrigation supply lines. Other uses include storm and sewer piping. If the manufacturer adds another step to the process, called CPVC, the pipe can be used for cold-water household use in most locations.

Pad-a term given to the flat spot on a graded lot where the condominium or house is to be built. A padded lot refers to a lot that has been graded flat in one or more elevations and usually certified by a civil engineer. It is also the material installed under the carpet.

Parapet-a low wall that extends above the edge of a roof and often found on the sides of decks and balconies.

Particle board-a mixture of wood chips, sawdust and a glue-like binder called resin for creation of a synthetic wood product. It is manufactured in boards like lumber, or sheets like plywood, and has a broad range of applications in residential construction. Examples are shelving, door cores, and backing (underlayment) for tile and vinyl flooring. A related product, called oriented strand board (OSB), is used as roof underlayment and shear panels.

Patio-see Flatwork.

Pavers-pieces of stone, concrete, or brick that are placed side-by-side to form walkways and driveways. Shapes can be square, rectangular, hexagonal or other geometric shapes. Depending on the specific use, pavers are set over a base of sand, concrete, or mortar.

Penny-a measurement of the size of nails. Derived from Old English where copper was used for both pennies and nails.

Perforated pipe-pipe that has holes or slots through the sidewall of the pipe to permit the collection of subterranean drainage water or the discharge of wastewater in a septic tank system leach field.

Pier-a column of concrete that extends down into the ground and is often attached to the underside of the grade beam. Sometimes an "independent" pier may be attached to the underside of the subfloor joists in the crawl space. The purpose of the pier is to provide additional load carrying capacity to the foundation.

Pitch-also known as slope, the amount of drop (or rise) of a building component such as a roof, or deck. For example a roof that has a 5 and 12 pitch means that for every 12 feet of horizontal measurement the roof would rise up 5 feet in vertical measurement.

Plant on-an architectural feature that is usually glued to or fastened to the exterior of a house to add dimension and character to walls and windows. Used frequently in stucco applications.

Plaster-see Stucco.

Plumb-a term given to a wall that is perfectly straight up and down. Out of plumb means that the wall is tilted to some measured extent.

Ponding-a condition where flat surfaces that are supposed to drain collect water in depressed areas called ponds (also called birdbaths).

Post-a vertical structural element larger than a stud used in the framing of a house. Posts are usually the vertical support for horizontal beams. Posts can also be found as a component in handrails.

Pot shelf-an architectural feature found on the inside and outside of some houses, used to permit the placement of pots. Often found in hallways and in bedrooms above closets, as well as on the exterior in front of windows.

Pre-emergent-a chemical that is applied to landscape areas in winter and spring prior to the growth of weeds to prevent weed seeds from sprouting.

Pressure treated-a chemical treatment given to lumber that may or will come in contact with the earth (ground). The process often gives a greenish or brownish color to the wood and linear perforations ("pickling marks") on the sides. Mudsills and fence posts are examples of lumber that should be pressure treated.

Primer-refers to the base coat or initial coat of a liquid, usually paint, sometimes resin, which penetrates and adheres to the coated object and provides a compatible surface for finish coats.

R-Value-the measurement of the ability of a substance to gain or lose heat. Insulation is rated by its R-Value. The higher the R-Value (like R-11, R-22, R-38 etc.), the greater ability to insulate.

Rafter-the common structural lumber used to create the frame of the roof. The rafters define the shape of the roof as well as the slope.

Rebar-the steel rods that are placed in a form, such as a foundation, to give added strength and resistance to prevent concrete cracking.

Refractory-a term given to ceramic or brick like material that is made to withstand heat. Many fireplaces have precast panels of refractory material at the sides and back.

Riser-the vertical, back piece of a stair step that separates one tread from another.

Roof-the upper most structural component of the house or the building frame. A number of other terms are associated with roofs:

- **Gable-**a simple design of pitched roofs having a high point (called the ridge) and a low point (at the eave).
- **Hip-**a gable roof that has been clipped back at its outer end, and with a sloped roof added to the clipped area.
- **Mansard-**a small, steeply pitched portion found around the perimeter of low pitched or flat roofs as an element of architectural enhancement.
- **Rake-**the line of the roof running from the ridge to the eave. Rakes can occur at the ends of gables, or where two sections of roof join in a hip.
- **Ridge-**the highest horizontal part of the roof.
- **Shed-**a pitched roof where the upper most part terminates at a wall, or a pitched roof that starts at the top of a wall and is pitched in only one direction (as opposed to a gable roof which is pitched in two directions).
- **Valley-**the opposite of **hip** (see above definition). The low point where two roof planes intersect.

Roof cover-while the roof is part of the house or building structure, the roof cover is the material that gives the water shedding or water repellency nature to the roof. Examples of roof covers are noted:

- **Asphalt composition or shingle-**made primarily by combining fiberglass or felt with a petroleum product and finishing the outer surface with granulated sand, stone, or other hard substance. Applied in strips about 3 feet long.
- **Built up roof-**also known as low pitch or flat roofs. The most common material used in this type of roof is hot asphalt (tar) mopped over a felt membrane and covered with gravel. Other materials used include rubber sheeting and elastomeric coatings.
- **Tile-**a term given to individual pieces made from mortar (called concrete) or terra cotta. The material can be colored in the manufacturing process and it comes glazed or unglazed. Shapes include flat pieces (known as shakes), interlocking "S" shapes, or semicircular barrels.
- **Wooden shake or wooden shingle-**usually made from split cedar logs and hand applied on the roof one at a time.

- **Other-**there are numerous other roof coverings that have limited use in new house construction. These include metal shingles with granular material glued on them, shakes made of cement and fiberglass, and reconstituted wood shakes.

Rosette-the two circular end pieces (usually plastic) mounted on the side wall of a closet. The purpose of a rosette is to provide the niche into which the closet pole is inserted. Also a rosette is the round portion of the door hardware used to trim out the hole bored through the door.

Scalloping-an unacceptable condition of finished boards (including flooring) where the saw has made irregular cuts or chips out of the surface of the board.

Screw drive-the method of operation of some garage door opener mechanisms. Also known as worm drive. The screw drive is a long steel rod that runs between the opener and the door header and it revolves in a clockwise and counterclockwise direction.

Seismic-a term frequently used in conjunction with earthquake activity. Seismic design, i.e. making the house stronger and less prone to damage in an earthquake, is a part of the Building Code. Some seismic building methods include tying the house to the foundation with long metal straps and using shear panels to keep the house from moving back and forth during an earthquake.

Sheathing-the part of the roof that covers the rafters. Sheathing is usually plywood or a wood type of product. Strip sheathings are strips of 1 x 3 inch or 1 x 4 inch boards that are nailed across the rafters to provide a nailing surface for shingles and shakes.

Sheetrock®-see Drywall.

Shower pan-the bottom part of a shower. It may have been installed as a single unit or tiled over a waterproofing system.

Siding-the exterior covering of a house. Many materials can be used for siding, including wood, brick, vinyl, aluminum, plaster (stucco), and cement board.

Sill-the bottom of a window or patio door that is often confused with the trim piece, known as the stool, which is placed on the sill. Another sill, known as the mudsill, is the first piece of horizontal framing that is bolted to the foundation. Mudsills are required to be of termite resistant wood.

Slab-a term given to flat concrete and is often used with a foundation type known as slab on grade; also used in reference to the floor of a garage or basement known as the garage slab and basement slab.

Slope-sometimes also referred to as pitch or "fall". The percentage or angle that a surface (such as a patio, driveway, or the grading around the house) drops, as one moves outward from the house. When dealing with plumbing pipes the term "fall" is used, which means the percentage or degree of inclination of the pipe.

Soffit-an architectural term given to a roof projection that has had the underside enclosed so that the rafters cannot be seen. Overhead decks and walkways may be constructed in a manner so as to have soffits.

Sole plate-the 2x4 or 2x6 (sometimes 4x4 or 4x6) section of lumber that is laid flat on the slab or subfloor and the wall studs are attached to the plate. In the case of a concrete slab, the sole plate and the mudsill are the same.

Spalling-the chipping or flaking of the exterior surface of a building material, usually concrete, that deeply pits the surface of the material. Concrete is known to spall in cold climates where there is repeated wetting and freezing of the surface. Cement plaster (stucco) can also spall for the same reason. Spalling can also occur in concrete when it is allowed to dry out (cure) too quickly.

Spark arrester-a metal screen-like device that is mounted on top of the chimney to prevent hot ashes from passing into the atmosphere and creating a fire hazard.

Splash block-a shallow trough with one open end that is placed under the discharge of a downspout to direct rainwater away from the foundation. Splash blocks are usually made of cast concrete, but they can also be made of cast fiberglass and metal.

Spores-microscopic organisms that are capable of rapid reproduction and give rise to a new adult molds, mildews, and fungi. Found in mushrooms, ferns, mosses, as well as other organic material.

Stile- the right and left side pieces of a door or cabinet that run from top to bottom.

Stool-the piece of trim that sits horizontally on the sill of a window. Often accompanied with a companion piece underneath it known as an apron. "Stool" can also refer to the lower piece of a toilet. Two piece toilets have a tank to hold the flushing water and a stool to receive the waste.

Stoop-a step, or series of steps, plus a landing that leads to the exterior door of a house.

Storm collar-a piece of metal that looks like a clerical collar and is attached to the chimney cap or vent from a gas appliance. The flue runs through the storm collar.

Strike-that portion of door and cabinet hardware that is attached to the frame and receives the latch (through a hole in it) when the door is closed.

Stringer-the side boards on either side of a stairway. Unless the stairway is open, the treads run from one stringer across to the other.

Stucco-the exterior surface of a house that has been applied by troweling or spraying, to comprise a hard weather resistant surface. Stucco can be a form of mortar, known as cement plaster (sand and cement) or it can be a more synthetic material consisting of plastic resins and materials to bind them together. Many final textures are available for stucco including skip trowel, sand float, and brocade.

Stud-the common vertical structural pieces, usually wood, sometimes steel, which support the walls of a house. Studs are mostly 2 inches x 4 inches in cross dimension, although sometimes they can be 2 inches x 6 inches.

Subdrain-a drain that is placed underground to catch and divert subsurface water.

Subfloor-the flat flooring material that is connected to the floor joists. It is often made of plywood or several plywood substitutes. The finish floor, such as carpet, hardwood, tile, or linoleum, covers the subfloor.

Subpanel-a large electrical box with a metal or plastic door usually found mounted in the wall inside the house or garage. The subpanel contains the circuit breakers or fuses of the branch electrical circuits. Houses may have more than one subpanel. The main panel is the box on the outside of the house that contains the electric meter and possibly some circuit breakers.

Subsidence-see Displacement.

Subsurface water-water that passes underground through the soil, usually from a distant source and may cause soil to slide and swell, creating stability problems for houses.

Swale-a surface path for seasonal water flow that can be natural or man-made. Often swales are cut around houses as part of the finished grading process to allow rainwater to flow away from the house and out toward the street.

Sweat-the process by which copper piping is joined together. Using a torch, the parts to be joined are heated and the solder flows into the joint. This process is known as "sweating" pipes.

Swing-sometimes known as hand, the term describes whether a door swings to the right or the left as you face it and open it toward you. Left-hand doors open and swing to the left and right hand doors open and swing to the right. Swing is an important thing to know when replacing doorknobs.

Tack strip-a narrow strip of wood with specialized nails driven through it in the opposite direction of the anchor nails, designed to catch and hold the edge of carpet. Tack strips are about 1 inch wide and up to 8 feet long and are nailed to the subfloor or concrete floor around the perimeter of a room. Protruding through the wood strips are sharp ends of specialized tacks. These tacks grab the carpet backing as the carpet is stretched toward the wall.

Tannins-a substance found in many plants and trees that is acidic and dark in color. Tannins will leach when the material is wetted or crushed. Two materials that contain significant tannins are redwood and oak wood.

Threshold-a piece of wood, metal, or plastic that is placed on the bottom of the exterior door opening to direct water away from the opening.

Toe kick-a small piece of wood at the bottom of cabinets, usually about 4 inches high, which lifts the cabinet off the floor and is recessed behind the cabinet face.

Trap-the piece of waste pipe just below sinks (visible), and below tubs and showers (not visible), shaped like a "U" or a "P". Traps retain some of the waste water and prevent sewer gases from backing into the house.

Tread-the flat part of a step.

Trench Drain-a subterranean drainage trench that contains a perforated pipe at the bottom and is filled with a gravel mix. The term is often mistakenly interchanged with "French Drain" which is a gravel filled trench without a pipe

Trim-a generic term given to material that "finishes off" or dresses up a house. Various examples of trim are baseboard, door casings, window stools and aprons, crown molding, wood applied to the exterior around windows, and material that is applied to the house (usually wood) after the stucco or siding has been installed.

Truss-a structural component that has been engineered and manufactured to carry the weight of a floor or the weight of a roof. Trusses are often substituted for common floor joists and common rafters.

UL Label-a label affixed to electrical appliances that have passed the independent tests administered by Underwriters Laboratory.

Underlayment-sheet of material, usually plywood, particle board, or cement board that is placed underneath the product that covers them to give rigidity. Used in roofing and flooring applications. The underlayment, if coated, can serve as a membrane.

Useful life-the term given to how long a particular component or product is supposed to last. Useful lives are provided by manufacturers, by insurance companies, and by industry groups based upon actual experience and testing. If a product becomes obsolete, but is not worn out, it is also said that its useful life has passed.

Vapor barrier-a sheet membrane that has numerous applications to keep moisture from entering (or in some cases leaving) a house. Vapor barriers are installed on the exterior of the frame of a house prior to the application of siding or stucco. Building paper serves as a vapor barrier prior to the installation of lath and stucco. Concrete slabs are poured over a plastic vapor barrier to keep moisture in the ground moving up through the concrete via capillary action. In colder climates interior vapor barriers are put in the inside of exterior walls under the drywall to keep the humidity of the house at a constant level.

Vaulted ceiling-a ceiling that is not flat, but rather follows the pitch of the roof, or the underside of the truss.

Veneer-a thin layer of finished material applied over a much thicker layer of core material. It is a common practice for door, cabinets, and furniture manufactures to place a veneer of fine wood over a core of particle board as part of their manufacturing process. Veneers can also be brick or masonry products.

Vents-there are many types of vents found in houses. Here are some of the more common ones:

- **Attic-**attic vents are usually louvered, often round, and found underneath the gables of a roof. Attic vents allow heat to escape during summer months.
- **Foundation-**foundation vents are installed with pier and grade beam foundations. These vents allow air to circulate and moisture to escape.
- **Plumbing-**plumbing vents are pipes that stick up through the roof and allow wastewater to pass through the house plumbing without becoming air locked.
- **Soffit-**vents that are found on the underside of soffits. They may be round, rectangular, or narrow and long.
- **Window-**that portion of the window that opens and closes is called the vent.
- **Other-**examples of other vents are exhaust fans, water heater flues, and cooktop vents.

Walkthrough-A practice used by Builders when a new house is delivered to the Homeowner. A representative of the Builder walks through the house with the Homeowner prior to delivery. Often the Builder will demonstrate the features of the house and give the Homeowner instructions on care and maintenance. This event is also a very important opportunity for the Homeowner to note any items that are not complete or appear to be unacceptable. For example, countertop scratches and marks on the walls will probably not be covered under a Builder's limited warranty once the Homeowner takes possession of the house.

Walkway-see Flatwork.

Wall-the exterior and interior vertical component system of a house. There are many types of walls and several examples are described here:

- **Bearing wall-**a wall that carries a portion of the weight of the house. Most exterior walls are bearing walls. Some interior walls are also bearing walls.
- **Headwall-**not a wall in a house, but a wall that has been constructed as part of a storm drain channel or piping system. The headwall is the concrete wall that serves as the beginning of a system where rain and storm water will flow from a channel into a system of piping.
- **Nonbearing wall-**a wall that is a partition between rooms, but does not carry the weight of any portion of the structure above it.
- **Party wall-**a wall where most likely two walls are constructed to separate one condominium from another or one townhouse from another. Also known as common walls, these walls must be constructed according to a specific standard in the Building Code.
- **Rated wall (Ceiling)-**a wall that has been constructed to meet certain fire resistive and noise transmission standards.
- **Shear wall-**a wall of a house that has been reinforced against back and forth movement (caused by earthquakes and wind forces) using sheets of plywood, oriented strand board, or other materials approved by the Building Code.

Water hammer-the action of water under high pressure, rushing through pipes and hitting a turn in the piping or a closed valve. Water hammer makes a banging noise in the piping. It can eventually break the piping connections and cause the piping to come loose. A common water hammer problem is the electric valves on a washing machine closing quickly between cycles.

Waterproofing-a term given to plastic and rubbery building materials that keep water from penetrating surfaces such as windows, retaining walls, and certain stucco surfaces.

Weatherstripping-material made of plastic, felt, rubber, and metal that are placed around the frames of doors and windows to provide a final seal against the intrusion of wind and rain.

Weep holes-a small hole found at the exterior side of most windows to allow rainwater to exit from the channel of the window onto the outside of the building.

Weep screed-a strip of metal, used as part of stucco applications, running parallel to the ground, about 6 inches off the ground where the stucco terminates. Rainwater that may be trapped behind the stucco will run down the building paper and exit through the weep screed.

Index

If a component or condition is not listed above, check the Table of Contents or Glossary Sections.

Bibliography and References

ASHRAE Handbook: Fundamentals, Atlanta, GA, American Society of Heating, Refrigerating and Air-Conditioning Engineers, 1963.

Ballast, David Kent, *Handbook of Construction Tolerances*, McGraw Hill, 1994.

Building Industry Association of San Diego County, *Top 25 Construction Problems and Their Resolution*, Construction Quality Task Force, 1993.

California, State of, Department of Real Estate, *Operating Cost Manual for Homeowner Associations,* September 1996 edition.

California, State of, Contractor's State License Board, *Workmanship Guidelines*, November 1982.

Concrete Performance Standards & Maintenance Guidelines, Concrete Committee of San Diego County, CA, 2001.

Gypsum Association, *Fire Resistance Design Manual,* GA-600-94, Washington DC.

Hassl, John J. and Peter Kuchinsky II, *Production Checklist for Builders and Superintendents*, NAHB Home Builder Press, Washington D.C., 2001.

Homeowners Booklet, New Home Warranty Program, State of New Jersey, Division of Codes and Standards, 1997.

Journal of Light Construction, *Troubleshooting Guide to Residential Construction*, Builderburg Group, 1997.

Maguire, Jack, *500 Terrific Ideas for Home Maintenance and Repair*, Galahad Books, NY, 1991.

Mold in Residential Buildings, NAHB Research Center, Inc., Washington D.C., 2001.

NRCA Roofing and Waterproofing Manual. Vols. 1 & 2. National Roofing Contractor's Association, Rosemont, IL, 1996.

Problems, Causes and Cures. National Wood Flooring Association, Ellisville, MO, 2000.

Residential Construction Performance Guidelines 2nd ed., NAHB Home Builder Press, Washington, DC, 2000.

Sacks, Alvin M., *Residential Water Problems*, NAHB Home Builder Press, Washington, DC, 1994.

Reynolds, Don, et al., *Residential & Light Commercial Construction Standards*, R. S. Means, Inc., Kingston, MA, 1998.

Tenenbaum, David J., *The Complete Idiot's Guide to Trouble Free Home Repair*, Alpha Books, NY, 1996.

Uniform Building Code, 1997 Edition, International Conference of Building Officials, Whittier, CA, 1997.